PLANT BASED *Diet* COOKBOOK FOR BEGINNERS

THE HEALTH BENEFITS OF EATING A PLANT BASED DIET.
600 HEALTHY AND DELICIOUS RECIPES TO HELP YOU LOSE WEIGHT, AND HEAL YOUR BODY

WHAT'S INSIDE

Copyright © 2020

All rights reserved. No part of this guide may be reproduced in any form without permission in writing from the publisher except in the case of brief quotations embodied in critical articles or reviews.

Table *of* content

Chapter One ——————————————————————————— 14

almond milk quinoa, quinoa and sweet potatoes, honey buckwheat coconut porridge, tempeh and potato, breakfast french toast, dairy-free pumpkin pancakes, protein blueberry bars, chickpea scramble breakfast basin, quinoa, oats, hazelnut and blueberry salad, buttered overnight oats, protein breakfast burrito, breakfast hummus toast, almond milk banana smoothie, nutritious toasted chickpeas, peanut butter oats, protein pancakes, savory vegan omelet, protein patties, vegan chickpea pancake, protein pudding, gluten-free tofu quiche, pumpkin oatmeal, breakfast berry quinoa, bean lentil salad with lime dressing, lentil arugula salad, serve with the crunchy bread,red cabbage and cucumber salad with seitan, red cabbage and cucumber salad with seitan.

Chapter Two ——————————————————————————— 38

Panzanella, Nutritious Beet Hummus, White Bean Soup with Green Herb Dumplings, Tomato-Braised Lentils with Broccoli Rabe, Caesar White Bean Burgers, Southwestern Quinoa Stuffed Peppers, Smoky Tempeh Burrito, Tofu Chickpea Stir-Fry with Tahini Sauce, Sweet and Sour Tempeh, Korean Braised Tofu, Red Lentil Tikka Masala, Easy Thai Red Tofu Curry, Barbecue Baked Seitan Strips, Easy Vegan Chilli Sin Carne, Teriyaki Tofu Stir Fry Over Quinoa, Vegan Fall Farro Protein Bowl, Black Bean, Quinoa Balls & Spiralized Zucchini, Mongolian Seitan (Vegan Mongolian Beef), Teriyaki Tempeh, Vegan Spinach Ricotta Lasagna, Vegan Samosa Pie, Lentil Roast with Balsamic Onion Gravy, Grilled Breaded Tofu Steaks & Spinach Salad, Sweet Potato & Black Bean Enchiladas, Edamame Fried Rice, Vegan Shepherd's Pie with Crispy Cauliflower Crust, Hearty Vegetarian Chili & Butternut Squash, Easy Banana Cacao Ice Cream, Flourless Walnut Kidney Bean Brownies, Raw Protein Thin Mints, Fudgy Cinnamon Chai Protein Bars, Black Bean Chocolate Orange Mousse, Chocolate Crispy Fruit Squares, Flourless Salted Caramel Chocolate Chip Cookies, Mango Chia Seed Pudding, Banana Bread Cookies, Simple Baked Cheesecake, Plant-Based Peanut Butter Cream Sweet Potato Brownies, Gluten-Free Pear & Banana Loaf, Plant-Based Blueberry Crisp, Raw Chickpea Cookie Dough, Whole Food Plant-Based Apple Crisp, Vegan Chocolate Beet Cake, Vegan Blueberry Flax Muffins, Cranberry Apple Cider Pie, Vegan Chocolate Avocado Pudding, Rosemary Fig Scones, Carrot Cake Waffles, High Protein Dessert Pizza with Raspberry Sauce, High Protein Rice Crispie Treats, Peanut Butter Chia Bars, Hidden Greens Chocolate Protein Shake, High Protein, Raw Vegan Carrot Cake.

Chapter Three — 66

Chocolate Raspberry Layer Cake, Chocolate Black Bean Smoothie, Vegan Vanilla Cashew Shake, Easy Peanut Butter Protein Bars, Vegan Chocolate Almond Protein Bars, Sweet Potato-Chickpea Patties & Sriracha-Yogurt Dip, Dark Chocolate Hemp Energy Bites, No-Bake Vegan Protein Bars, Runner Recovery Bites, High Protein Vegan Cheesy Sauce, Vegan High-Protein Queso, Vegan Buffalo Sauce, Vegan Ranch Dressing (Dipping Sauce), Vegan Smokey Maple BBQ Sauce, Vegan White Bean Gravy, Tahini Maple Dressing, Coconut Sugar Peanut Sauce, Coconut Sauce, Vegan Bean Pesto

4 WEEK MEAL PLAN — 75

Chapter Five — 88

Culiflower Wedges, Roasted Pumpkin & Brussels sprouts, Black Bean-Tomato Chili, Roasted Balsamic Red Potatoes, Easy Homemade Chunky Applesauce, Mushroom & Broccoli Soup, Avocado Fruit Salad with Tangerine Vinaigrette, General Tso's Cauliflower, Roasted Curried Chickpeas and Cauliflower, Chickpea Mint Tabbouleh, Smoky Cauliflower, Creamy Cauliflower Pakora Soup, Spice Trade Beans and Bulgur, Tofu Chow Mein, Chard and White Bean Pasta, Okra Roasted with Smoked Paprika, Spicy Grilled Broccoli, Sauteed Squash with Tomatoes and Onions, Garden Vegetable & Herb Soup

Chapter Six — 97

Healing Mushroom Soup New Instant Pot, Peaches and Cream Oatmeal Instant Pot, Roasted Red Pepper and Cauliflower Soup Instant Pot, Eggplant Sauce

Chapter Seven — 107

- week 1 — 108
- week 2 — 126
- week 3 — 147

Chapter Eight ── **167**

Vegan 'Bacon' Strips, Fudgy Double Chocolate Apple Muffins, Salted Caramel Apple, Lemon Cheesecake, Lemon-Oatmeal Cookies, Coconut Chocolate Mousse, Chocolate Cupcakes, Lemon Poppy Seed SconesBars, Brownies, No-Bake Lemon Tarts, Peanut Butter Caramel Rice Krispies, Peach Iced Tea, Guilt-Free Coconut Vanilla Macaroons, No-Bake Lemon Tarts, Peanut Butter Fudge, Takeaway-Style Vegan Korma, Black Bean & Avocado Tacos, Moroccan Stuffed Romano Peppers, Spicy Sesame & Edamame, Quick & Easy Tomato and Herb Gigantes Beans, Spelt Spaghetti with Avocado Pesto, Vegan Sausage Casserole; Bangers & Borlotti, Herby Giant Couscous with Asparagus and Lemon, Easy Seitan for Two, Quit-the-Cluck Seitan, Broccoli, Kale, Chili & Hazelnut Pizza, Cassoulet, Double-Garlic Bean and Vegetable Soup, Hummus Bisque, Mean Bean Minestrone, Sushi Rice and Bean Stew, Giardiniera Chili, Shorba (Lentil Soup), Split Pea Patties, Savory Edamame Mini Cakes, Quinoa Edamame Rolls, Spicy Chickpea Fries, Baked Falafel, Pudla, The Whole Enchilada, Mujaddara, Mediterranean Quinoa and Bean Salad, Tabbouleh Verde, Curried Bean and Corn Salad, Leek and Lemon Lentil Salad, Eat-it-Up Edamame Salad

Chapter Nine ── **202**

Crockpot Lasagna with Spinach Tofu, Crockpot Vegetarian Split Pea Soup, Black Bean Veggie Burger, Blueberry Tofu Smoothie, Fluffy 1-Bowl Sugar Cookies, Gluten-Free Black Beans Brownies, Tahini Chocolate Banana Soft Serve, Raw Oreos, Peanut Butter Cup Cookies, Gluten-Free Cinnamon Rolls

Conclusion ── **208**

DISCLAIMER

The information contained in this eBook is offered for informational purposes solely, and it is geared towards providing exact and reliable information in regards to the topic and issue covered. The author and the publisher does not warrant that the information contained in this e-book is fully complete and shall not be responsible for any errors or omissions.

The author and publisher shall have neither liability nor responsibility to any person or entity concerning any reparation, damages, or monetary loss caused or alleged to be caused directly or indirectly by this e-book. Therefore, this eBook should be used as a guide - not as the ultimate source.

The publication is sold with the idea that the publisher is not required to render accounting, officially permitted, or otherwise, qualified services. If advice is necessary, legal or professional, a practiced individual in the profession should be ordered.

In no way is it legal to reproduce, duplicate, or transmit any part of this document in either electronic means or printed format. Recording of this publication is strictly prohibited, and any storage of this document is not allowed unless with written permission from the publisher. All rights reserved.

The author owns all copyrights not held by the publisher. The trademarks that are used are without any consent, and the publication of the trademark is without permission or backing by the trademark owner. All trademarks and brands within this book are for clarifying purposes only and are not affiliated with this document.

INTRODUCTION

The Plant-Based Athlete-Getting Started

If you would like to improve the quality of your everyday life, boost the level of your energy, make your health better and prevent various diseases you might want to consider switching to a plant-based diet. Recent studies show that changing the way you eat can be a defining moment for living healthier and longer, helping the environment and animals, and having an overall better quality of life.A lot of people consider plant-based diet to be a strictly vegan diet, with altogether avoiding all animal products. Others think that vegetables, fruits, legumes, whole grains, and nuts should be the central part of their everyday diet, and animal products such as meat, fish, or dairy products can be consumed occasionally. A plant-based diet means eating foods that mostly or entirely made from plants, and it allows you to meet your nutritional needs by consuming foods in which none or close to none of the ingredients come from animals. A plant-based diet also focuses on healthful whole foods rather than processed foods.

Plant-based diets are becoming widely popular, and more and more people are switching to plant-based diets for a variety of reasons. Diets that are based on consumption of plant foods and are rich in beans, nuts, seeds, fruit and vegetables, whole grains, and cereal-based foods can provide all the nutrients needed for good health and offer affordable, tasty and nutritious alternatives to meat-based diets.

Scientific research provides evidence that switching to plant-based diets helps control, reduce and even reverse various chronic diseases. Analysis of the question given in the book called The China Study highlights the fact that plant-based diets that are also low in saturated fat, can help control weight and may reduce the risk of type 2 diabetes, cardiovascular and heart diseases, some types of cancer and other significant illnesses. There are also reports of having more energy, reduced inflammation, bigger fitness payoffs, and better overall health outcomes after switching to a plant-based diet.

However, as with any diet, this diet will require detailed planning and if thought through well, it can provide and support healthy living at every age and stage of life. Here are several steps that can help with switching and maintaining the plant-based diet:

- Start slowly by selecting a few easy to prepare plant-based meals that you enjoy and use them throughout the week. Once you try that and are satisfied with the outcome, you can expand further adding more dishes.
- Slowly lower the consumption of meat and processed foods. Start by reducing the proportion of animal-sourced foods in your every meal. Eat more salads, vegetables, and fruits. Then lower the consumption of dairy products if you plan on going 100% vegan and start replacing with plant-based alternatives.
- Once you are confident enough and satisfied with the results, you can try making one complete meal in your daily ration fully vegan.
- Next, you need to watch your protein intake. While our body needs to get 1 gram per 1 kg of weight every day, overconsumption of protein is not necessary and can even be harmful. And since plants have more than enough proteins, you might want to start watching them.
- You should be watching the products that you are consuming. Most of the commercial products on the market, like faux meat and cheese, are highly processed and contain the same nutrients as animal products, which make them health-damaging. That is why it is better to eat such foods once in a while.
- In general, it's best to stick to whole, intact foods as much as possible. There are lots of right products on the market today to stay healthy and adhere to the plant-based path.

Energy & Performance; Protein and Recovery

Plant-based diets are also becoming popular and widely accepted by professional athletes. There are several reasons for that.

Even athletes are prone to the risk of cardiovascular and heart diseases, and a plant-based diet is right in keeping heart healthy and problem-free, lowering blood pressure and cholesterol level.

Meat consumption and cholesterol from it can cause inflammation, which can result in lower athletic performance and slower recovery. Plant-based diet shows have anti-inflammatory effect. It also improves blood thickness, which results in more oxygen reaching muscles, which in turn improves athletic performance. It also makes arteries more flexible and more prominent in diameter resulting in better blood flow. One study shows that even one high-fat meal worsens arterial function for several hours. People that follow the plant-based diet get more antioxidants, which help in neutralizing free radicals that cause muscle fatigue, impaired recovery, and reduced athletic performance. A plant-based diet can reduce body fat, which can increase aerobic capacity that is vital to exercising through using more oxygen to fuel muscles. Studies indicate that athletes following the plant-based diet have increased maximum level of oxygen they can use while applying resulting in better endurance.

Muscle Protein Synthesis

Muscle Protein Synthesis is a process that is vital to the human body. Proteins are the compounds that are built from amino acids, which appear to be the building material for the creation of tissues in the human body, and Muscle Protein Synthesis is a naturally occurring process in which protein is produced to assist with the growth, repair and overall maintenance of human skeletal muscles. It is an opposing process to the Muscle Protein Breakdown, during which protein is being lost after exercising.

Muscle Protein Synthesis also closely correlates with exercising that muscles receive, as muscle growth can be achieved only through regular training and proper protein intake. Human skeletal muscles will not grow or get stronger without exercising, and in such case, Muscle Protein Synthesis will not be of any help and will only be doing ongoing repairs and maintenance of existing muscle tissues.

To accelerate muscle growth, improve athletic performance, endurance and recovery you will need to learn how to stimulate Muscle Protein Synthesis through the combination of exercise and appropriate diet.

There is a relationship between Muscle Protein Synthesis and Muscle Protein Breakdown and is called Protein Balance. To stimulate the growth of muscles a person needs to unsettle that protein balance, and to do that all that needs to be done is train hard, and the greater the intensity of exercising, the higher the Muscle Protein Synthesis. The correlation between diet and Muscle Protein Synthesis is not as straightforward as applying. Even if protein intake rises, Muscle Protein Synthesis increases for a short period. It is because body can only utilize a certain amount of amino acids that it receives, and everything above that certain amount will get broken down and excreted by the liver.

Macros & Micros

Macronutrients or macros and micronutrients or micros are molecules that the human body needs to survive, properly function and avoid getting ill. We need macros in large amounts as they are the primary nutrients for our body. There are three main macronutrients: carbohydrates, proteins, and fats. Micronutrients such as vitamins, minerals, and electrolytes are the other type of nutrients that human body requires, but in comparison to macros, micros are required in much smaller amounts.

Except for fad diets, the human body needs all three macronutrients and cutting out any of the macronutrients puts the risk of nutrient deficiencies and illness on human health.

Carbohydrates that you eat is a source of quick energy, they are transformed into glucose or commonly known as sugar, and are either used right after generated or stored as glycogen for later use.

Protein is there to help with growth, injury repair, muscle formation, and protection against infections. Proteins are the compounds that are built from amino acids, which appear to be the building material for the creation of tissues in the human body. And our body needs 20 various amino acids, 9 of which cannot be produced by our body, and thus must be received from outside sources.

Dietary fat is another essential macronutrient that is responsible for many essential tasks like absorbing the fat-soluble vitamins (A, D, E and K), insulating body during cold weather, surviving long periods without food, protecting organs, supporting cell growth and inducing hormone production.

Usually, to stay healthy, lose weight and for some other reasons we are told to count the number of calories that we intake entirely, forgetting to tell to track macronutrient intake. Calculating and monitoring macronutrient intake can help not only with making health better and reaching fitness goals but can also help you understand which types of foods improve your performance and which are bad for you. If you would like to get such a calculator, you can type in a Google search, and there you will get lots of information on the topic.

Plant-Based Protein Sources

There is a common misconception that vegetarian and vegan diets might be lacking a sufficient amount of protein. However, many dietitians and scientists say that vegetarian or vegan diets have more than enough nutrients in them if planned well. Nevertheless, all foods are different in their protein values, there is food that contains more protein, and there are those that contain less.

Legumes or commonly known as beans have high amounts of protein per serving and contain 15 grams of protein per cooked cup. They are also a great source of iron, complex carbohydrates, folate, fiber, phosphorus, manganese, and potassium. It can be used in a variety of recipes or eaten without anything else.

Nutritional yeast is another excellent source of protein. It has 14 grams of protein per 28 grams. It is also a great source of copper, magnesium, zinc, manganese and all B vitamins. It can be used in a variety of dishes and is sold as flakes and yellow powder.

Seitan, also known as wheat meat or wheat gluten, is quite a popular source of protein. It is produced from gluten and contains about 25 grams of protein per 100 grams, which makes a very rich plant protein source. Seitan can be sautéed, fried, and even grilled and, thus, is easy to incorporate in your favorite recipes.

Next, come lentils. They have 18 grams of protein per cooked cup. They also can be added to a whole variety of dishes. Lentils are also rich in iron, manganese, and folate.

Tempeh, tofu, and edamame are another great source of protein. They are made from whole soybeans, which means they provide all the essential amino acids. All three have 10-19 grams of protein per 100 grams, calcium, and iron. Edamame needs to be steamed or boiled before eating and can be eaten without anything else or incorporated into soups and salads. Tofu and tempeh can also be used in lots of recipes.

Hempseed is another excellent source of protein. It contains 10 grams of protein per 28 grams. It is a good source of iron, magnesium, selenium, zinc, omega-3 and omega-6 fatty acids. It can be added to smoothies, salad dressings, morning muesli, and protein bars.

Spelled and teff are from an ancient grains category. Teff is gluten-free, whereas spelled contains gluten. They have 10–11 grams of protein per cooked cup. Spelled and teff are rich in iron, zinc, magnesium, selenium, manganese, phosphorus, fiber, B vitamins, and complex carbs. They can be used in a whole variety of dishes.

Spirulina is a blue-green alga and is rich in protein. Two tablespoons will provide 8 grams of protein. It will also cover 22% of the daily iron and thiamin need and 42% of the daily requirement of copper. It is also a good source of riboflavin, magnesium, manganese, essential fatty acids and potassium.

Green peas have 9 grams of protein per cooked cup in them. Green peas are the right choice to get magnesium, iron, zinc, phosphorus, B vitamins and copper. One serving of green peas has enough in it to cover 1/4 of the daily need for vitamin A, C, K, fiber, manganese, folate, and thiamine. It can be used in a whole variety of recipes.

Quinoa and amaranth are ancient or gluten-free grains. They provide 8–9 grams of protein per cooked cup and are complete sources of protein. Amaranth and quinoa are also a good source of iron, complex carbs, fiber, phosphorus, magnesium, and manganese. It can be used in a whole variety of recipes.

Ezekiel bread and other bread made from sprouted grains like wheat, millet, barley, spelled, soybeans, and lentils are excellent choices of protein. 2 slices of Ezekiel bread contain 8 grams of protein. Sprouting can increase the bread's vitamin C, folate, soluble fiber, beta-carotene content and vitamin E. It may also slightly reduce the gluten content. It can be used in a whole variety of recipes.

Soy milk contains 7 grams of protein per cup and thus a good source of protein, but it's also an excellent source of calcium, vitamin D, and vitamin B12, but only fortified milk contains vitamin B12, so make sure to buy that one. It can be consumed on its own or used in a variety of recipes.

Oats and oatmeal are standard in almost everyone's diet. ½ cup of dry oats provides 6 grams of protein and 4 grams of fiber. It is also a great source of zinc, folate, magnesium, and phosphorus. Oats and oatmeal contain higher-quality protein than rice and wheat. It can be ground into flour and used in a wide variety of recipes as flour and flakes.

Wild rice has more protein than other long-grain rice varieties, including brown rice and basmati. One cooked cup provides 7 grams of protein. It is also a good source of manganese, phosphorus fiber, copper, B vitamins and magnesium. Wild rice is not stripped of its bran and, thus, can contain arsenic in it. Therefore washing wild rice before cooking is a must, and boiling it in a large amount of water should reduce the possible level of arsenic. It can be used in a wide variety of recipes.

Chia seeds provide 6 grams of protein and 13 grams of fiber per 35 grams. They are also a good source of iron, selenium, calcium, magnesium, antioxidants, and omega-3 fatty acids. It can be used in a wide variety of recipes.

Nuts, seeds, and products from them provide between 5–7 grams of protein per 28 grams. They are also a great source of iron, healthy fats, calcium, fiber, phosphorus, magnesium, vitamin E selenium, specific B vitamins, and antioxidants.

Chapter 1

Almond Milk Quinoa

SERVINGS: 1

METHOD

1. Add quinoa, cinnamon, almond milk, vanilla, and nutmeg to a pan and bring to a boil.
2. Reduce the heat to a simmer and cook for 15 minutes, covered. When cooked, fluff with a fork.
3. Transfer the quinoa to a bowl. Serve topped with bananas and peanut butter.

INGREDIENTS

- ½ cup quinoa
- ¾ cup almond milk, canned
- 2 bananas, sliced
- 1 teaspoon cinnamon
- 2 tablespoons peanut butter
- 1 teaspoon vanilla
- 1 nutmeg, crushed

20 MINUTES

INGREDIENTS

- ½ CUP QUINOA
- 2 SWEET POTATOES, SLICED
- 1 RED BEET
- 2 TABLESPOONS RAW WALNUTS, CHOPPED
- 2 TABLESPOONS COCONUT OIL, MELTED
- 1 TABLESPOON OLIVE OIL
- 1 TEASPOON BALSAMIC VINEGAR
- 1 LEMON JUICE
- LEMON ZEST
- PEPPER, SALT, TO TASTE

Quinoa and Sweet Potatoes

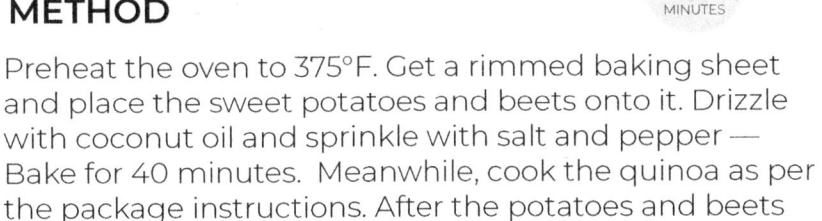

SERVINGS: 2

METHOD

Preheat the oven to 375°F. Get a rimmed baking sheet and place the sweet potatoes and beets onto it. Drizzle with coconut oil and sprinkle with salt and pepper — Bake for 40 minutes. Meanwhile, cook the quinoa as per the package instructions. After the potatoes and beets are baked, transfer them to a bowl to cool. Slice the beets into tiny pieces. Combine the prepared quinoa, beets, potatoes, and the rest of the ingredients in a large bowl, then serve.

40 MINUTES

Honey Buckwheat Coconut Porridge

SERVINGS: 2

METHOD

1. In a small pot, boil the coconut milk, honey, vanilla, and water. Stir in the ground buckwheat then reduce the heat to low.
2. Cook for 10 minutes, covered. Add extra liquid during the cooking if needed.
3. Transfer to a bowl and serve with shredded coconut, pecans, currants, and a drizzle of coconut syrup.

INGREDIENTS

- ¼ cup buckwheat, toasted, ground
- 1 tablespoon coconut, shredded
- 2 tablespoons pecans, chopped
- ½ cup + 2 tablespoons coconut milk
- 1 tablespoon raw honey
- ¾ teaspoon vanilla
- ¾ cup of water
- 2 tablespoons currants
- 1 drizzle coconut syrup

15 MINUTES

Tampeh and Potato

SERVINGS: 4

METHOD

1. Microwave the potatoes until done but still firm. Finely chop them when cool.
2. Preheat oil in a skillet over medium heat. Sauté onions until translucent. Add tempeh, potatoes and bell pepper and sauté, stirring constantly, over medium-high heat until golden brown.
3. Stir in the kale and seasoning, then cook, stirring constantly until the mixture is a bit browned. Occasionally add water to prevent sticking if necessary.
4. Sprinkle with pepper and salt to taste. Serve hot.

INGREDIENTS
- 1 package (8 oz) tempeh, finely diced
- 4 red potatoes
- 6 leaves lacinato kale, stemmed, chopped
- 2 tablespoons olive oil
- 1 medium onion, chopped
- 1 medium green bell pepper, diced
- 1 teaspoon smoked paprika
- 1 teaspoon seasoning, salt-free
- Ground pepper, salt, to taste

Breackfast French Toast

SERVINGS: 1

METHOD

Preheat the oven to 375°F. Get a rimmed baking sheet and place the sweet potatoes and beets onto it. Drizzle with coconut oil and sprinkle with salt and pepper — Bake for 40 minutes. Meanwhile, cook the quinoa as per the package instructions. After the potatoes and beets are baked, transfer them to a bowl to cool. Slice the beets into tiny pieces. Combine the prepared quinoa, beets, potatoes, and the rest of the ingredients in a large bowl, then serve.

INGREDIENTS
- 2 SLICES BREAD, GLUTEN-FREE
- 2 TEASPOONS CINNAMON
- 2 TABLESPOONS FLAXSEED, GROUND
- 6 OZ. SOY MILK
- 2 TEASPOONS VANILLA EXTRACT
- 1 SCOOP VEGAN PROTEIN POWDER

Breakfast French Toast

SERVINGS: 1

METHOD

1. Mix cinnamon, flaxseed, soy milk, vanilla extract, and protein powder in a deep baking dish. Deep the bread slices into the mixture to coat.
2. Preheat a non-stick frying pan over medium heat and toast the bread for 3 minutes per side. Enjoy!

INGREDIENTS

2 SLICES BREAD, GLUTEN-FREE
2 TEASPOONS CINNAMON
2 TABLESPOONS FLAXSEED, GROUND
6 OZ. SOY MILK
2 TEASPOONS VANILLA EXTRACT
1 SCOOP VEGAN PROTEIN POWDER

Dairy-Free Pumpkin Pancakes

SERVINGS: 12

METHOD

Combine almond milk and vinegar in a bowl. Let rest for 5 minutes. Mix flour, baking powder, baking soda, chia seeds, pumpkin pie spice, and salt in a separate bowl Whisk eggs into the almond milk, then stir in pumpkin puree, coconut oil, vanilla, and maple syrup. Pour the wet ingredients into the dry ingredients and mix until blended. Add in more almond milk if the batter is thick.
5. Place a non-stick frying pan over medium heat. Scoop out 1/3 of the batter and pour it into the pan. Cook for 1 minute, then flip to the other side and cook until golden brown. Do this with the remaining batter and serve.

INGREDIENTS

1-cup all-purpose flour, 2 teaspoons baking Powder, ½ cup pumpkin puree, 1 egg, 3 tablespoons chia seeds, 3 tablespoons coconut oil, melted, slightly cooled, 1 cup almond milk, 2 teaspoons vanilla extract, 1 tablespoon white vinegar, 1 tablespoon maple syrup, 1 teaspoon pumpkin pie spice, ½ teaspoon kosher salt

Protein Bluebarry Bars

SERVINGS: 16

METHOD

In a bowl, mix rolled oats, blueberries, almonds, flaxseed, walnuts, sunflower seeds, pistachios and pepitas together. Stir in apple sauce and maple syrup. Mix in almond butter, then pour the batter into a baking sheet lined with parchment paper (paper should be big enough to cover and hang over the baking sheet edges). Firmly press down the batter using your palms, then spread evenly.
Refrigerate for 1 hour. Remove from the freezer afterward and lift the batter from pan by lifting from the paper. Place on a working surface and gently remove the paper. Cut the dough into 16 bars and serve.

INGREDIENTS

- ½ cup dried blueberries
- 1 ½ cups rolled oats
- ¾ cup whole almonds
- 1/3 cup ground flaxseed
- 1/3 cup walnuts
- ¼ cup sunflower seeds
- ½ cup pistachios
- 1/3 cup pepitas
- ¼ cup apple sauce
- 1/3 cup maple syrup
- 1 cup almond butter

Chickpea Scramble Breakfast Basin

SERVINGS: 2

METHOD

Scoop out the chickpeas and a little bit of its water into a bowl. Slightly mash the chickpeas using a fork, intentionally omitting some. Stir in turmeric, pepper and salt until adequately combined. Sauté onions in olive oil until soft, then add garlic and cook for 1 minute. Stir in the chickpeas and sauté for 5 minutes.
For breakfast basin and serving: Get 2 breakfast basins. Layer the bottom of the basins with the combined greens. Top with chickpea scramble, parsley, and cilantro. Enjoy with avocado wedges.

INGREDIENTS

FOR CHICKPEA SCRAMBLE:
1 can (15 oz.) chickpeas, A drizzle olive oil, ¼ white onion, diced, 2 garlic cloves, minced, ½ teaspoon turmeric, ½ teaspoon pepper, ½ teaspoon salt
For breakfast basin:
1 avocado, wedged, Greens, combined, Handful parsley, minced, Handful cilantro, minced

Quinoa, Oats, Hazelnut and Blueberry Salad

SERVES
8

🕐 **35 MINUTES**

INGREDIENTS

- 1 cup golden quinoa, dry
- 1 cup oats, cut into pieces
- 2 cups blueberries
- 2 cups hazelnuts, roughly chopped, toasted
- ½ cup dry millet
- 2 large lemons, zested, juiced
- 3 tablespoons olive oil, divided
- ½ cup maple syrup
- 1 cup Greek yogurt
- 1 (1-inch) piece fresh ginger, peeled, cut
- ¼ teaspoon nutmeg

METHOD

Combine quinoa, oats and millet in a large bowl. Rinse, drain and set aside. Add one tablespoon olive oil into a saucepan and place over medium-high heat. Cook the rinsed grains in it for 3 minutes. Add 4 ½ cups water and salt. Add the zest of 1 lemon and ginger. When the mixture boils, cover the pot and cook in reduced heat for 20 minutes.

Remove from heat. Let rest for 5 minutes. Uncover and fluff with a fork. Discard the ginger and layer the grains on a large baking sheet. Let cool for 30 minutes. Transfer the grains into a large bowl and mix in the remaining lemon zest. Combine the juice of both lemons with the remaining olive oil in a separate bowl. Stir in the yogurt, maple syrup, and nutmeg. Pour the mixture into the grains and stir. Mix in the blueberries and hazelnuts. Refrigerate overnight, then serve.

Buttered Overnight Oats

INGREDIENTS

- ¾ cup rolled oats
- ½ teaspoon cinnamon
- 2 tablespoons chia seeds
- 1 ripe banana, mashed
- 2 tablespoons peanut butter
- ½ cup + 1 tbsp. water
- 1 cup vanilla almond milk, unsweetened
- 2 tablespoons maple syrup
- 1 pinch salt

SERVINGS: 1

5 MINUTES

METHOD

1. Get a mason jar and add oats, cinnamon, chia seeds and salt to it. Combine properly. Stir in almond milk, mashed banana, and ½ cup water.
2. Mix peanut butter and 1 tablespoon water in a bowl then add into the jar and stir. Stir in the maple syrup and refrigerate overnight. Serve.

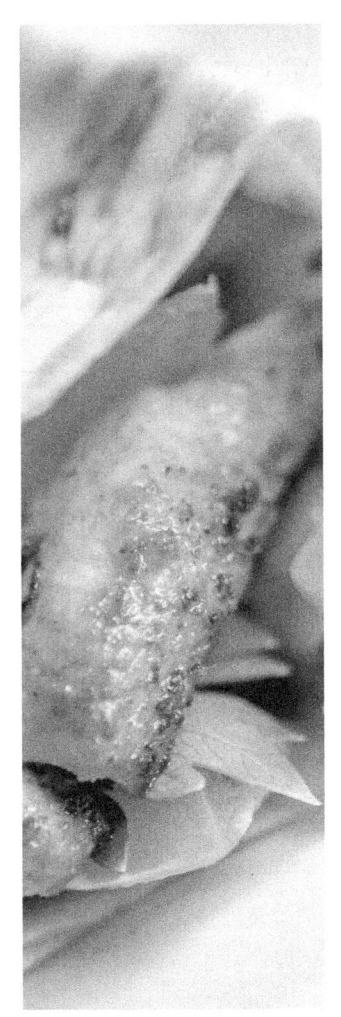

Protein Breakfast Burrito

SERVINGS: 4

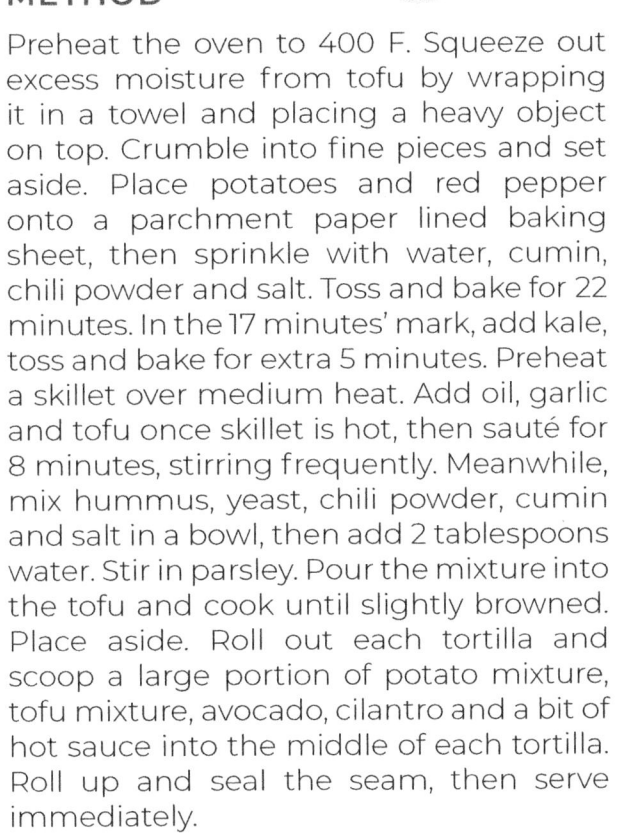

30 MINUTES

METHOD

Preheat the oven to 400 F. Squeeze out excess moisture from tofu by wrapping it in a towel and placing a heavy object on top. Crumble into fine pieces and set aside. Place potatoes and red pepper onto a parchment paper lined baking sheet, then sprinkle with water, cumin, chili powder and salt. Toss and bake for 22 minutes. In the 17 minutes' mark, add kale, toss and bake for extra 5 minutes. Preheat a skillet over medium heat. Add oil, garlic and tofu once skillet is hot, then sauté for 8 minutes, stirring frequently. Meanwhile, mix hummus, yeast, chili powder, cumin and salt in a bowl, then add 2 tablespoons water. Stir in parsley. Pour the mixture into the tofu and cook until slightly browned. Place aside. Roll out each tortilla and scoop a large portion of potato mixture, tofu mixture, avocado, cilantro and a bit of hot sauce into the middle of each tortilla. Roll up and seal the seam, then serve immediately.

INGREDIENTS

For tofu:

- 1 package (12 oz.) firm tofu
- ¼ cup parsley, minced
- 1 tablespoon hummus
- 1 teaspoon oil
- 1 teaspoon nutritional yeast
- ½ teaspoon cumin
- ½ teaspoon chili powder
- ¼ teaspoon salt
- 3 garlic cloves

For vegetables:

- 5 baby potatoes, sliced into pieces
- 2 cups kale, chopped
- 1 tablespoon water
- 1 medium red bell pepper, sliced thin
- ½ teaspoon ground cumin
- ½ teaspoon chili powder
- 1 pinch salt

For assembling: 4 large tortillas, 1 medium avocado, ripe, chopped, Hot sauce, Cilantro

Breakfast Hummus Toast

SERVINGS: 1

5 MINUTES

METHOD

Top the toasted breads with hummus, sunflower seeds and hemp seeds. Enjoy!

INGREDIENTS

- 2 slices wheat bread, sprouted, toasted
- ¼ cup hummus
- 1 tablespoon sunflower seeds, unsalted, roasted
- 1 tablespoon hemp seeds

INGREDIENTS

- 2 bananas, frozen
- ¾ cup almond milk
- 2 tablespoons peanut butter
- 2 tablespoons cacao powder

For topping:

- ½ banana, sliced
- Chocolate granola

Almond Milk Banana Smoothie

SERVINGS: 1

5 MINUTES

METHOD

1. Blend bananas, almond milk, peanut butter and cacao powder in a blender until smooth.
2. Transfer to a bowl and top with sliced banana and granola. Enjoy!

Nutritious Toasted Chickpeas

SERVINGS: 2

50 - 60 MINUTES

METHOD

Heat olive oil in a frying pan. Sauté shallots, stirring frequently until almost translucent. Add garlic then sauté until garlic is softened. Add the spices into the pan. Cook for 1 minute, stirring frequently. Add the tomatoes into the pan. Add some water, then cook on medium-low heat until a thick sauce forms. Stir in the chickpeas and cook for 3 minutes, then sprinkle with black pepper, sugar and salt. Top toasted bread with the chickpeas mixture and serve.

INGREDIENTS

2 cup chickpeas, cooked, 6 bread slices, toasted 2 large tomatoes, skinned, chopped, 2 tablespoons olive oil, 3 small shallots, diced, ½ teaspoon cinnamon, ¼ teaspoon smoked paprika, ½ teaspoon sweet paprika, 2 large garlic cloves, diced, ½ teaspoon sugar, Black pepper, to taste, ½ teaspoon salt

Almond Milk Chai Quinoa

INGREDIENTS

- ½ cup quinoa, rinsed
- 1 cup almond milk
- 1 chai tea bag

SERVINGS: 1

30 MINUTES

METHOD

1. Combine quinoa, almond milk and chai tea bag in a pan and bring to a boil. Remove the tea bag then reduce the heat. Cook, covered, for 20 minutes.
2. Remove from fire and leave covered 10 minutes. Enjoy!

Tomato Tofu Breakfast Tacos

SERVES 14

20 MINUTES

METHOD

1. Heat olive oil over medium heat in a large frying pan. Sauté the red onion and poblano pepper for 5 minutes.
2. In the meantime, blend the Roma tomatoes until properly chopped, but not thoroughly blended. Set aside.
3. To the frying pan, add smoked paprika, chili powder, red pepper and salt. Sauté for 1 minute. Add the Roma tomatoes and stir. Stir in the crumbled tofu, then cook for 10 minutes, stirring infrequently. Add the lime juice and cook for 1 minute. Remove from heat and season with ¼ teaspoon salt.
4. Top each tortilla with the tofu mixture and mashed avocado then enjoy.

INGREDIENTS

- 10 small corn tortillas, warmed
- 1 block (16 oz.) firm tofu, sprouted, drained, rinsed, crumbled
- 3 Roma tomatoes
- ½ tablespoon olive oil
- 1 lime juice
- ½ medium red onions, diced
- 1 tablespoon paprika, smoked
- 1 red bell pepper, roasted, chopped
- 1 poblano pepper, cored, diced
- 1 tablespoon chili powder
- ¾ teaspoon salt + ¼ tsp. to taste

For toppings: 1 ripe avocado, peeled, mashed with lime juice + salt

Peanut Butter Oats

SERVINGS: 2
METHOD

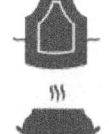

1. In a bowl, stir the oats, almond milk, peanut butter, and protein powder together.
2. Cover and refrigerate for 2 hours. Serve afterward.

INGREDIENTS

- 1 cup rolled oats
- 2 tablespoons peanut butter
- 1 ½ cups almond milk
- 1 scoop vanilla protein powder

INGREDIENTS

- 1 CUP ALL-PURPOSE FLOUR
- ¼ CUP BROWN RICE PROTEIN POWDER
- 1 TABLESPOON BAKING POWDER
- 2 TABLESPOONS MAPLE SYRUP
- 1 CUP OF WATER
- ½ TEASPOON SALT

Protein Pancakes

SERVINGS: 6
METHOD

1. In a bowl, combine all dry ingredients.
2. Mix in maple syrup and water, plus more water if necessary.
3. Preheat a non-stick frying pan over medium heat. Scoop a portion of the mixture into the pan and cook until bubbles form in the center of the pancake. Flip and cook for several more minutes. Do this with the remaining pancakes batter and enjoy!

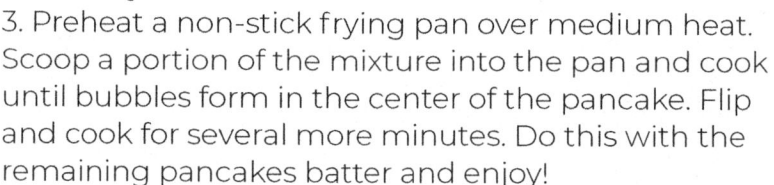

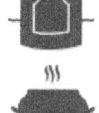

Savory Vegan Omelet

SERVINGS: 1
METHOD

Preheat the oven to 375 F. Heat an oven-safe skillet over medium heat then add olive oil and garlic. Cook garlic for 2 minutes. Add garlic and the remaining ingredients (except for the vegetables) to a food processor and mix until smooth and combined. Add 1 ½ tablespoons water. Set aside. Add more olive oil to the skillet. Add the vegetables and sprinkle with pepper and salt. Cook until done, then set aside. Turn off the heat. Ensure the skillet is coated with enough oil. Add ¼ of the vegetables and add the tofu mixture on top. Spread the tofu mixture across the entire skillet using a spoon but don't create gaps in it. Place on the stove and cook over medium heat for 5 minutes. Bake in the oven for 15 minutes. In the 13 minutes' mark, add the remaining vegetables on top the omelet and cook for extra 2 minutes. Remove from the oven. Fold over with a spatula and serve.

INGREDIENTS

For the Omelet:
- ¾ cup (5 oz.) firm tofu, drained, patted dry
- 1 teaspoon cornstarch
- 2 tablespoons nutritional yeast
- Olive oil
- 2 garlic cloves, minced
- ¼ teaspoon paprika
- Black pepper and salt

For the filling:
- 1 cup veggies (tomato, spinach, etc.), sliced

Protein Patties

SERVINGS: 5

METHOD

Preheat the oven to 300 F. Pulse all the ingredients in a food processor until smooth. Set aside. Brush the skillet with vegetable oil and place over medium heat. SPoon the mixture into the skillet. Shape into a patty using the back of the spoon, then season with salt, pepper, and paprika. Cook for 7 minutes flip over and cook for extra 7 minutes. Transfer to a baking sheet and bake for 15 minutes. Serve warm.

INGREDIENTS
- 1 can (15 oz.) chickpeas
- 1 teaspoon fennel seeds
- 1 teaspoon caraway seeds
- 1 tablespoon ground flax seeds
- 1 tablespoon tamari
- 2 tablespoons water
- 2 garlic cloves, peeled, chopped
- 1 teaspoon turmeric
- 1 teaspoon dried sage
- Pepper, salt, to taste

Vegan Chickpea Pancake

SERVINGS: 2

METHOD

1. Preheat a skillet over medium heat.
2. Mix the chickpea flour, baking powder, garlic powder, pepper, and salt in a bowl. Stir in the water. Mix for 15 seconds, then stir in onions and pepper.
3. Spray the skillet with non-stick cooking spray.
4. Pour in the batter and spread it out. Cook for 6 minutes flip carefully to the other side and cook for 5 minutes.
5. Serve with the desired toppings.

INGREDIENTS
- ½ cup chickpea flour
- ¼ teaspoon baking powder
- ½ cup + 2 tablespoons water
- 1 green onion, finely chopped
- ¼ cup red pepper, finely chopped
- 1/8 teaspoon ground black pepper
- ¼ teaspoon garlic powder
- ¼ teaspoon salt

Protein Pudding

SERVINGS: 1

METHOD

1. Combine all the ingredients in a jar. Close the lid and refrigerate for 2 hours.
2. Remove from the fridge and serve.

INGREDIENTS
- ¼ cup quinoa, cooked
- 2 tablespoons chia seeds
- 2 tablespoons hemp hearts
- ¾ cup cashew milk
- 2 tablespoons maple syrup
- ¼ teaspoon vanilla powder
- 1 pinch cinnamon

Gluten-Free Tofu Quiche

SERVINGS
8

90 MINUTES

INGREDIENTS

For the crust:
- 3 potatoes, grated
- 2 tablespoons vegan butter, melted
- ¼ teaspoon of sea salt
- ¼ teaspoon pepper

For the filling:
- 12 oz. extra-firm silken tofu, patted dry
- 1 cup broccoli, chopped
- ¾ cup cherry tomatoes halved
- 3 tablespoons hummus
- 2 tablespoons nutritional yeast
- 1 medium onion, diced
- 3 garlic cloves, chopped
- Black pepper, salt, to taste

METHOD

Preheat the oven to 450 F. Lightly spray a 10-inch pie pan with non-stick spray. Place 3 cups of grated potatoes onto a clean towel and squeeze out the excess moisture. Transfer to the pie pan. Drizzle with melted butter and sprinkle with salt and pepper. Toss to coat. Using your fingers, gently press the content into an even layer. Place into the oven and bake for 30 minutes. Take out the crust and set aside. Reduce the oven temperature to 400 F. Add vegetables and garlic to the baking sheet. Sprinkle with 2 tablespoons of olive oil, pepper, and salt. Toss properly to coat. Bake for 30 minutes, then set aside. Set the oven to 375°F. Mix tofu, hummus, nutritional yeast, black pepper and salt in a food processor.
Transfer the baked vegetables to a bowl. Add the tofu mixture and toss to coat. Add the mixture to the potato crust, then spread into an even layer.
Bake for 40 minutes at 375°F. Serve warm.

Pumpkin Oatmeal

INGREDIENTS

- ½ cup rolled oats
- ¼ cup pumpkin puree
- ½ cup almond milk
- ¼ teaspoon vanilla extract
- 3 tablespoon PB2
- ¼ teaspoon instant coffee granules
- ½ cup water + more if needed
- ½ teaspoon pumpkin pie spice
- Pinch of salt

SERINGS: 2

5 MINUTES

METHOD

1. Boil ½ cup milk + ½ cup water in a pan, then add oats. Cook for 2 minutes in medium heat. Stir in the pumpkin puree and cook for several minutes more.
2. Meanwhile, gradually add water to the PB2 and mix until you get the desired consistency. Add coffee, stir well to combine, and set aside.
3. As the liquid gets dissolved, stir in vanilla extract, pumpkin pie spice and a pinch of salt.
4. Once cooked to your desire, transfer to a bowl. Top with PB2 mixture and serve.

Breakfast Berry Quinoa

SERVINGS: 4

20 MINUTES

METHOD

1. Preheat the oven to 350 F and roast pecans for 6 minutes. Set aside for topping.
2. In a medium saucepan placed over high heat, bring water, milk, and quinoa to a bowl. Lower the temperature to medium-low and cook for 15 minutes, covered.
3. Remove from heat and let stand for 15 minutes, covered. Mix in the blackberries and cinnamon. Share the quinoa among four plates. Serve with pecan topping and a drizzle of agave nectar.

INGREDIENTS

- 1 cup quinoa, rinsed
- 2 cups fresh blackberries
- 1/3 cup pecans, chopped, toasted
- 4 teaspoons organic agave nectar
- 1 cup low-fat milk
- 1 cup of water½ teaspoon ground cinnamon

Bean Lentil Salad with Lime Dressing

SERVINGS: 5

⏱ 20 MINUTES

INGREDIENTS

- 1 cup green lentils, uncooked
- 15 oz. can black beans, rinsed, drained
- 2 Roma tomatoes, finely diced
- 2/3 cup cilantro, stemmed, roughly chopped
- ½ small red onion, finely diced
- 1 red bell pepper, finely diced

For the dressing:

- 1 lime, juiced
- 1 teaspoon Dijon mustard
- 2 garlic cloves, minced
- ½ teaspoon oregano
- 1 teaspoon cumin
- 1/8 teaspoon salt

METHOD

1. Cook lentils according to package instructions. Drain.
2. Mix all dressing ingredients in a small bowl and set aside.
3. Add the black beans, lentils, tomatoes, bell pepper and onions into a bowl. Sprinkle the dressing on top and toss to coat. Add the cilantro and toss lightly. Enjoy!

Lentil Arugula Salad

SERVINGS: 2

⏱ 7 MINUTES

INGREDIENTS

- 1 cup (15 oz) brown lentils, cooked
- 1 handful arugula, washed
- ¾ cup (100g) cashews
- 6 sun-dried tomatoes in oil, chopped
- 3 whole-wheat bread sliced, cut big pieces
- 2 tablespoons balsamic vinegar
- 3 tablespoons olive oil
- 1 onion
- 1 jalapeno pepper, chopped
- Pepper and salt, to taste

METHOD

Place a frying pan over low heat and roast the cashews for 3 minutes. Transfer to a salad bowl. Sauté onions in 1/3 olive oil for 3 minutes on low heat. Add jalapeno and dried tomatoes and cook for about 2 minutes. Transfer to a bowl. Add the remaining olive oil to the pan and fry the bread until crunchy. Sprinkle with pepper and salt. Set aside.   Add arugula to the bowl containing sautéed tomato mixture. Add lentils and toss to combine — season with pepper, salt and balsamic vinegar.
Serve with the crunchy bread.

Red Cabbage and Cucumber Salad with Seitan

SERVINGS: 1-2

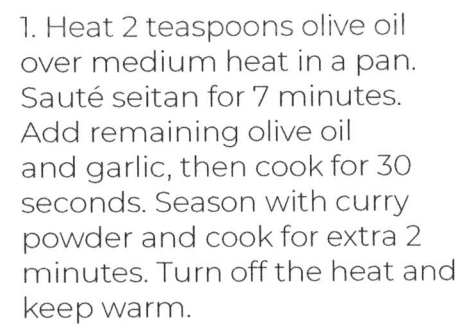

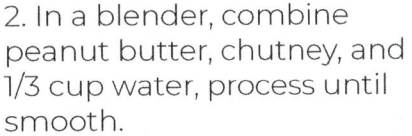

10 MINUTES

METHOD

1. Heat 2 teaspoons olive oil over medium heat in a pan. Sauté seitan for 7 minutes. Add remaining olive oil and garlic, then cook for 30 seconds. Season with curry powder and cook for extra 2 minutes. Turn off the heat and keep warm.
2. In a blender, combine peanut butter, chutney, and 1/3 cup water, process until smooth.
3. Place cabbage and cucumber into a bowl. Drizzle with the peanut butter mixture and toss properly. Top with seitan and green onions and serve.

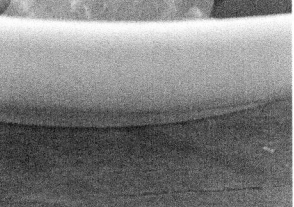

INGREDIENTS

For the salad:
- ½ small head red cabbage, shredded
- 1 package (8 oz.) seitan, cut into strips
- 1 small cucumber, sliced
- 3 green onions, thinly sliced
- 1 tablespoon olive oil
- 3 garlic cloves, minced
- ¾ teaspoon mild curry powder

For the dressing:
- 1/3 cup mango chutney
- 1/3 cup peanut butter

Protein Packed Chickpeas & Kidney Beans Salad

SERVINGS: 2

5 MINUTES

METHOD

1. Sauté onions in 1 tablespoon olive oil until golden. Add ginger, garlic, and chili and sauté till garlic is fragrant. Set aside to cool.
2. In a salad bowl, combine chickpeas, kidney beans, feta cheese, scallions, parsley, lemon juice, pepper, salt, cooled garlic mixture, and some olive oil. Toss well to combine correctly and enjoy!

INGREDIENTS

- 1 can chickpeas, drained, rinsed
- 1 can red kidney beans, drained, rinsed
- ½ cup feta cheese, crumbled
- 1 cup parsley, chopped
- Olive oil
- 1 lemon juice
- 3 scallions, chopped
- 1 small ginger, grated
- 1 medium onion, diced
- 2 garlic cloves, minced
- 1 pinch red chili flakes
- Black pepper and salt

Quick Chickpeas & Spinach Salad

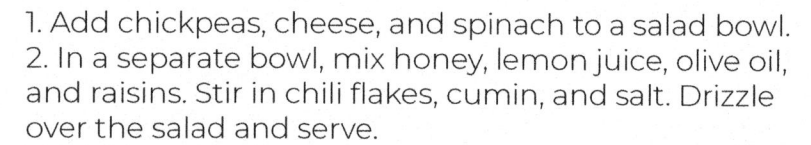

SERVINGS: 2

⏱ 7 MINUTES

METHOD

1. Add chickpeas, cheese, and spinach to a salad bowl.
2. In a separate bowl, mix honey, lemon juice, olive oil, and raisins. Stir in chili flakes, cumin, and salt. Drizzle over the salad and serve.

INGREDIENTS
- 1 can chickpeas, drained, rinsed
- 1 handful spinach
- 1 small handful raisins
- 3.5 oz. feta cheese, chopped
- 4 tablespoons olive oil
- 3 teaspoons honey
- ½ tablespoon lemon juice
- ½ teaspoon chili flakes
- ½ teaspoon cumin
- 1 pinch salt

Carrot Slaw & Tempeh Triangles

SERVINGS: 4

⏱ 5 MINUTES

METHOD

1. Heat olive oil in a skillet over high heat. Once hot, add tempeh, 1 ½ tbsp. Maple syrup and soy sauce. Cook for 5 minutes, flipping occasionally until the liquid is absorbed. Remove from heat and sprinkle with crushed walnut and pepper. Set aside and keep warm.
2. Toss carrots, tahini, lemon juice, remaining maple syrup, parsley, onions and spices in a mixing bowl for some minutes. Season with pepper and salt to taste.
3. Transfer to a serving bowl. Top with tempeh triangles and serve.

INGREDIENTS

8 oz tempeh, sliced into triangles, 4 cups carrots, shredded, ½ cup parsley, finely chopped, 1 tablespoon raw walnuts, crushed, 3 tablespoons grade B maple syrup, 1 teaspoon olive oil, ¼ cup lemon juice, 2 teaspoons soy sauce, 1 small onion, diced, 2 tablespoons tahini, 1/8 teaspoon black pepper, 1 tablespoon curry powder, Pepper and salt, to taste

---

Chili Tofu

SERVINGS: 8

⏱ 50 MINUTES

METHOD

Sauté tofu in vegetable oil over medium-high heat for 3 minutes.
Add in the onions, green pepper, mushrooms, garlic, cayenne, cumin, chili powder, pepper, and salt and cook for 5 minutes. Stir in tomato sauce, kidney beans, diced tomatoes with the liquid, and bring everything to a simmer. Cover and cook for an extra 45 minutes. Serve.

INGREDIENTS

1 package (14 oz.) firm tofu, 1 can (28 oz.) kidney beans, drained, 1 cup mushrooms, sliced, 1 can (28 oz.) tomatoes with liquid, diced, 1 can (14 oz.) tomato sauce, 3 tablespoons vegetable oil, 1 green bell pepper, diced, 1 onion, diced, ¼ teaspoon cayenne pepper, 3 tablespoons chili powder, ½ teaspoon cumin, 3 garlic cloves, minced, Pepper and salt, to taste

Lentil Soup (Vegan)

SERVINGS: 4

METHOD

1. Sauté onions and carrots in vegetable oil for 5 minutes. Mix in vegetable broth, lentils, bay leaves, pepper, and salt, stir well to combine.
2. Lower the heat to a simmer. Cook for 45 minutes, covered. Discard the bay leaves and serve.

INGREDIENTS
- 1 cup dry brown lentils
- 1 carrot, sliced
- 2 bay leaves
- 1 teaspoon vegetable oil
- 4 cups vegetable broth
- 1 onion, sliced
- ¼ teaspoon thyme, dried
- Pepper and salt, to taste

50 MINUTES

Hot Black Beans and Potato

SERVINGS: 5

METHOD

1. Cook garlic and onions in olive oil for 2 minutes. Add potatoes and carrots and cook for 6 minutes.
2. Lower the heat to medium-low and stir in the remaining ingredients. Cook for about 25 minutes, partially covered and stirring infrequently. Once done, serve.

INGREDIENTS

1 can (15 oz.) black beans, 2 small sweet potatoes, peeled, chopped, 2 medium carrots, sliced, 1 can (15 oz.) tomato sauce, 2 tablespoons olive oil, ½ cup of water, 1 small onion, diced, 2 garlic cloves, minced, 1/2 teaspoon cayenne, ½ teaspoon garlic powder, 1 tablespoon chili powder, 1 teaspoon cumin, ¼ teaspoon black pepper, ½ teaspoon salt

25 MINUTES

Low-Fat Bean Soup

SERVINGS: 4

METHOD

1. Pulse 1 can beans in a food processor until almost smooth.
2. Pour the mixture into a saucepan. Add the remaining can beans, vegetable broth, salsa, and chili powder into the pan.
2. Bring to a boil, and remove from the heat. Serve and enjoy!

INGREDIENTS
- 2 cans (15 oz each) black beans, undrained
- ½ cup of salsa
- 16 oz. vegetable broth
- 1 tablespoon chili powder

10 MINUTES

Protein Rich Vegetable Minestrone

INGREDIENTS
- ¼ cup white quinoa, uncooked
- 1 can (28 oz.) tomatoes, diced
- 1 cup carrots, sliced
- 1 ½ cups asparagus, chopped
- 1 cup packed kale, chopped
- ½ cup frozen peas
- 1 cup zucchini, chopped
- 2 bay leaves
- 1 tablespoon olive oil
- 4 cups of water
- 1 small white onion, diced
- 3 garlic cloves, minced
- 2 teaspoons Italian seasoning
- Pepper and salt, to taste

SERVings: 6

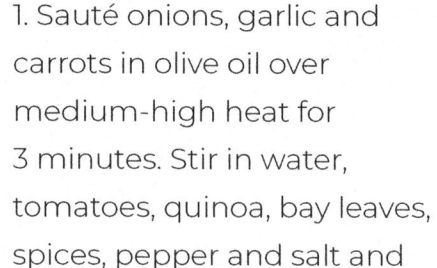

30 MINUTES

METHOD

1. Sauté onions, garlic and carrots in olive oil over medium-high heat for 3 minutes. Stir in water, tomatoes, quinoa, bay leaves, spices, pepper and salt and bring to a boil. Cover and simmer for 20 minutes.
2. Add the remaining vegetable and cook for 10 minutes. Taste and adjust seasonings if needed and serve hot.

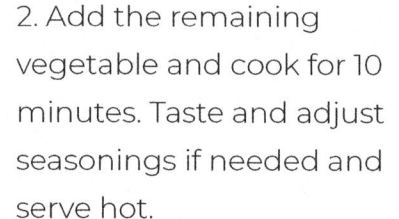

Quinoa P

SERVings: 4

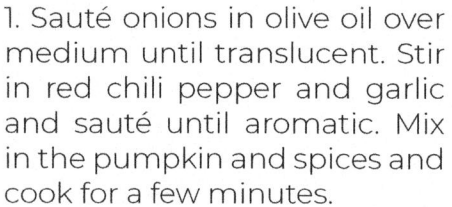

25 MINUTES

METHOD

1. Sauté onions in olive oil over medium until translucent. Stir in red chili pepper and garlic and sauté until aromatic. Mix in the pumpkin and spices and cook for a few minutes.
2. Pour in quinoa and 2 cups vegetable broth, then bring to a boil. Cook for extra 5 minutes, then add the remaining vegetable broth and cook until boiled. Stir in beans and bay leaves. Lower the heat and simmer for 10 minutes. Serve with avocados.

INGREDIENTS
- ½ cup quinoa
- 20 oz. can black beans, rinsed, drained
- 3 cups pumpkin, cubed
- 2 bay leaves
- 5 cups vegetable broth
- 1 tablespoon olive oil
- 1 onion, diced
- 5 garlic cloves, diced
- 1 red chili pepper, diced
- ½ teaspoon dried oregano
- 1 teaspoon ground cumin
- ½ teaspoon red pepper flakes, crushed

Red Lentil Soup with Farro

INGREDIENTS

- ½ cup red lentils
- ½ cup quick-cook farro
- 1 cup kale, stemmed, chopped
- 1 cup carrots, grated
- 2 tablespoons olive oil
- 5 cups vegetable broth
- 1 small onion, grated
- 1 small zucchini, grated
- 1 ½ teaspoon turmeric
- ½ teaspoon cumin
- ¼ teaspoon pepper
- 1 ½ teaspoons salt

For breadcrumbs:
- Eight slices French baguette, cubed
- Olive oil
- One garlic clove, minced
- Salt, to taste

SERVings: 4

32 MINUTES

METHOD

2. Add the chicken broth and bring everything to a boil. Add lentils and farro and cook for about 20 minutes over low heat.
3. In the meantime, pulse bread and garlic in a food processor until done. Transfer to a baking sheet and sprinkle with olive oil and salt — Bake for 7 minutes.
4. Once the lentil soup has cooked for 15 minutes, add kale and cook for 5 minutes. Serve topped with the breadcrumbs.

Moroccan Pumpkin Soup

SERVings: 4-5

50 MINUTES

METHOD

1. Cook garlic, onions and salt in olive oil over low heat for 3 minutes. Add all the spices and sauté until fragrant.
2. Stir in pumpkin, carrots, and peas. Pour in 6 cups of water and bring to a boil. Simmer for extra 30 minutes. Remove and discard the cinnamon stick.
3. Using an immersion blender, puree the soup until smooth, then let cool. Stir in the miso paste and serve just after that.

INGREDIENTS

- 3 lbs pumpkin, peeled, seeded, chopped
- 2 carrots, roughly chopped
- 1/3 cup split peas
- 3 tablespoons olive oil
- 3 tablespoons white miso paste
- 1 onion, diced
- 1 cinnamon stick
- 1 chili, finely chopped
- 1 garlic, finely chopped
- 1 small ginger, thinly sliced
- 1 ½ teaspoons cumin seeds

Mexican Chickpea & Tomatillos Pozole

INGREDIENTS

- 1 ½ cups chickpeas, cooked
- 10 tomatillos, peeled, washed
- 2 cups of water
- 1 cup cilantro, chopped
- 4 garlic cloves
- ¼ onion, sliced
- 1 whole serrano chile
- 1 teaspoon salt, or to taste

SERVings: 2-4

20 MINUTES

METHOD

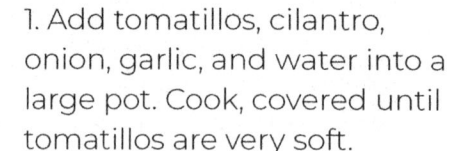

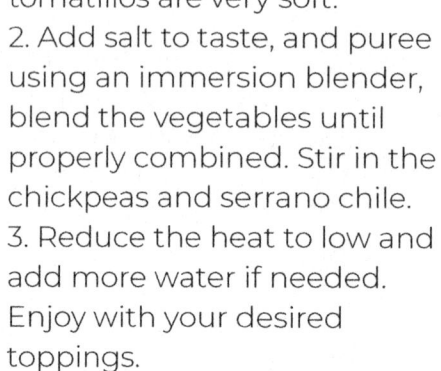

1. Add tomatillos, cilantro, onion, garlic, and water into a large pot. Cook, covered until tomatillos are very soft.
2. Add salt to taste, and puree using an immersion blender, blend the vegetables until properly combined. Stir in the chickpeas and serrano chile.
3. Reduce the heat to low and add more water if needed. Enjoy with your desired toppings.

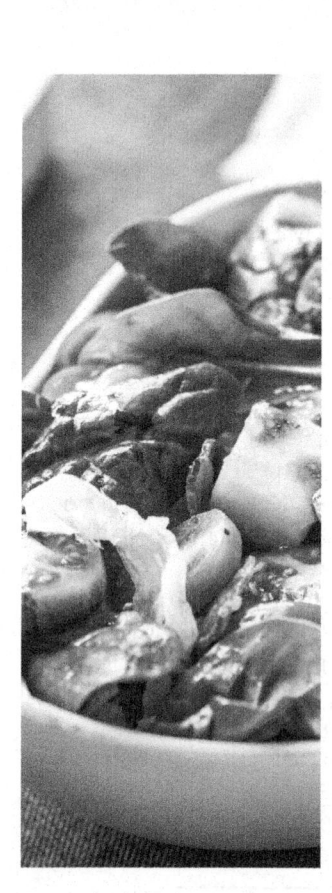

Tofu Bacon Bean Salad

SERVINGS: 4

15 MINUTES

METHOD

1. Divide all the ingredients between 4 plates and drizzle with lime juice dressing.
2. Toss well to combined. Enjoy immediately.

INGREDIENTS

- 12 slices Tofu Bacon, cut into pieces
- 1 can black beans, drained
- 1 large head romaine lettuce, washed, chopped
- 1 avocado, sliced
- 1 can organic corn
- 24 cherry tomatoes
- ½ cup cilantro, chopped
- Fresh lime juice, for dressing

Vegan French Onion Soup

SERVES
2-4

115 MINUTES

INGREDIENTS

For caramelized onions:
- 4 white onions
- ¼ cup olive oil

For the soup:
- 4 yellow onions
- 1 ½ cups French green lentils
- 1 cup fennel stalks, cut into thin slices
- 1 tablespoon tarragon leaves
- 1 bay leaf
- 3 vegetable bouillon cube, salt-free
- 2 tablespoons + ¼ cup olive oil
- 8 cups of water
- 6 tablespoons dry white wine
- 1 tablespoon Sherry vinegar
- 1 tablespoon fresh lemon juice
- ½ teaspoon black pepper
- 1 tablespoon + 1 teaspoon salt
- 2 tablespoons fresh thyme
- 2 garlic cloves, minced

METHOD

For the onions:

1. Slice onions into thin half circles. Cook on medium heat, infrequently stirring, for 20 minutes (without oil).
2. Pour in ¼ cup olive oil. Scrape the bottom of the pan using a wooden spatula. Stir and reduce the heat to medium-low. Cook for 20 minutes, stirring infrequently. Set aside.

For the soup:

1. In a separate pan, add one tablespoon wine. Deglaze the pan by scraping the bottom of the pan with a wooden spatula. Let rest for 10 minutes.
2. Pour in 2 more tablespoons wine, deglaze and cook for 10 minutes. Add an extra tablespoon wine, deglaze and turn the heat offseason with salt.
3. Combine lentils, water, bay leaf, and two sprigs thyme in a large pot. Cook until it boils. Simmer on medium-low heat for extra 20 minutes. Remove and discard the bay leaf and thyme sprigs.
4. Meanwhile, sauté sliced fennel stalks and garlic in olive oil over medium-low heat until garlic is fragrant.
5. Add tarragon, bouillon cubes, and two tablespoons thyme. Mash the bouillon. Stir the ingredients, then add one tablespoon wine. Cook the stalks, frequently stirring until they turn golden. Pour in the remaining wine. Scrape the bottom of the pan with a spatula, then cook for some minutes more.
6. Pour the sautéed fennel stalk mixture and the caramelized onions into the cooked lentils. Mix in 2 tablespoons water, sherry vinegar, lemon juice, pepper, and salt, then cook for some minutes before serving.

Rice Noodles Salad for Summer

INGREDIENTS
- 1 can (8 oz.) rice noodles
- 1 cup carrots, shredded
- 1/3 cup peanuts
- 2 scallions, chopped
- ½ teaspoon black sesame seeds
- ½ red bell pepper, thinly sliced

For the dressing:
- 1/3 cup peanut butter
- 3 tablespoons sriracha
- 1 tablespoon rice vinegar
- 2 tablespoons hot water
- 2 garlic cloves, minced

SERVINGS: 2
5 MINUTES

METHOD

1. Prepare noodles according to package instructions. Drain and rinse with cold water to cool. Set aside.
2. Mix all the dressing ingredients in a bowl and set aside.
3. Toss the noodles with the rest of the ingredients. Mix with the peanut butter dressing and serve.

Protein Power Salad

SERVINGS: 4
25 MINUTES

METHOD

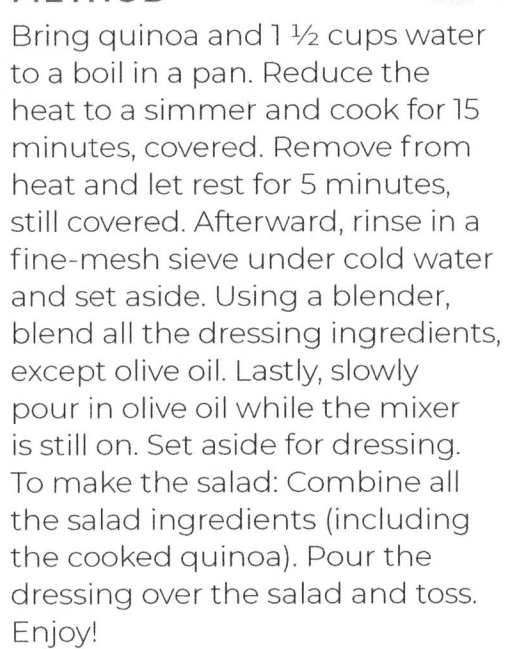

Bring quinoa and 1 ½ cups water to a boil in a pan. Reduce the heat to a simmer and cook for 15 minutes, covered. Remove from heat and let rest for 5 minutes, still covered. Afterward, rinse in a fine-mesh sieve under cold water and set aside. Using a blender, blend all the dressing ingredients, except olive oil. Lastly, slowly pour in olive oil while the mixer is still on. Set aside for dressing. To make the salad: Combine all the salad ingredients (including the cooked quinoa). Pour the dressing over the salad and toss. Enjoy!

INGREDIENTS

For the salad:
¾ cup red quinoa, rinsed, uncooked, 1 cup cherry tomatoes, halved, 4 cups mild green, 1 cup hothouse cucumber, chopped, cup kalamata olives halved, 1/3 cup toasted Marcona almonds, 1/3 cup prepared Lemon Oregano Vinaigrette

For the dressing:
2 tablespoons lemon juice, 2 tablespoons white wine vinegar, 1/3 cup extra virgin olive oil, 1 tablespoon + 1 teaspoon maple syrup, 1 tablespoon oregano leaves, 1½ teaspoons Dijon mustard, 1 garlic clove, ⅛ teaspoon black pepper, ⅛ teaspoon salt

Mushrooms Lemon Salad

INGREDIENTS

- 4 cups Swiss brown and button mushrooms, sliced
- ½ cup French green lentils
- 2 tablespoons parsley, roughly chopped
- ½ cup arugula
- 1 ½ tablespoon lemon juice
- 5 tablespoons extra virgin olive oil
- 2 cups of water
- ½ shallot, chopped
- 2 garlic cloves, minced
- ¼ teaspoon chili flakes
- Pepper and salt, to taste

SERVINGS: 2

40 MINUTES

METHOD

Bring lentils and 2 cups water to a boil in a pan. Simmer for 25 minutes. Drain and set aside. Cook mushrooms part by part in a frying pan (without oil), over medium heat for 3 minutes, flipping over half-way through. Set aside. Sauté shallots in 2 teaspoons olive oil over medium-low heat until slightly golden. Add in the mushrooms, chili flakes, and garlic and cook for 2 minutes. Set aside. Drizzle the salad with the remaining olive oil and lemon juice. Sprinkle with pepper and salt to taste. Top with parsley and arugula, then serve!

Vegan Cauliflower Soup

SERVINGS: 6

25 MINUTES

METHOD

Preheat the oven to 375°F. Get a rimmed baking sheet and place the sweet potatoes and beets onto it. Drizzle with coconut oil and sprinkle with salt and pepper — Bake for 40 minutes. Meanwhile, cook the quinoa as per the package instructions. After the potatoes and beets are baked, transfer them to a bowl to cool. Slice the beets into tiny pieces. Combine the prepared quinoa, beets, potatoes, and the rest of the ingredients in a large bowl, then serve.

INGREDIENTS

- 1 head (3-pound) cauliflower, cut into florets
- 2 cups split peas, cooked
- 2 tablespoons dietary yeast
- 2 tablespoons olive oil
- 7 cups of water
- 1 ½ yellow onions, chopped
- 1 ½ teaspoon ground turmeric
- Black pepper, to taste
- 1 ½ teaspoon salt

All-in-One Roasted Squash and Freekeh Lunch Salad

SERVES
4

⏰ 20 MINUTES

INGREDIENTS

For the squash:
- 1 butternut squash, peeled, diced
- 1 tablespoon maple syrup
- 2 tablespoons olive oil
- ½ teaspoon black pepper
- 1 teaspoon kosher salt

For the freekeh and kale:
- 1 cup freekeh, uncooked
- 8 cups kale, chopped
- 1 tablespoon olive oil
- 2 ½ cups water
- ¼ teaspoon ground nutmeg
- ¼ teaspoon red pepper flakes, crushed
- 2 teaspoons garlic, minced
- ¼ teaspoon black pepper
- 1 ½ teaspoon kosher salt

For the dressing:
- 1 tablespoon maple syrup
- 2 tablespoon apple cider vinegar
- 1 tablespoon orange juice
- ½ cup olive oil
- ½ cup dried cranberries
- ½ cup toasted walnuts, chopped, halved
- 2 teaspoons Dijon mustard
- ¼ teaspoon black pepper
- 1 teaspoon kosher salt

METHOD

1. For the squash: Preheat the oven to 400°F. Place the squash on a baking sheet and sprinkle with 1 tbsp. Maple syrup, 2 tablespoons olive oil, pepper and salt to taste. Toss properly and bake for 20 minutes, turning halfway through.
2. For the freekeh: Boil 2 ¼ cups water in a pan, sprinkle with ½ teaspoon salt. Lower the heat to medium-low and cook freekeh, covered, for 20 minutes. Turn off the heat and leave covered for 5 minutes, then fluff and set aside.
3. For the kale: Sauté kale in 1 tablespoon olive oil over medium heat for 5 minutes, stirring frequently. Add garlic, nutmeg, red pepper flakes, pepper, and salt. Stir and cook for 1 minute.
4. For the dressing: Combine maple syrup, vinegar, orange juice, mustard, pepper, and salt in a bowl. Gently pour in olive oil while mixing until well incorporated.
5. To make the salad: In the kale skillet, stir in the butternut squash, freekeh, cranberries, and walnuts. Drizzle some of the dressing on top and toss softly to coat. Transfer to serving plates, drizzle with the remaining dressing, and serve.

Chapter 2

Panzanella

SERVINGS: 4

METHOD

1. Heat the oven to 375 F. Drizzle bread with olive oil and season with salt and bake for about 11 minutes
2. Brush tofu with some olive oil, place on a baking pan and bake for about 7 minutes on each side. Cut into ½-inch slices and place into a bowl.
3. Mix peanut butter, vinegar, sesame oil, garlic, pepper flakes and ¼ teaspoon salt in a bowl. Add hot water to make thin the mixture. Add more pepper or salt to taste if needed.
4. Drizzle tofu generously with the mixture and toss well to combine. Add the bread and toss slightly. Spread onto a serving dish and leave to cool slightly. Top with tomatoes and sprouts, and then serve.

INGREDIENTS

- 2 slices multi-grain bread, cut into 1-inch cubes
- 12 oz. extra-firm tofu, sliced into 4 pieces
- ½ cup sun-dried tomatoes
- 1 ½ cups sprouts
- 1/3 cups peanut butter
- 2 tablespoons olive oil
- 2 tablespoons apple cider vinegar
- ½ teaspoon toasted sesame oil
- 2/3 cup hot water
- 1 garlic clove
- ¼ teaspoon red pepper flakes
- Pinch of salt

Nutritious Beet Hummus

SERVINGS: 8

METHOD

1. Peel the chickpeas then puree in a blender. Add the beets and puree well until smooth. Add lemon juice, tahini, garlic, salt, and ice water and blend for 3 minutes. Add more salt and lemon juice if necessary
2. Transfer to a serving plate, top with sesame seed and serve

INGREDIENTS

- 1 can (14 oz.) chickpeas, drained, rinsed
- 1 raw golden beet, peeled, quartered
- 2 tablespoons tahini
- Sesame seeds
- 6 tablespoons fresh lemon juice
- 4 garlic cloves
- ¼ teaspoon salt
- ½ cup of ice water

White Bean Soup with Green Herb Dumplings

SERVINGS: 6
25 MINUTES

INGREDIENTS

White Bean Soup:
- 1 can (14 oz.) cannellini beans, drained, rinsed
- ½ cup whole wheat pastry flour
- 2 carrots, peeled and diced
- 3 tablespoons olive oil
- 5 cups of water
- 1 big onion, finely chopped
- 1 teaspoon salt

Green Herb Dumplings:
- 1 cup herbs (scallions, dill, basil), chopped
- 2 tablespoons pesto
- 1 ½ cups whole wheat pastry flour
- 2 teaspoons baking powder
- 1 ¼ cup milk
- ½ teaspoon salt

METHOD

Heat olive oil in a pot over medium-high heat, then fry onions and carrots in it for about 7 minutes. Stir in flour and cook for 3 minutes. Add water and salt and boil for 6 minutes. Stir in beans and boil while you prepare the herbs. Mix milk and pesto properly in a bowl then add herbs. In a separate bowl, combine flour, baking powder, and salt. Add the milk mixture, then mix properly to combine. Add a large tablespoon of this mixture into the boiling soup. Cover and cook for 7 minutes. Flip each dumpling then cook for extra 7 minutes. Top with more herbs and serve hot.

Tomato-Braised Lentils with Broccoli Rabe

SERVINGS: 4
50 MINUTES

METHOD

Heat 2 tablespoon olive oil in a pan. Cook onions for 8 minutes over low heat and season to taste. Add minced garlic and cook for 1 minute more. Add tomato paste, lentils, and a splash of stock. Turn the heat to medium and cook until the stock is absorbed. Add the rest of the stock and cook for 30 minutes. Bring a pot of water to a boil. Add broccoli rabe and cook for 2 minutes. Remove and add to an ice bath to cool down. Drain. Heat the remaining oil in a pan. Add broccoli rabe and garlic cloves — season and cook for 3 minutes. Add chopped tomato to the lentils and cook for 3 minutes. Add the butter and cream. Add basil leaves, add sautéed broccoli rabe on top and serve.

INGREDIENTS

- 1 onion, chopped
- 1 garlic clove, minced
- 4 tablespoons olive oil
- 1 tablespoon tomato paste
- 1 ½ cups French lentils
- 3 cups vegetable stock
- 1 bunch broccoli rabe
- 1 garlic clove, sliced
- 1 tomato, chopped
- 2 tablespoons butter
- ½ cup heavy cream
- Handful basil leaves, torn
- Salt and pepper, to taste

Caesar White Bean Burgers

SERVINGS
4

20 MINUTES

INGREDIENTS

- 2 (14 oz) cans white beans, rinsed and drained
- ½ onion, diced
- 2 tablespoons olive oil
- 2 garlic cloves, minced
- 1/3 cup vegan Parmesan cheese, shredded
- ½ cup breadcrumbs
- 1 flax egg
- ¼ cup parsley leaves, chopped
- 1 tablespoon anchovy paste
- 3 tablespoons lemon juice
- 2 teaspoons Dijon mustard
- 2 teaspoons Worcestershire sauce
- 4 hamburger buns
- ¼ teaspoon salt and pepper

METHOD

1. Heat 1 tablespoon oil in a pan over medium heat. Add the onion and cook for about 3-4 minutes. Add garlic and cook for 1 minute more. Remove the pan from heat.
2. Blend beans in a blender until broken down. Add onion, breadcrumbs, parsley, vegan cheese, flax egg, lemon juice, Worcestershire, anchovy paste, mustard, salt, and pepper to the bowl and mix well to combine. Cover and refrigerate for 2 hours.
3. Divide the mixture into 4 parts and shape each one into ½" patty.
4. Heat the remaining oil in a pan over medium heat. Add the patties. Cook for 6 minutes flip and cook the other side for 6 minutes.
5. Place patties on the buns and serve.

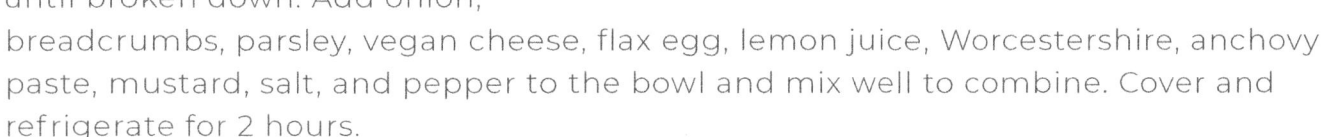

Southwestern Quinoa Stuffed Peppers

SERVES
8

30 MINUTES

INGREDIENTS

- 1 tablespoon olive oil
- 1 cup quinoa, rinsed
- 1 yellow onion, diced
- 2 tablespoons tomato paste
- 1 ½ teaspoon chili powder
- 1 ½ teaspoon ground cumin
- 2 garlic cloves, chopped
- 2 cups of water
- 8 red bell peppers
- 15 oz. can black beans, drained and rinsed
- ½ cup cilantro, chopped
- 1 ½ cups corn kernels
- 1 teaspoon salt
- Black pepper, to taste

METHOD

1. Heat the oven to 375°F and place a rack in the middle. Add 1 cup of water to the baking dish and set aside.
2. Heat 1 tablespoon oil in a pan over medium heat. Add onion, season to taste, and cook for 8 minutes.
3. Add quinoa and cook for 2 minutes. Add garlic, chili powder, tomato paste, and cumin and cook for 2 minutes. Add 2 cups water and one teaspoon salt and mix well. Bring everything to a boil. Reduce the heat to low, cover and cook for 15 minutes.
4. Cut a circle around each bell pepper stem. Remove any seeds and membranes from it. Drizzle each one with oil and season with salt and pepper and set aside.
5. Let quinoa stand for 5 minutes once done. Fluff with a fork add cilantro, beans, and corns and stir well — season with salt and pepper.
6. Divide the mixture among peppers. Top with the caps. Transfer the stuffed peppers into the baking dish. Cover tightly with foil.
7. Bake for 1 hour. Let rest for 5 minutes. Serve and enjoy.

Smoky Tempeh Burrito

SERVINGS
4

50 - 60 MINUTES

INGREDIENTS

- 15 oz. can black beans
- ½ teaspoon cumin powder
- 1 cup uncooked brown rice
- Water
- 10 oz. tempeh
- 1 tablespoon avocado oil
- ½ white onion, diced
- 1 tablespoon olive oil
- 2 garlic cloves, minced
- 15 oz. tomato sauce
- 1 whole chipotle in adobo sauce
- 1 tablespoon adobo sauce
- Red cabbage, sliced

METHOD

Add 1" water to a saucepan and bring to a simmer. Add the steamer basket on top and add tempeh to the basket. Steam for 15 minutes. Cube and set aside. Heat a skillet over medium heat. Add oil and onion. Cook for 3 minutes add garlic and cook for 2 minutes. Add chipotle pepper, adobo sauce, and tomato sauce and mix. Heat until starts to bubble, reduce the heat and simmer for 4 minutes. Transfer the sauce to a blender and blend on high until smooth. Transfer the sauce back to the skillet and heat over low heat. Add the black beans to a pan and heat over medium heat. Once boils, reduce the heat, add cumin, and add salt.
Heat a skillet over medium heat. Add oil and cubed steamed tempeh and cook for 8 minutes until crisp. Add to the red sauce and mix well.
Cover with the lid for 3 minutes, remove and simmer over low heat. Divide everything among 4 serving bowls. Add red cabbage. Serve and enjoy.

Tofu Chickpea Stir-Fry with Tahini Sauce

SERVINGS
4

INGREDIENTS

- ¼ cup tahini
- 2 tablespoons soy sauce
- 2 teaspoons honey
- 1/3 cup water
- 1 teaspoon ginger, minced
- 2 tablespoons rice vinegar
- 1 cup cooked chickpeas, drained and rinsed
- 1 tablespoon peanut oil
- ½ red onion, sliced
- 2 teaspoons ginger, chopped
- 1 red bell pepper, cored, seeded and diced
- 8 oz baked tofu, cubed
- 4 cups cooked rice
- Sesame seeds, toasted
- Minced chives

METHOD

1. Mix the first 6 ingredients to make the sauce and place near the stove.
2. Preheat oil in a skillet over medium heat. Add chickpeas and cook for about 2 minutes. Add the ginger and cook for 1 minute more.
3. Add peppers and onions and cook for 3 minutes. Add baked tofu and cook for 5 minutes.
4. Add tahini sauce over tofu and cook the mixture for 1 minute. Add to the cooked rice, sprinkle with sesame seeds and top with minced chives.
5. Serve and enjoy!

Sweet and Sour Tempeh

INGREDIENTS
- 1 brown onion
- 1 packet tempeh, gluten-free
- 1 teaspoon sesame oil
- 1 tablespoon sunflower oil
- ½ bell pepper
- 1/3 cup rice vinegar
- 1 tablespoon ketchup
- 4 tablespoons coconut sugar
- 1 teaspoon tamari
- 2 teaspoons cornstarch
- 4 teaspoons water
- Handful of snow peas

SERVINGS: 2

20 MINUTES

METHOD
1. Dissolve cornstarch in water.
2. Mix rice vinegar, ketchup, coconut sugar and tamari in a pan placed over medium heat. Bring to a boil. Remove from heat, add cornstarch mixture, and set aside.
3. Cut tempeh into squares. Cut bell peppers into slices and prepare the snow peas. Add sesame and sunflower oil into a pan. Fry tempeh until brown.
4. Dice onion and add to the tempeh and cook until browned. Add prepped veggies and cook for about 3 minutes. Add the sauce, mix well to coat well, and cook for 2 minutes.
Serve and enjoy.

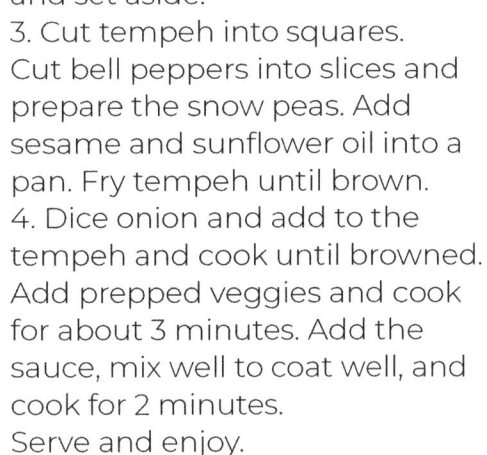

Korean Braised Tofu

SERVINGS: 4

10 MINUTES

METHOD
Add onion slices in a pan and add tofu on top. Mix soy sauce, Korean chili powder, sake, and sugar in a bowl and add over tofu slices. Cover pan. Increase heat to high and cook until it boils. Turn heat to medium-high and cook for 5 minutes, baste with sauce. Remove lid, increase heat to high and cook until sauce reduces. Transfer to a plate, garnish with sesame seeds and serve.

INGREDIENTS
- 14 oz. block firm tofu, cut into 16 squares
- 1 tablespoon sugar
- 1 scallion, thinly cut
- 1 onion, thinly cut
- 3 tablespoons soy sauce
- 1 tablespoon Korean chili powder
- 4 tablespoons sake
- Sesame seeds, toasted

Red Lentil Tikka Masala

INGREDIENTS
- 1 onion, diced
- 2 tablespoons olive oil
- 3 garlic cloves, minced
- 1 jalapeno pepper, minced
- 1 tablespoon ginger, grated
- 1 ½ tablespoons garam masala
- 1 tablespoon tomato paste
- 1 tablespoon coconut sugar
- 28 oz can tomatoes, crushed
- 1 cup red lentils
- 1 ½ cups vegetable broth
- ½ cup of coconut milk
- ¼ cup cilantro, chopped
- Salt and pepper, to taste

SERVINGS: 5
30 MINUTES

METHOD

1. Cook onions and jalapeno pepper in hot olive oil in a pan until soft. Add garam masala, garlic, ginger, and tomato paste and stir for 1 minute.
2. Add coconut sugar, tomatoes, and vegetable broth. Mix well and add red lentils.
3. Bring to a simmer, turn the heat down and cook for about 30 minutes.
4. Add cilantro and coconut milk and mix. Serve and enjoy.

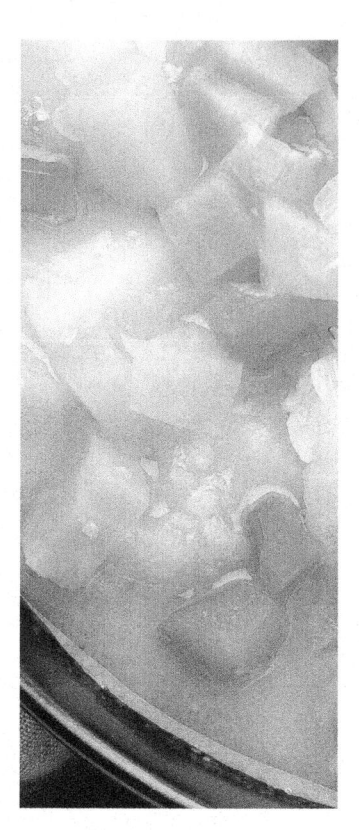

Teriyaki Glazed Tofu Steaks

SERVINGS: 3
15 MINUTES

METHOD

1. Mix all ingredients except oil and tofu in a bowl to make the sauce. Cut tofu into 1/2" thick slices.
2. Coat a pan with oil and heat over medium-high. Add the tofu steaks. Flip and cook until crust is brown from all sides. Leave last batch in pan and add half of teriyaki sauce.
3. Coat the tofu steaks thoroughly with the sauce and cook for 2 minutes. Repeat with the remaining tofu steaks and sauce. Serve and enjoy.

INGREDIENTS
- 14 oz. block tofu
- 1 teaspoon garlic, minced
- 1/2 teaspoon ginger, grated
- 1 tablespoon lemon juice
- 4 tablespoons soy sauce
- 2 tablespoons maple syrup
- 1 tablespoon rice vinegar
- 1/4 teaspoon corn starch
- 1/4 teaspoon Dijon mustard
- Oil

Easy Thai Red Tofu Curry

SERVES
4

30 MINUTES

INGREDIENTS

- 4 garlic clove, minced
- 2 tablespoons sesame oil
- 4 tablespoons soy sauce
- 3 tablespoons rice vinegar
- 1 tablespoon brown sugar
- 1 teaspoon red pepper flakes
- 3 tablespoons corn starch
- 1 yellow onion, minced
- 1 teaspoon ginger, grated
- 1 red bell pepper, sliced
- 1 cup Cremini mushrooms, sliced
- 3 tablespoons red curry paste
- 13 oz. coconut milk
- 1 tablespoon sambal oelek
- 1 lime, zest and juice
- 8 Thai basil leaves, ribboned
- Cooked rice

METHOD

Drain and press the tofu for 30 minutes. Mix 1 garlic clove, 3 tablespoons soy sauce, 2 tablespoons sesame oil, 1 tablespoon brown sugar, rice vinegar, red pepper flakes and corn starch in a bowl. Cut tofu into cubes and add to the freezer bag, add the marinade and refrigerate for 30 minutes. Transfer tofu to a bowl and add cornstarch. Mix well. Heat coconut oil in a pan over medium heat. Fry tofu cubes for 2 minutes on each side. Transfer to a bowl. Add ¼ cup water to the pan and bring to a simmer. Add garlic, ginger and minced onion and turn the heat to medium. Cook for 5 minutes. Add mushrooms and red bell pepper. Add 3 tablespoons red curry paste and mix well.

Add coconut milk, lime juice and zest and soy sauce. Mix well and cook for 15 minutes. Serve with rice.

Barbecue Baked Seitan Strips

SERVES
4

60 MINUTES

INGREDIENTS
- ½ cup nutritional yeast
- 3 cups vital wheat gluten
- 1 ½ teaspoon smoked paprika
- 1 ½ tablespoon garlic powder
- 1 teaspoon onion powder
- ½ teaspoon dried oregano
- ½ teaspoon dried basil
- 3 ½ cups vegetable broth
- 2 cups vegan barbecue sauce
- 5 tablespoons olive oil
- 5 tablespoons maple syrup
- 3 tablespoons soy sauce
- 1 teaspoon liquid smoke
- 1 teaspoon garlic powder
- 1 ½ teaspoons black pepper

METHOD

Preheat the oven to 390F. Mix gluten, yeast, 1 ½ tablespoon garlic powder, 1 teaspoon smoked paprika, 1 teaspoon onion powder, ½ teaspoon black pepper, ½ teaspoon oregano and ½ teaspoon basil in a bowl. Mix 1 cup BBQ sauce, 2 tAblespoons maple syrup, 1 ½ cups vegetable broth, 2 tablespoons olive oil and 1 tablespoon soy sauce in a bowl. Add liquid to dry ingredients and mix well. Knead the mixture until the dough is formed. Let rest.
4. Mix the remaining broth, BBQ sauce, maple syrup, olive oil, soy sauce, liquid smoke, black pepper, garlic powder, and smoked paprika in a bowl and mix well to make a marinade.
5. Place dough on a flat surface and flatten. Add a little oil and roll out to 1" thick and rectangle shape. Add 1 cup marinade to a tray and place dough on top. Cover with the remaining marinade. Bake for 1 hour adds 1 cup broth if it dries in between. Serve and enjoy.

Easy Vegan Chilli Sin Carne

INGREDIENTS

- 3 garlic cloves, minced
- 2 tablespoon olive oil
- 2 celery stalks, chopped
- 1 red onion, sliced
- 2 red peppers, chopped
- 2 carrots, peeled and chopped
- 1 teaspoon chili powder
- 1 teaspoon ground cumin
- 1 lb canned tomatoes, chopped
- 14 oz can red kidney beans, drained and rinsed
- 3 1/2 oz split red lentils
- 14 oz frozen soy mince
- 1 cup vegetable stock
- salt and pepper, to taste
- basmati rice, cooked

SERVINGS: 6

METHOD

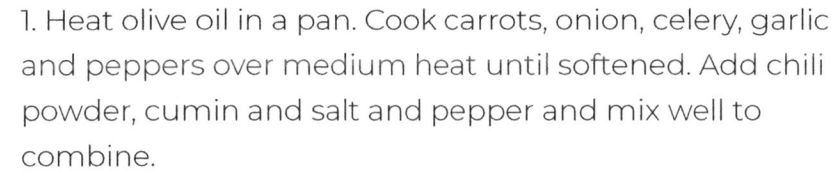

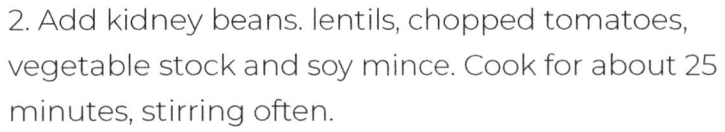

1. Heat olive oil in a pan. Cook carrots, onion, celery, garlic and peppers over medium heat until softened. Add chili powder, cumin and salt and pepper and mix well to combine.
2. Add kidney beans. lentils, chopped tomatoes, vegetable stock and soy mince. Cook for about 25 minutes, stirring often.
3. Serve with basmati rice.

Teriyaki Tofu Stir Fry Over Quinoa

SERVINGS: 4

METHOD

Cut tofu block in half. Squeeze to remove excess liquid. Cut into 1/2" thick cubes and fry in 1 teaspoon cooking oil on medium-high heat until lightly brown on all sides. Add 1 tablespoon tamari and toss. Set aside. Mix 3 tablespoon tamari, sesame oil, rice vinegar, garlic cloves, ginger, coconut sugar, corn starch and water in a bowl for sauce. Cut asparagus into 2" long pieces and dice other veggies. Heat 1 teaspoon cooking oil in a pan over medium-high heat. Cook diced veggies until crispy. Add in the tofu. Add in the sauce. Lower heat and cook until sauce thickens. Turn off heat and add over the cooked quinoa. Serve and enjoy.

INGREDIENTS

- 1 lb. asparagus
- 14 oz. firm tofu
- 2 tablespoon green onions, chopped
- 4 tablespoon tamari
- 2 teaspoon cooking oil
- 1 tablespoon sesame oil
- 5 garlic cloves, minced
- 1 1/2 tablespoon rice vinegar
- 1/2 tablespoon ginger, grated
- 1/4 cup coconut sugar
- 1/2 cup water
- 2 teaspoon cornstarch
- 4 cups quinoa, cooked

Vegan Fall Farro Protein Bowl

INGREDIENTS

- 1 cup carrots, diced
- 1 cup sweet potatoes, diced
- 15 oz. can chickpeas, drained and rinsed
- 1 1/2 cups water
- 2 teaspoons cooking oil
- 4 oz. smoky tempeh strips
- 1/2 cup farro, uncooked
- 2 cups mixed greens
- 2 tablespoon almonds, roasted
- 1/4 cup hummus
- 4 lemon wedges
- salt and pepper, to taste

SERVINGS: 2
METHOD
45 MINUTES

Preheat the oven to 375F and prepare a baking sheet. Mix carrots and sweet potatoes with 1 teaspoon cooking oil and salt and pepper in a bowl. Spread on one half of the baking sheet. Mix chickpeas, remaining oil, 1/8 teaspoon black pepper and pinch salt in a bowl. Spread on the second half of the baking sheet. Add tempeh strips on the baking sheet and roast all for 30 minutes. Flip and shuffle everything at half point. Add farro grains, water, and pinch of salt to a pot and place over medium heat. Cover, bring to a boil and reduce the heat and cook for 25 minutes. Divide farro, greens, and roasted tempeh, chickpeas, and potatoes among 4 bowls. Top with wedges, almonds, and hummus. Serve and enjoy.

Black Bean, Quinoa Balls & Spiralized Zucchini

SERVINGS: 4
METHOD
55 MINUTES

Add 1 cup water and quinoa to a pot and cook for about 15 minutes. Drain water and let cool. Add black beans to a bowl and mash with a fork. Add sesame seeds, quinoa, oat flour, Sriracha, yeast, tomato paste and spices and mix well. Shape the mixture into balls. Place on a lined baking sheet. Bake at 400 F for 40 minutes. Add 1/2 cup cherry tomatoes, sun-dried tomatoes, apple cider vinegar, garlic clove, pine nuts, yeast, basil, oregano and salt and pepper to a blender and blend until creamy to make the sauce. Spiralize zucchinis and add to a bowl. Add tomato sauce and 1/2 cup cherry tomatoes to the bowl and add 5 quinoa balls per serving. Serve and enjoy!

INGREDIENTS

4 zucchinis, 1/4 cup sesame seeds, 1 can black beans, 1/2 cup quinoa, 2 tablespoon tomato paste, 1/4 cup oat flour, 1/2 tablespoon Sriracha, 2 tablespoon nutritional yeast, 1 teaspoon garlic powder, 1 1/2 tablespoon herbs, chopped, 1 tablespoon apple cider vinegar, 1 cup cherry tomatoes, halved, 1/2 cup sun-dried tomatoes, 1 garlic clove, 2 tablespoon pine nuts, toasted, 2 tablespoon nutritional yeast, 1 teaspoon oregano, A handful basil, salt and pepper, to taste

Mongolian Seitan (Vegan Mongolian Beef)

INGREDIENTS

- 2 tablespoon + 2 teaspoon vegetable oil
- 3 garlic cloves, minced
- 1/2 teaspoon ginger, minced
- 1/3 teaspoon red pepper flakes
- 1/2 cup soy sauce
- 2 teaspoons corn starch
- 2 tablespoons cold water
- 1/2 cup + 2 tablespoons coconut sugar
- 1 lb homemade seitan
- Rice, cooked, for serving

SERVINGS: 6

30 MINUTES

METHOD

Heat 2 teaspoons vegetable oil in a pan over medium heat. Add garlic and ginger and mix well. Add red pepper flakes after 30 seconds and cook for 1 minute. Add coconut sugar and soy sauce and mix well. Reduce the heat to medium-low and cook for 7 minutes. Mix cornstarch and water and add to the pan and mix well to combine. Cook for 3 minutes reduce the heat to lowest and simmer. Heat the remaining oil in a skillet over medium-high heat. Add the seitan and cook for 5 minutes. Reduce the heat and add the sauce to the pan. Mix well to coat every seitan piece and cook until all sauce adheres. Remove from heat. Serve with rice.

Teriyaki Tempeh

SERVINGS: 4

40 MINUTES

METHOD

Cut tempeh into triangles and steam for 10 minutes. Add vegetable broth, 1 tablespoon tamari, 1/2 teaspoon garlic powder and onion powder in a bowl and mix well to combine. Pour marinade over tempeh. Let rest for 20 minutes. Add olive oil to the pan and cook tempeh for 4 minutes per side. Mix the remaining tamari, sesame oil, maple syrup, sriracha, apple cider vinegar, remaining garlic powder and cornstarch in a bowl. Add cooked tempeh to this sauce and mix well. Add covered tempeh back to the pan. Heat for 30 seconds per side turn the heat off and add the remaining sauce into the pan. Let rest for 1 minute. Top with sesame seeds and serve.

INGREDIENTS

1 tablespoon olive oil,
8 oz. organic tempeh,
5 tablespoon tamari, 3 tablespoon vegetable broth, 1/4 teaspoon onion powder,
1 teaspoon garlic powder, 1 teaspoon sesame oil,
2 tablespoon maple syrup, 1 teaspoon apple cider vinegar,
1 teaspoon sriracha,
1/2 teaspoon cornstarch, sesame seeds

Vegan Spinach Ricotta Lasagna

INGREDIENTS

- 1 lb firm tofu
- 2 tablespoons olive oil
- 5 garlic cloves
- 1 tablespoon mustard
- 2 lemons, juiced
- 1 teaspoon salt
- A pinch nutmeg
- A pinch black pepper
- 1/3 cup margarine
- 1/3 cup flour
- 3 cup soy sauce
- 2 teaspoon dried oregano
- 3/4 cup passata
- 1 lb frozen spinach
- 2/3 lb lasagna sheets

SERVING: 4

METHOD

70 MINUTES

Defrost the spinach. Add olive oil, garlic cloves, lemon juice, nutmeg, mustard, black pepper and 1/2 teaspoon salt to a blender and blend until smooth. Break the tofu into chunks and add to the blender. Blend until crumbly. Melt margarine in a pan, add flour and mix well. Add soy milk and 1/2 teaspoon salt and keep whisking. Mix passata, dried oregano, salt, and pepper in a bowl. Prepare lasagne by starting with a layer of lasagna noodles and top with the tofu mixture. Next top with the sauce. Top last lasagne sheet with both sauces to fully cover the pasta. Bake for 40 minutes at 375°F. Serve and enjoy.

Vegan Samosa Pie

SERVINGS: 4

METHOD

35 MINUTES

Preheat the oven to 350F and let filo pastry come to room temperature. Cook potatoes in boiling water in a pot until soft. Drain and mash. Heat oil in a pan and cook garlic and onion until soft. Add coriander, curry powder and chili powder and cook for 1 minute then add soy mince. Add 1 drop water and cook for 10 minutes on medium heat. Mix mash mixture with soy mince and season with salt and pepper. Transfer to a baking dish and smooth in one layer. Layer filo pastry on top of the mince mixture, one sheet at a time and use oil to grease. Slice 4 slits on top. Cook in the oven for 20 minutes. Serve and enjoy.

INGREDIENTS

- 3 tablespoon vegetable oil
- 1 onion, diced
- 2 potatoes, peeled and diced
- 1 cup frozen green peas
- 3 garlic cloves, minced
- 9/10 lb. frozen soy mince
- 1 tablespoon dried coriander
- 2 tablespoon curry powder
- 1 teaspoon chili powder
- 1 pack filo pastry
- Salt and pepper, to taste

Lentil Roast with Balsamic Onion Gravy

INGREDIENTS

3 tablespoon vegetable oil, 3 garlic cloves, minced, 1 onion, minced, 2 Portobello mushrooms, chopped, 1 carrot, grated, 4 tablespoons tamari soy sauce, 2 tablespoons mixed dry herbs, 4 tablespoons yeast, 14 oz cooked kidney beans, rinsed, 14 oz cooked puy lentils, rinsed, 1 1/3 cup rolled oats, 1 vegetable stock cube, 1 red onion, sliced, 1 tablespoon coconut sugar, 1 tablespoon arrowroot powder, 3 tablespoons balsamic vinegar, 1 cup red wine, black pepper, to taste.

SERVINGS: 6

60 MINUTES

METHOD

Preheat the oven to 350F and prepare a lined loaf tin. Heat 1 tablespoon vegetable oil in a pan and cook onion and garlic until soft. Add carrot and mushroom and cook for 5 minutes more. Add kidney beans, puy lentils, 1 tablespoon tamari sauce, herbs, yeast, oats, and little pepper and mash to combine. Transfer to the loaf tin and bake for 45 minutes. Add 1/2 liter of vegetable stock with a stock cube and set aside. Add 2 tablespoons vegetable oil to a pan and add onion and coconut sugar and cook for 10 minutes. Add arrowroot powder and stir to combine. Add balsamic vinegar, wine and tamari sauce and cook until stock is reduced. Add vegetable stock and cook for 10 minutes. Serve with the bread loaf.

Grilled Breaded Tofu Steaks & Spinach Salad

SERVINGS: 2

25 MINUTES

METHOD

Add spinach, olive oil, lemon juice, pine nuts and salt and pepper to a bowl and toss well to make the spinach salad. Set aside. Squeeze water out of the tofu. Cut the block into 3 layers and slice across to make 6 triangles — drain water. Pat dry the tofu to remove excess water. Mix tomato paste, soy sauce, miso paste, maple syrup and sesame oil in a bowl and mix well to combine. Add breadcrumbs to a separate dish. Dip tofu steaks in the sauce and coat with breadcrumbs repeat with every piece. Grease a ribbed grill pan. Preheat the grill to medium-high and cook tofu steaks for 13 minutes, flip over and cook for 10 minutes on another side. Serve and enjoy.

INGREDIENTS

- 1/2 block firm tofu
- 1 teaspoon tomato paste
- 1 tablespoon soy sauce
- 1 teaspoon miso paste
- 1 teaspoon sesame oil
- 1/4 cup breadcrumbs
- 1/2 teaspoon maple syrup
- 2 cups baby spinach
- 1 tablespoon olive oil
- 1 tablespoon lemon juice
- 1 tablespoon pine nuts
- Salt and pepper, to taste

Sweet Potato & Black Bean Enchiladas

SERVINGS: 5

INGREDIENTS

- 1 teaspoon olive oil
- 1 onion, diced
- 5 garlic cloves, minced
- 1 jalapeno, seeded and diced
- 10 oz. can diced tomatoes with green chilies
- 2 1/2 cups sweet potatoes, peeled and cut into 1/2" cubes
- 1 1/2 cups canned black beans, drained and rinsed
- 1/4 cup cilantro
- 1/2 teaspoon chili powder
- 1 1/2 teaspoon ground cumin
- 10 whole wheat flour tortillas
- 2 cups Mexican cheese, shredded
- 2 tablespoon vegetable oil
- 1 1/2 cups tomato sauce
- 1/2 teaspoon chipotle chili powder
- 3/4 cup chicken broth
- 3 chipotle chilies in adobo sauce
- Salt and black pepper, to taste

METHOD

Preheat the oven to 400F. Spread 1/4 cup red enchilada sauce on the bottom of a baking dish. Heat olive oil in a skillet over medium-high heat. Add onions, 3 garlic cloves and jalapeno and cook for 2 minutes. Add diced tomatoes, cubed sweet tomatoes, cilantro, black beans, 1 teaspoon cumin, chili powder, 1/4 cup water and salt and pepper — cover and cook for 10 minutes over medium-low heat. Add 1/3 cup filling in the center of each tortilla, roll and place seam side down on the baking dish. Add 3/4 cup enchilada sauce and cheese over it. Cover with foil and bake for 10 minutes. Top with cilantro. Add onion and garlic to the pan placed over medium-low heat and cook for 30 seconds. Add chicken broth, tomato sauce, chili powder, cumin, chipotle chilies and salt and pepper. Bring to boil. Reduce the heat and cook for 7 minutes. Serve enchiladas with sauce.

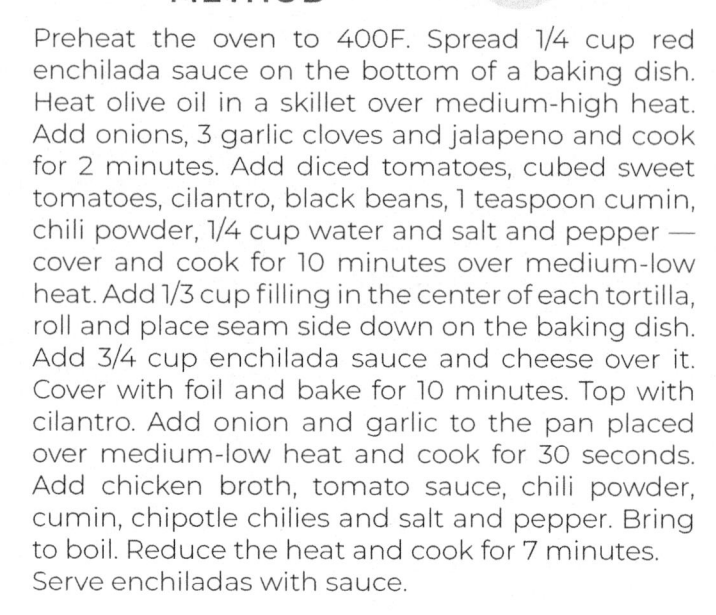

Edamame Fried Rice

SERVINGS: 4

METHOD

1. Heat oil in a skillet over medium heat. Add bell peppers and scallion whites and cook for about 3-4 minutes. Add garlic and edamame and cook for 30 seconds more.
2. Crack the eggs into the skillet and fry until cooked and scrambled. Add soy sauce. Add rice and stir well to combine.
3. Top with scallion greens and serve.

INGREDIENTS

- 3 tablespoon vegetable oil
- 1 red bell pepper, diced
- 4 scallions, sliced, white and green parts separated
- 2 garlic cloves, chopped
- 1 cup shelled edamame
- 2 eggs
- 2 cups long-grain white rice, cooked
- 2 tablespoon soy sauce

Vegan Shepherd's Pie with Crispy Cauliflower Crust

SERVINGS: 4

80 MINUTES

INGREDIENTS

- 1 tablespoon coconut oil
- 3/4 cup brown lentils, uncooked
- 2 celery stalks, diced
- 2 cups savoy cabbage, chopped
- 1 carrot, diced
- 1 cup of water
- 1 garlic clove, minced
- 1 tablespoon balsamic vinegar
- 1 tablespoon vegan Worcestershire sauce
- 1 tablespoon tomato paste
- 1/8 teaspoon ground cloves
- 2 tablespoon olive oil
- 1/2 head cauliflower, chopped
- 1 teaspoon salt
- black pepper, to taste

METHOD

Preheat the oven to 375F. Add lentils to a pan and cover with water. Bring to a boil, reduce the heat to medium and cook for about 30 minutes. Drain and set aside. Steam cauliflower until tender. Add to a blender with olive oil, 1/2 teaspoon salt, pepper and blend until smooth. Heat coconut oil in a skillet over medium heat. Add celery, carrot, cabbage, and garlic. Cook for about 8 minutes. Add reserved cooked lentils, vinegar, water, Worcestershire, tomato paste, cloves, salt, and pepper. Pour the filling mixture into a ceramic baking dish. Add dollops of cauliflower crust on top and spread evenly. Bake for about 30 minutes serve and enjoy!

Hearty Vegetarian Chili & Butternut Squash

SERVINGS: 6

95 MINUTES

METHOD

1. Heat oil in a pan over medium heat. Add poblano, onions, carrot, celery, garlic, chili powder, jalapeno, cumin, oregano, paprika, salt, and pepper. Cook for about 10 minutes, stirring often.
2. Add broth, tomatillos, and Worcestershire sauce and bring everything to a boil. Add potatoes, butternut squash, pinto beans, and white beans, Cook for about 1 hour.
3. Add cilantro, lime juice, and corn, Cook for 2 minutes.
4. Serve with sour cream, tortilla chips, and lime wedges.

INGREDIENTS

8 oz. Yukon Gold potatoes, peeled and chopped, 2 cups vegetable broth, 2 tablespoon olive oil, 1 onion, chopped, 1 poblano chile pepper, seeded and chopped, 3 tablespoon lime juice, 1 tablespoon Worcestershire sauce, 1 carrot, chopped, 1 ribs celery, chopped, 1 jalapeno, seeded and diced, 4 garlic cloves, minced, 1 teaspoon dried oregano, 2 cans whole tomatillos, drained and chopped, 1 butternut squash, peeled and chopped, 1 can white beans, drained and rinsed, 1 can pinto beans, drained and rinsed, 1/2 cup frozen corn, thawed, 1/4 cup cilantro, chopped, 1 tablespoon chili powder, 1 tablespoon paprika, 1 teaspoon ground cumin, 1 teaspoon salt, 1/2 teaspoon pepper, sour cream, lime wedges, tortilla chips

Easy Banana-Cacao Ice Cream

SERVINGS: 4

METHOD

1. Blend the first 8 ingredients in a blender on high speed.
2. Transfer the mixture to a container and place it into the freezer. Freeze for about 4-8 hours, stirring every 1 hour.
3. Serve topped with cacao nibs, ground flax seeds, chia seeds, and almonds.

INGREDIENTS

1 tablespoon raw cacao powder, 2 bananas, frozeN, 1 teaspoon maca powder, 1 teaspoon maple syrup, 2 teaspoons natural peanut butter, 1 scoop vegan chocolate protein powder, pinch cinnamon, splash almond milk, chia seeds, ground flax seeds, almonds, chopped, cacao nibs

---

Flourless Walnut Kidney Bean Brownies

SERVES: 20

METHOD

1. Preheat the oven to 345 F and drain and rinse kidney beans.
2. Add the beans and the remaining ingredients into a blender and process well until smooth. Line a brownie dish with parchment paper and add the butter to it. Spread evenly.
3. Bake for 30 minutes, remove and let cool. Cut into squares and serve.

INGREDIENTS

- 1/2 cup cacao powder
- 14 oz. can kidney beans
- 1 teaspoon vanilla extract
- 1/8 cup natural date syrup
- 1/3 cup coconut sugar
- 1 teaspoon baking powder
- 2 flax eggs
- 1/4 cup coconut oil, melted
- 1/3 cup walnut pieces
- pinch Himalayan salT

Raw Protein Thin Mints

SERVINGS: 10

METHOD

1. ADD ALL INGREDIENTS TO A BOWL AND MIX WELL TO COMBINE. TRANSFER TO A TRAY AND REFRIGERATE.
2. STORE IN A FREEZER UNTIL HARD TO TOUCH. SERVE.

INGREDIENTS

- 2 1/2 tablespoons cocoa
- 1 teaspoon vanilla extract
- 3/4 cup protein powder
- 1/2 teaspoon stevia, liquid
- 7 tablespoons coconut oil, melted
- 1 teaspoon peppermint extract

Fudgy Cinnamon Chai Protein Bars

INGREDIENTS

- 6 dates, soaked in 1/4 cup boiling water
- 15 oz. can chickpeas, drained and rinsed
- 1 teaspoon bourbon vanilla
- 1 tablespoon chai tea leaves infused in boiling water with dates
- 2 1/2 tablespoons coconut oil
- 3/8 teaspoon stevia powder
- 2 1/2 tablespoon vegan vanilla protein powder
- 1 1/2 teaspoons cinnamon
- 4 tablespoons coconut flour

SERVINGS: 6
10+CHILL MINUTES

METHOD

1. Mix soaked dates, chickpeas, vanilla, tea, coconut oil, cinnamon, stevia powder, and vanilla protein powder in a blender and blend until smooth.
2. Add coconut flour and blend until it thickens. Transfer to a loaf pan and place into a freezer.
3. Let sit until firm then transfer to the fridge 30 minutes before serving.
4. Slice into squares and serve.

Black Bean Chocolate Orange Mousse

SERVINGS: 6
10 MINUTES

METHOD

1. Add black beans and dates to a blender and blend on high for 1 minute. Add the brown rice syrup, coconut oil, milk and cacao powder and blend for 1 minute until smooth.
2. Add in the orange zest. Transfer the mixture to 6 espresso cups, add cacao nibs and little orange zest.
3. Place into the refrigerator until ready and serve.
the ingredients in a large bowl, then serve.

INGREDIENTS

- 2 tablespoons coconut oil, melted
- 8 tablespoons brown rice
- 15 oz. can black beans, drained and rinsed
- 1 7/10 oz. pitted dates
- 5 tablespoons cacao powder
- 1 orange zest
- 4 tablespoons milk, non-dairy
- 1 teaspoon cacao nibs

Chocolate Crispy Fruit Squares

SERVINGS: 9-12 SQUARES

METHOD

1. Blend raisins and dates in a blender for 30 seconds. Add sesame seeds and walnuts and blend for 20 seconds. Add chocolate chips and cereal. Mix well to combine.
2. Transfer the mixture to a glass dish and press it into the bottom of the dish. Cover and refrigerate for 1 hour.
3. Cut into square bars and serve.

INGREDIENTS

- 1 cup raisins
- 1 cup dates
- 2 tablespoons sesame seeds
- 1/2 cup walnuts, chopped
- 1/4 cup dark chocolate chips, dairy-free
- 1 cup of rice cereal, puffed

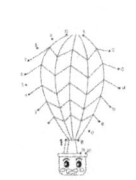

Flourless Salted Caramel Chocolate Chip Cookies

SERVINGS: 8 COOKIES

METHOD

Preheat the oven to 350°F and soak dates in water for 30 minutes and drain the dates. Mix sea salt, dates, 2 tablespoon water in a blender and blitz until caramel forms. Remove. Mix vanilla, baking powder and cashew butter in the blender. Add caramel to this mixture and pulse to combine. Add chocolate chips and pulse well. Transfer to a parchment paper lined baking sheet. Bake for about 10 minutes. Let cool and remove. Serve and enjoy!

INGREDIENTS

- 5 Medjool dates, pits removed
- 1 cup cashew butter
- 2 tablespoon water
- 1 teaspoon vanilla extract
- 1/4 teaspoon baking powder
- 1/4 cup dark chocolate chips
- 1/4 teaspoon sea salt

Mango Chia Seed Pudding

SERVINGS: 4

METHOD

ADD CHIA SEEDS, VANILLA, CARDAMOM, COCONUT MILK, AND COCONUT NECTAR INTO A BOWL AND MIX WELL. STIR WELL, COVER, AND REFRIGERATE. PLACE THE MANGO UPRIGHT AND SLICE RIGHT AND LEFT SIDE VERTICALLY SO THAT THE CENTER REMAINS. SLICE THE SIDES AND DISCARD THE STONES. PUSH MANGO SKIN INSIDE AND CUT INTO CRISSCROSS GRIDS. RUN KNIFE BENEATH THE GRID TO SEPARATE THE FLESH FROM SKIN. BLEND THE MANGO IN A BLENDER UNTIL PUREED PUREE. MIX MANGO AND CHIA SEEDS AND SERVE.

INGREDIENTS

- 1/2 cup chia seeds
- 2 cups of coconut milk
- 1 teaspoon vanilla extract
- 2 mangoes
- 1/4 teaspoon cardamom
- 3 tablespoon coconut nectar

Banana Bread Cookies

SERVINGS: 18

METHOD

Preheat the oven to 350F. Mash bananas in a bowl and add maple syrup and peanut butter. Mix well. Add chia seeds, oats, cinnamon and nutmeg and mix well. Add the chocolate chips. Shape the batter into the balls and place on the baking sheet, Flatten with a spoon and bake for 15 minutes.
Serve and enjoy.

INGREDIENTS
- 2 tablespoon maple syrup
- 2 ripe bananas
- 1/2 cup peanut butter
- 2 cups quick-cook oats
- 1 tablespoon chia seeds
- 1 teaspoon cinnamon
- 1/4 cup mini chocolate chips
- 1/2 teaspoon salt
- A dash nutmeg

Simple Baked Cheesecake

SERVINGS: 6-8

METHOD

1. Preheat the oven to 350F and oil a springform pan and set aside.
2. Blend 1 1/2 cup cashews, dates and cashew butter in a blender until a crumble forms. Transfer to the oiled pan and press down to shape a crust. Set aside.
3. Blend the rest of the ingredients until very smooth. Add over the crust. Bake in a preheated oven for 45 minutes remove and cool completely.
4. Slice and serve.

INGREDIENTS
- 8 Medjool dates pitted
- 1 1/2 cup cashews
- 2 tablespoon cashew butter
- 1 cup vanilla coconut yogurt
- 1 cup raw cashews, presoaked and drained
- 1 lemon juice
- 6 tablespoon agave
- 1 teaspoon vanilla extract
- 1 tablespoon psyllium husk
- 1/2 teaspoon raw ground vanilla bean
- 1 teaspoon salT

Plant-Based Peanut Butter Cream Sweet Potato Brownies

SERVINGS: 10

METHOD

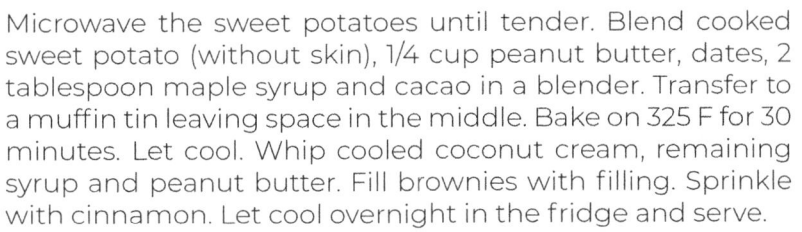

Microwave the sweet potatoes until tender. Blend cooked sweet potato (without skin), 1/4 cup peanut butter, dates, 2 tablespoon maple syrup and cacao in a blender. Transfer to a muffin tin leaving space in the middle. Bake on 325 F for 30 minutes. Let cool. Whip cooled coconut cream, remaining syrup and peanut butter. Fill brownies with filling. Sprinkle with cinnamon. Let cool overnight in the fridge and serve.

INGREDIENTS
- 2 SWEET POTATOES
- 1/4 CUP + 3 TABLESPOON PEANUT BUTTER
- 8 DATES, SOAKED AND PITTED
- 4 TABLESPOONS MAPLE SYRUP
- 8 OZ. COCONUT CREAM, CHILLED
- 1/4 CUP CACAO
- A PINCH CINNAMON

Gluten-Free Pear & Banana Loaf

INGREDIENTS

- 3/4 cup oat flour
- 3/4 cup chickpea flour
- 2 teaspoons baking powder
- 3/4 teaspoon baking soda
- 3/4 cup almond meal
- 1/2 teaspoon ground cinnamon
- 1 1/2 cups ripe pears, peeled, chopped and divided
- 3/4 cup ripe banana, sliced
- 1 tablespoon lemon juice
- 6 tablespoons maple syrup
- 1 1/2 teaspoon vanilla extract
- 1/4 teaspoon salt

SERVINGS: 1 LOAF

45 MINUTES

METHOD

1. Preheat the oven to 350F and line a loaf pan with parchment paper.
2. Mix oat flour, almond meal, chickpea flour, cinnamon, baking soda, baking powder, and salt and set aside.
3. Blend 3/4 cup chopped pear, maple syrup, lemon juice, banana, and vanilla until smooth. Transfer the mixture to the dry ingredients and mix. Add the remaining chopped pears.
4. Transfer the batter to the prepared pan and spread evenly — Bake for 45 minutes.
5. Let fresh, slice and serve.

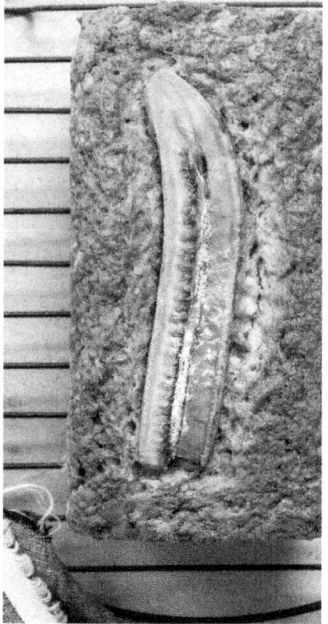

Plant-Based Blueberry Crisp

SERVINGS: 12

55 MINUTES

METHOD

Preheat the oven to 375F. Add blueberries to a baking dish. Squeeze lemon juice over them. Blend 1 cup oats, flax seeds, 1/2 cup almonds, 2 tablespoon cinnamon and 1 teaspoon salt. Add 1 cup oats, 1/2 teaspoon salt, 1/2 cup almonds, 1/2 lemon zest, 1/4 cup water and 1/2 cup maple syrup in a bowl and mix. Add the remaining maple syrup over the berries. Add blended oat mixture, wet oat mixture, 1/4 cup water, remaining lemon zest and 2 tablespoon cinnamon in this order over the berries. Bake for 35 minutes. Serve and enjoy.

INGREDIENTS

- 2 cups oats
- 7 cups blueberries
- 1 cup maple syrup
- 1 lemon, juiced and zested
- 1 cup almonds, sliced
- 2 tablespoons flax seeds
- 1/2 cup water
- 4 tablespoons cinnamon
- 1 1/2 teaspoons salt

Raw Chickpea Cookie Dough

SERVINGS: 2

METHOD

1. ADD ALL INGREDIENTS TO A BLENDER EXCEPT THE RAISINS AND BLEND UNTIL SMOOTH. TRANSFER TO A BOWL.
2. FOLD IN THE RAISINS. SERVE AND ENJOY.

INGREDIENTS

- 1 tablespoon vanilla extract
- 1 can chickpeas, drained and rinsed
- 1 tablespoon peanut butter
- 3 tablespoon maple syrup
- 1/4 cup raisins
- 1 dash sea salt
- few tablespoons water

Whole Food Plant-Based Apple Crisp

SERVINGS: 8

METHOD

1. Preheat the oven to 350F.
2. Mix water, lemon juice, 2 teaspoons cinnamon, 2 tablespoon maple syrup and dash sea salt in a bowl and pour over the apples in a dish.
3. Microwave the apple mixture on high for 5 minutes. Blend 1 cup oats until coarse. Add the remaining ingredients and blend until mixed well.
4. Add the crumbled mixture over the apples and bake for 40 minutes. Serve and enjOY.

INGREDIENTS

- 3/4 cup water
- 6 apples, sliced
- 1 tablespoon + 2 teaspoon cinnamon
- 1 tablespoon lemon juice
- 6 tablespoon maple syrup
- 1 1/2 cups oats
- 1 cup walnuts
- A pinch sea salt

Vegan Chocolate Beet Cake

SERVINGS: 10

METHOD

1. Preheat the oven to 375F.
2. Melt 1/4 cup coconut oil and chocolate chips over boiling water. Mix flax eggs and sugar in a bowl until combined well. Add beets, remaining coconut oil, vanilla and chocolate mixture.
3. Add baking soda, flour and salt in the beet mixture and combine well — transfer mixture to a greased Bundt pan and bake for 1 hour. Remove from the oven, let cool and serve.

INGREDIENTS

- 1 cup coconut oil
- 1/2 cup semisweet chocolate chips
- 1 cup sugar
- 2 cups cooked beets, pureed
- 3 flax eggs
- 2 teaspoons baking soda
- 2 cups all-purpose flour
- 2 teaspoons vanilla
- 1/4 teaspoon salt

Vegan Blueberry Flax Muffins

INGREDIENTS

- 1/4 cup ground flax
- 2 cups oat flour
- 2 teaspoons baking powder
- 1 teaspoon vanilla extract
- 4 tablespoons coconut oil, melted
- 1 teaspoon vinegar
- 1 cup almond milk
- 1/2 cup brown sugar
- 1/2 cup applesauce
- 1 1/2 cups blueberries
- 1/3 cup maple syrup
- 1/4 teaspoon salt

SERVINGS: 12

50 MINUTES

METHOD

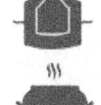

1. Preheat the oven to 375 F.
2. Mix vinegar and almond milk in a bowl and let rest for 10 minutes. Mix flaxseed, flour, salt, baking powder and cinnamon in a bowl and combine well.
3. Add coconut oil, applesauce, sugar and almond milk and vinegar mixture to the flour. Mix gently and fold in the blueberries.
4. Grease a muffin tray. Fill each of 12 tins with 3/4 way with batter. Bake for 30 minutes. Serve and enjoy.

Cranberry Apple Cider Pie

SERVINGS: 6-7

60 MINUTES

METHOD

Preheat the oven to 400F. Mix tap water, maple syrup, and cranberries in a pan. Bring to a boil, then reduce heat to medium-low and stir for 10 minutes. Remove from heat and add orange juice and zest. Let cool.

Peel and slice apples into pieces. Mix with 1/3 cup sugar, 1/4 teaspoon salt, 1/2 teaspoon cinnamon, 1/4 teaspoon pumpkin pie spice, and 1 1/2 tablespoons flour. Whisk the remaining flour, salt, cinnamon and pumpkin pie spice in a bowl. Add butter and mix until crumbly. Add ice water and mix well until the dough forms. Shape the dough into 2 balls, one bigger than other ones. Roll the bigger ball into the crust and place it on a pie pan. Mix cranberry sauce and apple filling and add to the pan with the dough. Roll out the other dough ball. Cut the crust into strips and make a top. Press down the edges and sprinkle with sugar and cinnamon. Bake for 45 minutes. Let cool completely. Serve and enjoy.

INGREDIENTS

- 1/2 cup tap water
- 2 cups cranberries
- 1 orange zest and juice
- 1/3 cup maple syrup
- 1/3 cup sugar
- 4 cups apples, peeled and sliced
- 3/4 teaspoon cinnamon
- 1/2 teaspoon pumpkin pie spice
- 2 cups + 1 1/2 tablespoons all-purpose flour
- 1 1/4 teaspoon salt
- 2 2/3 tablespoons vegan butter
- 6 tablespoons of ice water

Vegan Chocolate Avocado Pudding

SERVINGS: 6

METHOD

1. ADD ALL INGREDIENTS TO A BLENDER AND BLEND UNTIL FULLY COMBINED AND SMOOTH.
2. TRANSFER TO A BOWL, ADD TOPPINGS AND SERVE.

INGREDIENTS
- 1 large banana
- 1 1/2 avocados
- 1/4 cup any sweetener
- 1/2 cup cacao powder
- 1/4 cup almond milk, unsweetened
- mixed berries for topping

20 MINUTES

Rosemary Fig Scones

SERVINGS: 8

METHOD

1. Preheat the oven to 350F.
2. Mix rosemary, lemon zest and milk in a bowl and set aside.
3. Mix coconut sugar, brown rice flour, baking powder, coconut oil and salt in a bowl. Add coconut oil into the flour mixture and stir to combine. Add dried figs into it.
4. Mix dry and wet ingredients and make the dough. Roll out the dough into a circle about 1 1/2" thick. Cut the dough into 8 pieces.
5. Transfer the pieces to a parchment-lined baking sheet and bake for 18 minutes. Serve, enjoy.

INGREDIENTS
- 1/4 cup coconut sugar
- 2 cups brown rice flour
- 1/2 cup coconut oil, cold
- 1 tablespoon baking powder
- 1 cup non-dairy milk
- 3 tablespoons rosemary, chopped
- 1 tablespoon lemon zest
- 1/2 cup dry figs, chopped
- 1/4 teaspoon salt

40 MINUTES

Carrot Cake Waffles

SERVINGS: 4

METHOD

1. Preheat waffle iron. Mix almond milk and vinegar in a bowl. Add warm water to the flax seeds to make the flax egg.
2. Mix the dry ingredients and combine well. Add almond milk mixture, coconut, and crushed pineapple to it and mix.
3. Add the grated carrots and flax egg. Scoop the batter into the waffle iron and cook until crispy and golden.
4. Serve and enjoy.

INGREDIENTS

1 cup flour, gluten-free, 2 tablespoons coconut sugar, 1/2 teaspoon cinnamon, 1 teaspoon baking powder, 1 1/2 tablespoons ground flax seeds, 3/4 cup almond milk, 1 teaspoon apple cider vinegar, 1/2 cup carrots, gratEd, 2 1/2 tablespoons warm water, 1/4 cup pineapple, crushed, 2 tablespoon coconut flakes, 1 pinch ground ginger, 1 pinch salt

15 MINUTES

High Protein Dessert Pizza with Raspberry Sauce

INGREDIENTS

- 1/4 cup chickpea flour
- 1/4 cup cacao powder
- 1 packet Plant Fusion Lean Chocolate Brownie Flavor
- 3 tablespoons maple syrup
- 2 tablespoons coconut oil
- 1/2 teaspoon vanilla extract
- 1 cup coconut cream
- 1 lemon, zested
- 12 oz. raspberries
- 1 tablespoon lemon juice

SERVINGS: 4
30 MINUTES

METHOD

Preheat the oven to 350F. Mix Plant Fusion Lean, chickpea flour and cacao powder in a bowl. Mix 2 tablespoons maple syrup and coconut oil. Add to the dry ingredients and mix until smooth. Roll out the dough into a circle. Place onto a parchment paper. Bake for 14 minutes and let cool. Mix raspberries, lemon zest, and juice in a pot. Bring to a boil and cook until jam-like consistency forms and let cool. Beat coconut milk in a bowl on high for 2 minutes. Add vanilla extract and maple syrup and beat until well mixed. Cut the pizza crust into 8 pieces, top with raspberries, raspberry jam and coconut cream and serve.

High Protein Rice Crispie Treats

SERVINGS: 8 TREATS
10 MINUTES

METHOD

1. Grease an 8 cup muffin tin. Mix protein powder and cereal in a bowl.
2. Heat a pan over medium heat. Cook the syrup and nut butter until mixtures start bubbling. Cook for 30 seconds longer.
3. Add over cereal mixture and stir well. Add to the prepared muffin cups. Press it down into the bottom of the cups.
4. Cool completely, remove and serve.

INGREDIENTS

- 1/4 cup vanilla plant-based protein powder
- 2 cups crisp rice cereal
- 3 tablespoons brown rice syrup
- 3 tablespoons creamy nut butter

Peanut Butter Chia Bars

SERVINGS: 2

METHOD

1. Mix chia, water, vanilla, honey and PB2 in a bowl.
2. Transfer to a container and flatten. Chop almonds and add to the bars.
3. Serve and enjoy!

INGREDIENTS

- 2 tablespoon chia seeds
- 2 1/2 tablespoon PB2
- 1 tablespoon water
- 3 drops vanilla extract
- 1 tablespoon almonds, chopped
- 1/2 teaspoon honey

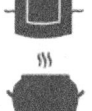

Hidden Greens Chocolate Protein Shake

SERVINGS: 3 CUPS

METHOD

1. Blend all ingredients until smooth.
2. Serve in chilled cups.

INGREDIENTS

- 1 cup frozen kale
- 1 1/2 cups almond milk, unsweetened
- 2 tablespoons hulled hemp seeds
- 3 Medjool dates pitted
- 2 tablespoons cocoa powder
- 1 banana
- 1 tablespoon avocado
- A dash cinnamon

High Protein, Raw Vegan Carrot Cake

SERVINGS: 4

METHOD

1. Blend the first 10 ingredients in a blender until smooth. Add the blended mix to a cake pan. Bake for about 45-50 minutes.
2. Blend the remaining ingredients in a blender until smooth. Add water if needed.
3. Add frosting over cake and serve.

INGREDIENTS

1/2 cup dried coconut, 2 carrots, 1/2 cup ground almonds, 2 tablespoon orange zest, 2 tablespoon orange juice, 1 teaspoon cinnamon, 2 teaspoon stevia, 1/4 teaspoon ground nutmeg, 1/2 cup pecans, 3 tablespoon vanilla protein powder, 2 tablespoons lemon juice, 2 cups soaked cashews, 2 tablespoon maple syrup, 2 tablespoon coconut oil, Water

Chapter 3

Chocolate Raspberry Layer Cake

SERVES
12

INGREDIENTS

- 1/2 cup chocolate protein powder
- 1 1/2 cups wholemeal flour
- 2 teaspoons baking powder
- 1 cup cacao powder
- 1 teaspoon baking soda
- 1/2 cup cashews + 1 1/2 cup water
- 1/2 cup coconut nectar
- 1/2 cup coconut oil, melted
- 2 teaspoon vanilla extract
- 2 tablespoon apple cider vinegar
- 3/4 teaspoon sea salt
- 1 cup dates
- 1 cup cashews
- 2/3 cup water
- 2 cups raspberries

60 MINUTES

METHOD

1. Preheat the oven to 350 F and grease a cake tin.
2. Grind almonds into flour and mix with chocolate protein powder, 1/2 cup cacao powder, 2 teaspoon baking powder, 1 teaspoon baking soda, 1/2 teaspoon salt and 1/2 cup cashews.
3. Blend coconut nectar, oil, apple cider vinegar and vanilla extract in a blender. Combine the dry and wet ingredients together. Bake for 45 minutes. Remove, let cool 10 minutes then cool completely on a wire rack.
4. Blend the remaining ingredients except for raspberries in a blender until smooth to make ganache. 5. Slice the cake in half, spread half of the ganache on the bottom, place 1 cup raspberries on top, add another half of cake, another half of ganache and the remaining raspberries on top. Let rest for 30 minutes and serve.

Chocolate Black Bean Smoothie

SERVINGS: 1

METHOD

1. Add all ingredients to a blender and blend until smooth.
2. Transfer to a glass cup and serve.

2 MINUTES

INGREDIENTS
- 1 cup cauliflower, frozen
- 1 banana, frozen
- 1/2 cup black beans
- 1 cup almond milk
- 1/2 Medjool dates
- 1 tablespoon cocoa powder
- 1 tablespoon hemp seeds
- 1 teaspoon ground cinnamon

Vegan Vanilla Cashew Shake

INGREDIENTS
- 1/3 cup raw cashews
- 1 banana
- 1 tablespoon maple syrup
- 1/3 cup water
- 1/2 teaspoon vanilla extract
- 1 cup of ice cubes
- 1 tablespoon chia seeds
- A pinch salt

SERVINGS: 1

METHOD

1. Add all ingredients to a blender. Blend on low until mixed well. Blend on high for 30 seconds until pureed.
2. Transfer to a glass cup and serve.

5 MINUTES

Easy Peanut Butter Protein Bars

SERVINGS: 4-8

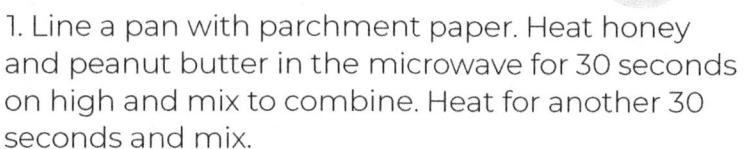

METHOD

1. Line a pan with parchment paper. Heat honey and peanut butter in the microwave for 30 seconds on high and mix to combine. Heat for another 30 seconds and mix.
2. Add protein powder and oats until mixed well. Spread on the prepared pan.
3. Refrigerate for 1 hour. Remove and cut into 12 bars.
4. Serve and enjoy.

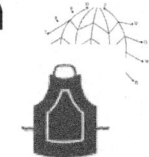

5 MINUTES

INGREDIENTS
- 3/4 cup honey
- 1 cup peanut butter
- 1 1/2 cups quick oats
- 1 cup vanilla protein powder

Vegan Chocolate Almond Protein Bars

INGREDIENTS

- 1 teaspoon cinnamon
- 1 cup raw almonds
- 1 1/2 cups rolled oats
- 1/3 cup maple syrup
- 5 oz. vanilla protein powder
- 1/4 cup chocolate chips, dairy-free
- 1/4 teaspoon salt

SERVINGS: 4

10 MINUTES

METHOD

1. Line a square pan with parchment paper. Chop 1/4 cup almonds and set aside.
2. Add remaining almonds and salt to a blender and blend for few minutes. Add cinnamon, protein powder, oats, and maple syrup and blend until smooth.
3. Transfer mixture to the pan and spread. Top with the chopped almonds.
4. Add chocolate chips in a bowl and microwave until melted. Add chocolate over the bars and refrigerate for 20 minutes.
5. Cut into bars and serve.

Sweet Potato-Chickpea Patties & Sriracha-Yogurt Dip

SERVES 14

15 MINUTES

METHOD

Add garbanzo beans to a bowl and mash until all beans are mashed. Peel and grate the sweet potato and add to the bowl. Grate the onion slightly larger and add to the bowl. Add parsley, garlic, egg, panko, paprika, 1 teaspoon cumin and fine salt in the bowl and mix well. Take 1/4 cup mixture and form into 1/2" thick patties. Heat half oil in a pan over medium heat. Place half of the patties and cook for 4 minutes per side. Remove to a plate and repeat with remaining oil and patties. Mix Sriracha sauce, yogurt, kosher salt and remaining cumin in a bowl. Serve patties with the sauce.

INGREDIENTS

1 sweet potato, 3 tablespoon vegetable oil, 15 oz. can garbanzo beans, drained and rinsed, 1/4 cup panko breadcrumbs, 1/2 yellow onion, 2 garlic cloves, minced, 1 egg, beaten, 2 tablespoons parsley leaves, chopped, 1 1/8 teaspoon ground cumin, 1/2 teaspoon smoked paprika, 2 teaspoons fine salt, 1/2 cup Greek yogurt, 1 1/2 teaspoons Sriracha sauce, 1/4 teaspoon kosher salt

Dark Chocolate Hemp Energy Bites

INGREDIENTS

- 2 cups raw walnuts
- 1 cup Medjool dates, pitted
- 3 tablespoon hemp seeds
- 6 tablespoon cacao powder
- 3 tablespoon almond butter
- 1 tablespoon coconut oil, melted
- 1/4 teaspoon sea salt

SERVINGS: 20 BITES

25 MINUTES

METHOD

Add dates to a blender and blend until small bits remain. Take out and set aside. Add walnuts to a blender and blend until smooth. Add hemp seeds, cacao powder, and sea salt. Blend to combine. Add dates back to blender with coconut oil and almond butter. Blend until combined. Refrigerate for 10 minutes. Take out tablespoon amounts and form into 20 balls. Serve and enjoy.

No-Bake Vegan Protein Bars

SERVINGS: 9 BARS

40 MINUTES

METHOD

Line a baking pan with parchment paper and set aside.
Heat a pot over medium-high heat. Pop amaranth by adding 3 tablespoons at a time and cook for 10 seconds and remove repeat and transfer to a bowl and set aside. Add maple syrup and almond butter to a bowl and mix well. Add protein powder and stir. Add popped amaranth a little at a time until a dough forms. Stir. Transfer the mixture to the baking pan and spread evenly. Lay parchment paper on top and press down to make an even layer. Place in the freezer for 15 minutes. Cut into bars and serve.

INGREDIENTS

- 1 cup almond butter
- 2 tablespoon maple syrup
- 1/3 cup amaranth
- 3 tablespoon vanilla vegan protein powder

Runner Recovery Bites

SERVINGS: 12

METHOD

Drain sunflower and pumpkin seeds and add to a blender. Blend until a paste forms. Add dates and blend to mix. Add the remaining ingredients except hemp seeds and blend until a dough forms. Roll 1 tablespoon dough into balls with hands. Roll the ball in hemp seeds until covered. Transfer the prepared balls to a plate and freeze until firm. Serve and enjoy.

INGREDIENTS

1/4 cup pumpkin seeds, soaked for 1 hour, 1/3 cup oats, 1/4 cup sunflower seeds, soaked for 1 hour, 5 dates, 1 teaspoon maca powder, 1 tablespoon goji berries, 1 teaspoon coconut, shredded and unsweetened, 1 tablespoon coconut water, 1 teaspoon vanilla extract, 1 tablespoon protein powder, 1 tablespoon maple syrup, 1/4 cup hemp seeds, A pinch sea salt

---

High Protein Vegan Cheesy Sauce

SERVINGS: 2 CUPS

METHOD

1. Add all ingredients to a blender and blend until smooth. Combine well. Add more milk as desired.
2. Refrigerate for 24 hours.
3. Serve and enjoy.

INGREDIENTS

- 1 1/4 CUPS UNSWEETENED PLANT-BASED MILK
- 1 BLOCK TOFU
- 1 TEASPOON ONION POWDER
- 2 TEASPOON GARLIC POWDER
- 1/2 CUP NUTRITIONAL YEAST
- 1/4 TEASPOON TURMERIC
- 3/4 TEASPOON SALT

Vegan High-Protein Queso

SERVINGS: 2

METHOD

1. Add tofu, yeast, starch, lemon juice, salt, garlic powder, turmeric and onion powder and blend until well mixed.
2. Add water as desired. Heat in a microwave for 30 seconds.
3. Serve and enjoy.

INGREDIENTS

- 1/4 cup nutritional yeast
- 1/2 block tofu
- 3 tablespoon lemon juice
- 1/4 teaspoon tapioca starch
- 1/4 teaspoon garlic powder
- 1/4 teaspoon turmeric
- 1/4 teaspoon onion powder
- 1/4 cup water
- 1/2 teaspoon salt

Vegan Buffalo Sauce

SERVINGS: 1 CUP

METHOD

1. Mix soy milk, hot sauce, sugar, vinegar, sugar, pepper, tomato sauce and garlic granules in a pan and cook over medium heat for 10 minutes.
2. Let cool and serve.

INGREDIENTS
- 1/2 cup soy milk
- 1 cup hot sauce
- 1/2 cup vinegar
- 1/2 teaspoon pepper
- 2 tablespoons sugar
- 1/2 teaspoon garlic granules
- 1 tablespoon tomato sauce

INGREDIENTS
- 2 tablespoons lemon juice
- 14 oz. silken tofu
- 1 tablespoon yellow mustard
- 1 tablespoon apple cider vinegar
- 1 teaspoon onion granules
- 1 tablespoon agave
- 1 teaspoon garlic granules
- 2 tablespoons parsley, minced
- 2 tablespoons dill, minced
- 1/2 teaspoon Himalayan salt

Vegan Ranch Dressing
(Dipping Sauce)

SERVINGS: 8

METHOD

1. Add all ingredients except parsley and dill to a blender and blend until smooth at high speed.
2. Add dill and parsley and blend until mixed.
3. Serve chilled.

Vegan Smokey Maple BBQ Sauce

SERVINGS: 8

METHOD

1. Add all ingredients to a bowl. Mix them until well combined.
2. Serve and enjoy.

INGREDIENTS
- 1 tablespoon maple syrup
- 1/2 cup ketchup
- 1 teaspoon garlic powder
- 1 teaspoon liquid smoke

Vegan White Bean Gravy

SERVINGS: 2 1/2 CUPS

METHOD

1. Add all ingredients except flour, herbs, and salt to a blender and blend on high speed until smooth.
2. Add this mixture to a pan placed over medium heat. Add salt, herbs, and flour, whisk all the time — Cook for 5 minutes.
3. Serve and enjoy.

INGREDIENTS

1 cup of soy milk, 1 cup vegetable broth, 1 cup white beans, rinsed and drained, 1 tablespoon nutritional yeast, 3 tablespoons tamari, 1 teaspoon garlic granules, dried, 2 teaspoons onion granules, dried, 2 tablespoons all-purpose flour, 1 tablespoon combination thyme, oregano, dill, minced, 1/4 teaspoon black pepper, 1/4 teaspoon Himalayan salt

Tahini Maple Dressing

SERVINGS: 4 OZ

METHOD

1. Add all the ingredients to a bowl, Stir well to combine, until well mixed.
2. Use as a dressing for the salad or other dishes. Store in a fridge.

INGREDIENTS

- ¼ cup tahini
- 1 ½ tablespoons maple syrup
- 2 teaspoons lemon juice
- ¼ cup of water
- 1/8 teaspoon Himalayan pink salt

Coconut Sugar Peanut Sauce

SERVINGS: 1 1/2 CUPS

METHOD

1. In a bowl, combine all the ingredients until properly combined. Serve as a topping for the salad or other dishes.
2. Store in a fridge.

INGREDIENTS

- 4 tablespoons coconut sugar
- 6 tablespoons powdered peanut butter
- 1 tablespoon chili sauce
- 2 tablespoons liquid aminos
- ¼ cup of water
- 1 teaspoon lime juice
- ½ teaspoon ginger powder

Coconut Sauce

SERVINGS: 3
METHOD

1. Boil the carrots for 10 minutes in a pan.
2. Blend the cooked carrots, lentils, onion, garlic, yeast and coconut milk in a blender until smooth. Stir in pepper and salt.
3. Pour the mixture into a saucepan and cook for 2 minutes, stirring frequently.
4. Pour the sauce over the cooked pasta or salad servers.

INGREDIENTS

- ½ cup red lentils, cooked
- 4 carrots, peeled, chopped
- 1 cup (250 ml) coconut milk, canned
- 3 tablespoons nutritional yeast
- ½ onion, diced
- 2 garlic cloves, minced
- Pepper and salt, to taste

15 MINUTES

Vegan Bean Pesto

SERVINGS: 2
METHOD

1. Blend all the ingredients (except the seasonings) in a blender until smooth.
2. Sprinkle with pepper and salt to taste, then blend for 1 extra minute. Enjoy with pasta.

INGREDIENTS

- 1 can (15 oz.) white beans, drained, rinsed
- 2 cups basil leaves, washed, dried
- ½ cup non-dairy milk
- 2 tablespoons olive oil
- 3 tablespoons nutritional yeast
- 1 garlic clove, peeled
- Pepper and salt to taste

5 MINUTES

4 WEEK MEAL PLAN

WEEK 1

Day 1

BREAKFAST   Almond Milk Quinoa
LUNCH   Bean Lentil Salad with Lime Dressing
DINNER   Tomato-Braised Lentils with Broccoli Rabe
DESSERT   Easy Banana-Cacao Ice Cream

Day 2

BREAKFAST   Quinoa and Sweet Potatoes
LUNCH   Lentil Arugula Salad
DINNER   Caesar White Bean Burgers
DESSERT   Flourless Walnut Kidney Bean Brownies

Day 3

BREAKFAST   Honey Buckwheat Coconut Porridge
LUNCH   Red Cabbage and Cucumber Salad with Seitan
DINNER   Southwestern Quinoa Stuffed Peppers
DESSERT   Raw Protein Thin Mints

Day 4

BREAKFAST	Tempeh and Potato
LUNCH	Protein Packed Chickpeas and Kidney Beans Salad
DINNER	Tofu Chickpea Stir-Fry with Tahini Sauce
DESSERT	Peanut Butter Chia Bars

Day 5

BREAKFAST	Breakfast French Toast
LUNCH	Quick Chickpeas and Spinach Salad
DINNER	Smoky Tempeh Burrito Bowls
DESSERT	Hidden Greens Chocolate Protein Shake

Day 6

BREAKFAST	Dairy-Free Pumpkin Pancakes
LUNCH	Carrot Slaw and Tempeh Triangles
DINNER	Sweet and Sour Tempeh
DESSERT	Fudgy Cinnamon Chai Protein Bars

Day 7

BREAKFAST

Protein Blueberry Bars

LUNCH

Chili Tofu

DINNER

Korean Braised Tofu

SNACK

Chocolate Black Bean Smoothie

WEEK 2

Day 1

BREAKFAST   Chickpea Scramble Breakfast Basin
LUNCH   Lentil Soup (Vegan)
DINNER   Red Lentil Tikka Masala
DESSERT   Black Bean Chocolate Orange Mousse

Day 2

BREAKFAST   Quinoa, Oats, Hazelnut and Blueberry Salad
LUNCH   Hot Black Beans and Potato
DINNER   Red Lentil Tikka Masala
DESSERT   Chocolate Crispy Fruit Squares

Day 3

BREAKFAST   Buttered Overnight Oats
LUNCH   Low-Fat Bean Soup
DINNER   Easy Thai Red Tofu Curry
DESSERT   Flourless Salted Caramel Chocolate Chip Cookies

Day 4

BREAKFAST Protein Breakfast Burrito
LUNCH Protein Rich Vegetable Minestrone
DINNER Teriyaki Glazed Tofu Steaks
DESSERT Vegan Vanilla Cashew Shake

Day 5

BREAKFAST Breakfast Hummus Toast
LUNCH Quinoa Pumpkin Soup
DINNER Easy Vegan Chilli Sin Carne
DESSERT Vegan Vanilla Cashew Shake

Day 6

BREAKFAST Almond Milk Banana Smoothie
LUNCH Red Lentil Soup with Farro
DINNER Teriyaki Tofu Stir Fry Over Quinoa
DESSERT Mango Chia Seed Pudding

Day 7

BREAKFAST

Nutritious Toasted Chickpeas

LUNCH

Moroccan Pumpkin Soup

DINNER

Vegan Fall Farro Protein Bowl

SNACK

Easy Peanut Butter Protein Bars

WEEK 3

Day 1

BREAKFAST — Almond Milk Chai Quinoa
LUNCH — Mexican Chickpea and Tomatillos Pozole
DINNER — Black Bean and Quinoa Balls and Spiralized Zucchini
DESSERT — Banana Bread Cookies

Day 2

BREAKFAST — Tomato Tofu Breakfast Tacos
LUNCH — Modernized French Onion Soup
DINNER — Mongolian Seitan (Vegan Mongolian Beef)
DESSERT — Simple Baked Cheesecake

Day 3

BREAKFAST — Peanut Butter Oats
LUNCH — Tofu Bacon Bean Salad
DINNER — Teriyaki Tempeh
DESSERT — Gluten-Free Pear and Banana Loaf

Day 4

BREAKFAST   Protein Pancakes
LUNCH   Rice Noodles Salad for the Summer
DINNER   Vegan Spinach Ricotta Lasagne
DESSERT   Dark Chocolate Hemp Energy Bites

Day 5

BREAKFAST   Savory Vegan Omelet
LUNCH   Protein Power Salad
DINNER   Vegan Samosa Pie
DESSERT   Vegan Chocolate Almond Protein Bars

Day 6

BREAKFAST   Protein Patties
LUNCH   'Roomy' Lemon Salad
DINNER   Lentil Roast with Balsamic Onion Gravy
DESSERT   Plant-Based Blueberry Crisp

Day 7

BREAKFAST

Vegan Chickpea Pancake

LUNCH

All-in-One Roasted Squash and Freekeh Lunch Salad

DINNER

Grilled Breaded Tofu Steaks with Spinach Salad

SNACK

Sweet Potato-Chickpea Patties with Sriracha-Yogurt Dip

WEEK 4

Day 1

BREAKFAST Protein Pudding
LUNCH Vegan Cauliflower Soup
DINNER Sweet Potato and Black Bean Enchiladas
DESSERT Raw Chickpea Cookie Dough

Day 2

BREAKFAST Gluten-Free Tofu Quiche
LUNCH Panzanella
DINNER Edamame Fried Rice
DESSERT Whole Food Plant-Based Apple Crisp

Day 3

BREAKFAST Pumpkin Oatmeal
LUNCH Nutritious Beet Hummus
DINNER Vegan Shepherd's Pie with Crispy Cauliflower Crust
DESSERT Vegan Chocolate Beet Cake

Day 4

BREAKFAST Breakfast Berry Quinoa
LUNCH White Bean Soup with Green Herb Dumplings
DINNER Hearty Vegetarian Chili with Butternut Squash
DESSERT Peanut Butter Chia Bars

Day 5

BREAKFAST Almond Milk Quinoa
LUNCH Bean Lentil Salad with Lime Dressing
DINNER Tomato-Braised Lentils with Broccoli Rabe
DESSERT Runner Recovery Bites

Day 6

BREAKFAST Quinoa and Sweet Potatoes
LUNCH Lentil Arugula Salad
DINNER Caesar White Bean Burgers
DESSERT Vegan Blueberry Flax Muffins

Day 7

BREAKFAST

Honey Buckwheat Coconut Porridge

LUNCH

Red Cabbage and Cucumber Salad with Seitan

DINNER

Southwestern Quinoa Stuffed Peppers

SNACK

No-Bake Vegan Protein Bars

Chapter 5

Culiflower Wedges

SERVINGS: 4
METHOD

Remove leaves and trim originate from cauliflower. Cut cauliflower into eight wedges. Blend turmeric and pepper pieces. Brush wedges with oil; sprinkle with turmeric blend. Grill, secured, over medium-high warmth or cook 4 in. from heat until cauliflower is delicate, 9 minutes on each side. Whenever wanted, shower with lemon juice and extra oil and present with pomegranate seeds.

62 MINUTES

INGREDIENTS
1 huge head cauliflower
1 teaspoon ground turmeric
1/2 teaspoon squashed red pepper chips
2 tablespoons olive oil
Lemon juice, extra olive oil, & pomegranate seeds, discretionary

---

INGREDIENTS
1 medium pie pumpkin (around 3 pounds), stripped and cut into 3/4-inch 3D shapes, 1 pound new Brussels grows, cut and split the long way, 4 garlic cloves, meagerly cut, 1/3 cup olive oil, 1 tablespoons balsamic vinegar, 1 teaspoon ocean salt, 1/2 teaspoon coarsely ground pepper, 2 tablespoons minced crisp parsley

Roasted Pumpkin & Brussels sprouts

SERVINGS: 8
METHOD

1. Preheat broiler to 400°. In an enormous bowl, consolidate pumpkin, Brussels sprouts, and garlic. In a little bowl, whisk oil, vinegar, salt, and pepper; shower over vegetables and hurl to cover.
2. Move to a lubed 15x10x1-in. Preparing container. Cook 35-40 minutes or until delicate, blending once. Sprinkle with parsley.

50 MINUTES

Black Bean-Tomato Chili

SERVINGS: 6
METHOD

1.In a Dutch broiler, heat oil over medium-high warmth. Include onion and green pepper; cook and mix 8-10 minutes or until delicate. Include garlic and seasonings; cook brief longer.
2. Mix in extra fixings; heat to the point of boiling. Lessen heat; stew, secured, 20-25 minutes to enable flavors to mix, blending incidentally. SERVE.

45 MINUTES

INGREDIENTS
2 tablespoons olive oil, 1 huge onion, cleaved, 1 medium green pepper, cleaved, 3 garlic cloves, minced, 1 teaspoon ground cinnamon, 1 teaspoon ground cumin, 1 teaspoon bean stew powder, 1/4 teaspoon pepper, 3 jars (14-1/2 ounces each) diced tomatoes, undrained, 2 jars (15 ounces each) dark beans, washed and depleted, 1 cup squeezed orange or juice from 3 medium oranges

Roasted Balsamic Red Potatoes

SERVINGS: 6

METHOD

1. Preheat stove to 425°. Hurl potatoes with oil and seasonings; spread in a 15x10x1-in. skillet.
2. Broil 25 minutes, blending midway. Sprinkle with vinegar; cook until potatoes are delicate, 5-10 minutes.

INGREDIENTS

2 pounds little red potatoes, cut into wedges
2 tablespoons olive oil
3/4 teaspoon garlic pepper mix
1/2 teaspoon Italian flavoring
1/4 teaspoon salt
1/4 cup balsamic vinegar

Easy Homemade Chunky Applesauce

SERVINGS: 5 CUPS

METHOD

1. Strip, center and cut every apple into 8 wedges. Cut each wedge across down the middle, place in a huge pan. Include remaining fixings.
2. Heat to the point of boiling. Diminish excitement; stew, secured until wanted consistency is come to, 15-20 minutes, mixing once in a while.

INGREDIENTS

7 medium McIntosh, Empire or different apples (around 3 pounds)
1/2 cup sugar
1/2 cup water
1 tablespoon lemon juice
1/4 teaspoon almond or vanilla concentrate
Fueled by Chicory

Mushroom & Broccoli Soup

SERVINGS: 8

METHOD

Cut broccoli florets into reduced down pieces. Strip and hack stalks. In an enormous pot, heat oil over medium-high warmth; saute mushrooms until delicate, 4-6 minutes. Mix in soy sauce; expel from skillet. In the same container, join broccoli stalks, carrots, celery, onion, garlic, soup, and water; heat to the point of boiling. Diminish heat; stew, revealed, until vegetables are relaxed, 25-30 minutes. Puree soup utilizing a drenching blender. Or then again, cool marginally and puree the soup in a blender; come back to the dish. Mix in florets and mushrooms; heat to the point of boiling. Lessen warmth to medium; cook until broccoli is delicate, 8-10 minutes, blending infrequently. Mix in lemon juice.

INGREDIENTS

1 bundle broccoli (around 1-1/2 pounds)
1 tablespoon canola oil, 1/2 pound cut crisp mushrooms, 1 tablespoon diminished sodium soy sauce, 2 medium carrots, finely slashed, 2 celery ribs, finely slashed, 1/4 cup finely slashed onion, 1 garlic clove, minced, 1 container (32 ounces) vegetable juices, 2 cups of water, 2 tablespoons lemon juice

Avocado Fruit Salad with Tangerine Vinaigrette

INGREDIENTS

3 medium ready avocados, stripped and meagerly cut
3 medium mangoes, stripped and meagerly cut
1 cup crisp raspberries
1 cup crisp blackberries
1/4 cup minced crisp mint
1/4 cup cut almonds, toasted

DRESSING:

1/2 cup olive oil
1 teaspoon ground tangerine or orange strip
1/4 cup tangerine or squeezed orange
2 tablespoons balsamic vinegar
1/2 teaspoon salt
1/4 teaspoon naturally ground pepper

SERVINGS: 8

25 MINUTES

METHOD

1. Mastermind avocados and organic product on a serving plate; sprinkle with mint and almonds. In a little bowl, whisk dressing fixings until mixed; shower over a plate of mixed greens.
2. To toast nuts, prepare in a shallow container in a 350° stove for 5-10 minutes or cook in a skillet over low warmth until softly sautéed, mixing every so often.

General Tso's Cauliflower

SERVINGS:

45 MINUTES

METHOD

In an electric skillet or profound fryer, heat oil to 375°. Consolidate flour, cornstarch, salt, and heating powder. Mix in club soft drink just until mixed (hitter will be slender). Plunge florets, a couple at once, into the player and fry until cauliflower is delicate and covering is light dark colored, 8-10 minutes. Channel on paper towels. For the sauce, whisk together the initial six fixings; race in cornstarch until smooth. In a huge pot, heat canola oil over medium-high warmth. Include chilies; cook and mix until fragrant, 2 minutes. Include a white piece of onions, garlic, ginger, and orange get-up-and-go; cook until fragrant, around 1 moment. Mix soy sauce blend; add to the pan. Heat to the point of boiling; cook and mix until thickened, 4 minutes. Add cauliflower to sauce; hurl to cover. Present with rice; sprinkle with daintily cut green onions.

INGREDIENTS

Oil for profound fat fricasseeing
1/2 cup generally useful flour, 1/2 cup cornstarch, 1 teaspoon salt, 1 teaspoon preparing powder, 3/4 cup club pop, 1 medium head cauliflower, cut into 1-inch florets (around 6 cups),
1/4 cup squeezed orange,
3 tablespoons sugar, 3 tablespoons soy sauce, 3 tablespoons vegetable stock,
2 tablespoons rice vinegar,
2 teaspoons sesame oil, 2 teaspoons cornstarch, 2 tablespoons canola oil, 2 to 6 dried pasilla or other hot chilies, cleaved, 3 green onions, white part minced, green part daintily cut,
3 garlic cloves, minced,
1 teaspoon ground new gingerroot, 1/2 teaspoon ground orange get-up-and-go 4 cups hot cooked rice

Roasted Curried Chickpeas and Cauliflower

SERVINGS: 4

METHOD

1. Preheat broiler to 400°. Spot initial 7 fixings in an enormous bowl; hurl to cover. Move to a 15x10x1-in. preparing containers covered with cooking shower.
2. Cook until vegetables are delicate, 30-35 minutes, blending every so often. Sprinkle with cilantro.

INGREDIENTS

2 pounds potatoes (around 4 medium), stripped and cut, into 1/2-inch solid, shapes, 1 little head, cauliflower, broken into florets (around 3 cups), 1 can (15 ounces) chickpeas or garbanzo beans, flushed and depleted
3 tablespoons olive oil, 2 teaspoons curry powder, 3/4 teaspoon salt, 1/4 teaspoon pepper, 3 tablespoons minced crisp cilantro or parsley

---

INGREDIENTS

1 cup bulgur, 2 cups of water, 1 cup new or solidified peas (around 5 ounces), defrosted, 1 can (15 ounces), Chickpeas or garbanzo beans, washed and depleted, 1/2 cup minced new parsley, 1/4 cup minced new minT, 1/4 cup olive oil, 2 tablespoons julienned sun-dried tomatoes (not stuffed in oil), 2 tablespoons lemon juice, 1/2 teaspoon salt, 1/4 teaspoon pepper

Chickpea Mint Tabbouleh

SERVINGS: 4

METHOD

1. In a huge pot, consolidate bulgur and water; heat to the point of boiling. Decrease heat; stew, secured, 10 minutes. Mix in crisp or solidified peas; cook, secured, until bulgur and peas are delicate, around 5 minutes.
2. Move to an enormous bowl. Mix in outstanding fixings. Serve warm, or refrigerate and serve cold.

Smoky Cauliflower

SERVINGS: 8

METHOD

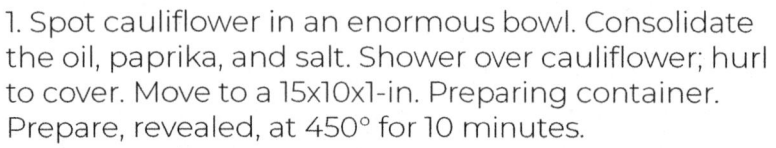

1. Spot cauliflower in an enormous bowl. Consolidate the oil, paprika, and salt. Shower over cauliflower; hurl to cover. Move to a 15x10x1-in. Preparing container. Prepare, revealed, at 450° for 10 minutes.
2. Mix in garlic. Prepare 14 minutes longer or until cauliflower is delicate and daintily cooked, mixing every so often. Sprinkle with parsley.

INGREDIENTS

1 huge head cauliflower, broken into 1-inch florets (around 9 cups)
2 tablespoons olive oil
1 teaspoon smoked paprika
3/4 teaspoon salt
2 garlic cloves, minced
2 tablespoons minced new parsley

Creamy Cauliflower Pakora Soup

INGREDIENTS
1 huge head cauliflower, cut into little florets
5 medium potatoes, stripped and diced
1 huge onion, diced
4 medium carrots, stripped and diced
2 celery ribs, diced
1 container (32 ounces) vegetable stock
1 teaspoon garam masala
1 teaspoon garlic powder
1 teaspoon ground coriander
1 teaspoon ground turmeric
1 teaspoon ground cumin
1 teaspoon pepper
1 teaspoon salt
1/2 teaspoon squashed red pepper chips
Water or extra vegetable stock
New cilantro leaves
Lime wedges, discretionary

SERVINGS: 8
METHOD
40 MINUTES

1. In a Dutch stove over medium-high warmth, heat initial 14 fixings to the point of boiling. Cook and mix until vegetables are delicate, around 20 minutes. Expel from heat; cool marginally. Procedure in groups in a blender or nourishment processor until smooth. Modify consistency as wanted with water (or extra stock). Sprinkle with new cilantro. Serve hot, with lime wedges whenever wanted.
2. Stop alternative: Before including cilantro, solidify cooled soup in cooler compartments. To utilize, in part defrost in cooler medium-term. Warmth through in a pan, blending every so often and including a little water if fundamental. Sprinkle with cilantro. Whenever wanted, present with lime wedges.

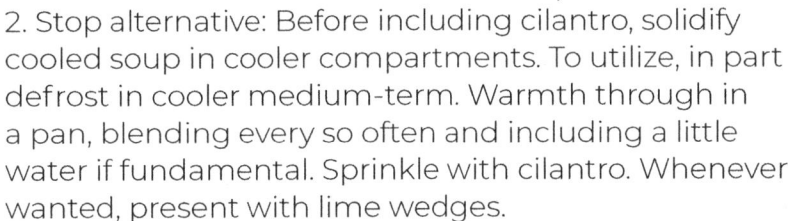

Spice Trade Beans and Bulgur

SERVES 14
METHOD
240 MINUTES

1. In a large skillet, heat 2 tablespoons oil over medium-high warmth. Include onions and pepper; cook and mix until delicate, 3-4 minutes. Include garlic and seasonings; cook brief longer. Move to a 5-qt. slow cooker.
2. In the same skillet, heat remaining oil over medium-high warmth. Include bulgur; cook and mix until daintily caramelized, 2-3 minutes or until softly sautéed.
3. Include bulgur, tomatoes, stock, darker sugar, and soy sauce to slow cooker. Cook, secured, on low 3-4 hours or until bulgur is delicate. Mix in beans and raisins; cook 30 minutes longer. Whenever wanted, sprinkle with cilantro.

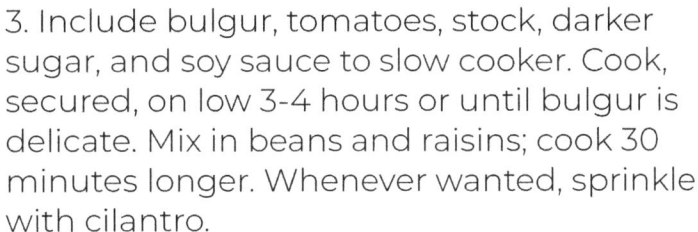

INGREDIENTS
3 tablespoons canola oil, isolated, 2 medium onions, slashed, 1 medium sweet red pepper, slashed
5 garlic cloves, minced
1 tablespoon ground cumin, 1 tablespoon paprika, 2 teaspoons ground ginger, 1 teaspoon pepper, 1/2 teaspoon ground cinnamon, 1/2 teaspoon cayenne pepper, 1-1/2 cups bulgur, 1 can (28 ounces) squashed tomatoes, 1 can (14-1/2 ounces) diced tomatoes, undrained, 1 container (32 ounces, vegetable juices, 2 tablespoons darker sugar, 2 tablespoons soy sauce
1 can (15 ounces) garbanzo beans or chickpeas, flushed and depleted, 1/2 cup brilliant raisins, Minced crisp cilantro, discretionary

Tofu Chow Mein

INGREDIENTS
8 ounces uncooked entire wheat holy messenger hair pasta
3 tablespoons sesame oil, separated
1 bundle (16 ounces) extra-firm tofu
2 cups cut new mushrooms
1 medium sweet red pepper, julienned
1/4 cup decreased sodium soy sauce
3 green onions daintily cut

SERVINGS: 4
METHOD
30 MINUTES

Cook pasta as per bundle headings. Channel; flush with cold water and channel once more. Hurl with 1 tablespoon oil; spread onto a preparing sheet and let remain around 60 minutes. In the meantime, cut tofu into 1/2-in. 3D shapes and smudge dry. Enclose by a clean kitchen towel; place on a plate and refrigerate until prepared to cook. In an enormous skillet, heat 1 tablespoon oil over medium warmth. Include pasta, spreading equitably; cook until the base is daintily caramelized, around 5 minutes. Expel from skillet. In the same skillet, heat remaining oil over medium-high warmth; pan sear mushrooms, pepper, and tofu until mushrooms are delicate, 3-4 minutes. Include pasta and soy sauce; hurl and heat through. Sprinkle with green onions.

Chard and White Bean Pasta

SERVINGS: 8
METHOD
40 MINUTES

Cook pasta as indicated by bundle headings. Channel, holding 3/4 cup pasta water. In a 6-qt. stockpot, heat oil over medium warmth; saute leeks and onion until delicate, 5-7 minutes. Include garlic and sage; cook and mix 2 minutes. Include potato and chard; cook, secured, over medium-low warmth 5 minutes. Mix in beans, seasonings and held pasta water; cook, secured, until potato and chard are delicate, around 5 minutes. Include pasta, basil, and vinegar; hurl and warmth through. Present with sauce.

INGREDIENTS
1 bundle (12 ounces) uncooked entire wheat or darker rice penne pasta, 2 tablespoons olive oil, 4 cups cut leeks (a white bit as it were), 1 cup cut sweet onion, 4 garlic cloves, cut , 1 tablespoon minced crisp savvy or 1 teaspoon scoured sage, 1 enormous sweet potato, stripped and cut into 1/2-inch solid shapes, 1 medium bundle Swiss chard (around 1 pound), cut into 1-inch cuts, 1 can (15-1/2 ounces) extraordinary northern beans, flushed and depleted, 3/4 teaspoon salt, 1/4 teaspoon bean stew powder, 1/4 teaspoon squashed red pepper drops, 1/8 teaspoon ground nutmeg, 1/8 teaspoon pepper, 1/3 cup finely slashed crisp basil, 1 tablespoon balsamic vinegar, 2 cups marinara sauce, warmed

Okra Roasted with Smoked Paprika

SERVINGS: 12

⏱ 35 MINUTES

METHOD

1. PREHEAT STOVE TO 400°. HURL TOGETHER ALL FIXINGS. MASTERMIND IN A 15X10X1-IN. HEATING SKILLET; COOK UNTIL OKRA IS DELICATE AND SOFTLY SAUTÉED, 30-35 MINUTES.

INGREDIENTS

- 3 pounds new okra cases
- 3 tablespoons olive oil
- 3 tablespoons lemon juice
- 1-1/2 teaspoons smoked paprika
- 1/4 teaspoon garlic powder
- 3/4 teaspoon salt
- 1/2 teaspoon pepper

Spicy Grilled Broccoli

SERVES: 6

⏱ 30 MINUTES

METHOD

Cut every broccoli pack into 6 pieces. In a 6-qt. stockpot, place a steamer container more than 1 in. of water. Spot broccoli in a bushel. Heat water to the point of boiling. Decrease warmth to keep up a stew; steam, secured, 4-6 minutes or until fresh delicate. In an enormous bowl, whisk marinade fixings until mixed. Include broccoli; delicately hurl to cover. Let stand, secured, 15 minutes. Channel broccoli, saving marinade. Flame broil broccoli, secured, over medium warmth, or cook 4 in from heat 6-8 minutes or until broccoli is delicate, turning once. Whenever wanted, present withheld marinade.

INGREDIENTS

- 2 PACKS BROCCOLI

MARINADE:
- 1/2 CUP OLIVE OIL
- 1/4 CUP JUICE VINEGAR
- 1 TEASPOON ONION POWDER
- 1 TEASPOON GARLIC POWDER
- 1 TEASPOON SMOKED PAPRIKA
- 1/2 TEASPOON SALT
- 1/2 TEASPOON SQUASHED RED PEPPER PIECES
- 1/4 TEASPOON PEPPER

Sauteed Squash with Tomatoes and Onions

SERVINGS: 8

⏱ 20 MINUTES

METHOD

1. In a huge skillet, heat oil over medium-high warmth. Include onion; cook and mix until delicate, 2-4 minutes. Include zucchini; cook and mix 3 minutes.
2. Mix in tomatoes, salt, and pepper; cook and mix until squash is delicate, 4-6 minutes longer. Present with an opened spoon.

INGREDIENTS

- 2 tablespoons olive oil
- 1 medium onion, finely hacked
- 4 medium zucchini, hacked
- 2 huge tomatoes, finely hacked
- 1 teaspoon salt
- 1/4 teaspoon pepper

Garden Vegetable & Herb Soup

INGREDIENTS
2 tablespoons olive oil
2 medium onions, hacked
2 huge carrots, cut
1 pound red potatoes (around 3 medium), cubed
2 cups of water
1 can (14-1/2 ounces) diced tomatoes in sauce
1-1/2 cups vegetable soup
1-1/2 teaspoons garlic powder
1 teaspoon dried basil
1/2 teaspoon salt
1/2 teaspoon paprika
1/4 teaspoon dill weed
1/4 teaspoon pepper
1 medium yellow summer squash, split and cut
1 medium zucchini, split and cut

SERVINGS: 8
METHOD

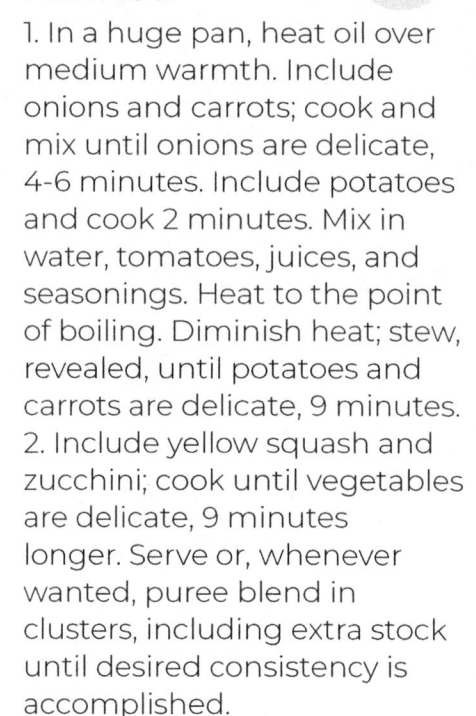

1. In a huge pan, heat oil over medium warmth. Include onions and carrots; cook and mix until onions are delicate, 4-6 minutes. Include potatoes and cook 2 minutes. Mix in water, tomatoes, juices, and seasonings. Heat to the point of boiling. Diminish heat; stew, revealed, until potatoes and carrots are delicate, 9 minutes.
2. Include yellow squash and zucchini; cook until vegetables are delicate, 9 minutes longer. Serve or, whenever wanted, puree blend in clusters, including extra stock until desired consistency is accomplished.

Cauliflower with Roasted Almond & Pepper Dip

SERVINGS: 10
METHOD

In a 6-qt. stockpot, bring water, 1/2 cup oil, 1/2 cup sherry, salt, sound leaf and pepper pieces to a bubble. Include cauliflower. Diminish heat; stew, revealed, until a blade effectively embeds into focus, 15-20 minutes, turning part of the way through cooking. Evacuate with an opened spoon; channel well on paper towels. Preheat broiler to 450°. Spot cauliflower on a lubed wire rack in a 15x10x1-in. heating dish. Prepare on a lower broiler rack until dim brilliant, 39 minutes. In the meantime, place almonds, bread morsels, tomatoes, cooked peppers, parsley, garlic, paprika, salt, and pepper in a nourishment processor; beat until finely cleaved. Include remaining sherry; process until mixed. Keep preparing while step by step, including remaining oil in a constant flow. Present with cauliflower.

INGREDIENTS
10 cups water, 1 cup olive oil, isolated, 3/4 cup sherry or red wine vinegar, isolated, 3 tablespoons salt, 1 cove leaf, 1 tablespoon squashed red pepper drops, 1 enormous head cauliflower, 1/2 cup entire almonds, toasted, 1/2 cup delicate entire wheat or white bread morsels, toasted, 1/2 cup fire-simmered squashed tomatoes, 1 container (8 ounces) broiled sweet red peppers, depleted, 2 tablespoons minced new parsley, 2 garlic cloves, 1 teaspoon sweet paprika, 1/2 teaspoon salt, 1/4 teaspoon newly ground pepper

Chapter 6

WHOLE FOODS RECIPES

Whole food recipes can be tricky to master. Regularly you wind up attempting to cook with fixings that you are new to, which implies that quite possibly your family probably won't care for the dish... the unique flavors and surfaces can be altogether different from what you are accustomed to eating. However, don't stress, because there are numerous entire nourishments plans accessible online that are both healthy and delectable!

The main thing you have to consider is the nutrition of the food that you are getting ready. Numerous individuals comprehend that they have to eat increasingly healthy foods, yet they are uncertain of the motivation behind why. Sound nourishments in their standard structure are excellent sources of fiber, nutrients, and minerals.

You can build your general wellbeing by eating foods, for example, leafy foods, entire grains, nuts and seeds, beans and vegetables, and healthy fats. These nourishments contain supplement thick calories, which implies that they will give your body a high measure of sustenance when you eat them in their regular structure.

At the point when you are searching for whole foods recipes, it is ideal to discover plans that contain natural recipes. There are numerous incredible recipes, including prepared products (utilizing entire wheat flour), bean dishes, vegetable dishes, and natural product-based treats. At the point when you are changing to a more advantageous eating plan, you will be astonished to perceive what numbers of choices are accessible.

Below are healthy Whole food recipes to try:

Healing Mushroom Soup New Instant Pot

SERVINGS
10

INGREDIENTS

110 MINUTES

- 1 box cut white mushrooms (226 grams)
- 1/2 box Shtik mushrooms (226 grams), stems expelled, end disposed of and stems hacked
- 100 grams Enoki mushrooms (Half of a little pack)
- One medium white onion, cleaved
- 3 celery stalks, cleaved
- 3 garlic cloves, crushed
- 1 carrot, cut into slight circles or slashed into shapes
- Little bunch watercress, cleaved
- Bone stock to arrive at the 6 cup mark within the Instapot
- 3 tbsp grease or warmth stable fat of decision
- 1 tbsp minced crisp ginger
- 1 tbsp fish sauce
- 2 crisp straight leafs
- 1 tsp dried oregano
- 1/2 tsp dried thyme
- 1 tsp nectar
- 1-2 tbsp collagen* (discretionary)
- Juice from half of a lime
- Foul salt to taste
- Collagen Hydrolysate (Green holder if utilizing Great Lakes brand)

METHOD

1. Attachment in the Instant Pot and press the "Sauté" work.
2. Include your fat of decision, onions, carrots, and celery to the pot and sauté until they start to relax and turn translucent. Include a liberal spot of foul salt to bring out flavors and discharge juices.
3. Following five minutes, include the white mushrooms and keep on cooking until delicate, 5 additional minutes.
4. When the veggies are delicate, include the garlic and ginger, mix and cook for a moment or two until fragrant.
5. Include the fish sauce, sound leaves, and flavors and consolidate well.
6. Add the rest of the mushrooms to the pot, Shiitake, and Enoki
7. Pour in the stock to the 6 cup stamp and tenderly mix to consolidate.
8. Press the "Keep Warm/Cancel" catch to stop the sauté mode.
9. Spot the top on the Instant Pot and lock the cover. Contort the steam discharge handle on the cover to "Fixing".

More Directions:

1. Press the "manual" catch to switch the cooking mode. Set the cooking time for 7 minutes. Note that the soup will cook for longer than seven minutes as it requires some investment for the compel cooker to arrive at the wanted weight. The brief clock will begin once a legitimate weight is accomplished.
2. When the soup is finished cooking, the Instant Pot will consequently change to the "Keep Warm" mode and will flag finished with signals. When you hear the blares, the soup has cooked for the full seven minutes at the total weight. Give the soup a chance to stay in the "Keep Warm" mode for 10 minutes and afterward press "Drop."
3. Turn the steam discharge handle on the cover to "Venting." I generally put on my broiler glove as a precautionary measure as a modest quantity of steam will escape from the venting opening.
4. When the weight has discharged, cautiously open the Instant Pot.
5. Mix in the nectar and the juice of half of new lime.
6. Taste for flavoring. Include progressively foul salt (if necessary)
7. Include collagen powder, if utilizing, to include additional protein.
8. Tenderly mix in the cleaved watercress and let sit for one moment.
9. Scoop soup into bowls. On the off chance that you are attempting to build you solid fats, mix in one tbsp to each bowl of either grass encouraged to spread, coconut oil, fed fat or ghee before serving.

Peaches and Cream Oatmeal Instant Pot

SERVINGS
12

75 MINUTES

INGREDIENTS

- 2 ready peaches, set + hacked
- 1/4 cup unadulterated maple syrup
- 1/4 tsp ground cinnamon
- 1/8 cup separated water
- 2 cups nut milk of decision
- 1 cup separated water
- Touch of ocean salt
- Cinnamon stick (discretionary)
- 1 cup natural without gluten steel-cut oats
- 1-4 tbsp grass-encouraged spread (or coconut oil for dairy-free)
- 1/4-1/2 cup full fat cream (or coconut milk for dairy-free)
- Extra cream or dairy-free milk of decision for serving
- Extra unadulterated maple syrup for serving
- 1-3 new ready peaches, set and diced
- Hacked nuts, seeds or dried product of choice for fixings

METHOD

1. In a blender, puree the hacked peaches, maple syrup, cinnamon, and 1/8 cup water. Empty peach puree into an estimating cup.

2. Fitting in the Instant Pot. Include the oats, 2 cups nut milk, 1 cup sifted the water, a touch of ocean salt and a discretionary cinnamon stick.

3. Mix and afterward place the top on the Instant Pot and lock the cover. Bend the steam discharge handle on the cover to "Fixing".

4. Press the "manual" catch to pick the cooking mode. Utilize the bolts to change the cooking time to 3 minutes. Note that the cereal will cook for longer than 3 minutes as it requires some investment for the constrain cooker to arrive at the wanted weight. The brief clock will begin once an appropriate weight is accomplished.

5. When the cereal is finished cooking, the Instant Pot will naturally change to the "Keep Warm" mode and will flag finished with signals. When you hear the blares, the oats have cooked for the full 3 minutes at total weight. Give the oats a chance to stay in the "Keep Warm" mode until the weight normally discharges and afterward press "Drop."
6. Wind the steam discharge handle on the top to "Venting," but since you discharged the weight usually there will be no steam.

7. Open the Instant Pot and mix in necessary measure of margarine or coconut oil and the peach fluid from the blender. Taste and modify sweetness as per taste.

8. Let sit for a couple of moments to cool marginally at that point include the 1/4-1/2 cup of cream or coconut/nut milk of decision

9. Overlay in crisp diced peaches and present with extra milk of choice and fixings of decision

Roasted Red Pepper and Cauliflower Soup Instant Pot

SERVINGS
9

66 MINUTES

INGREDIENTS

- 1 head cauliflower, cut into florets
- 5 garlic cloves, crushed
- 4 green onions, slashed
- 1 340 ml container of simmered red peppers, diced (approx. 3 peppers)
- 1 14oz container of finely slashed tomatoes (I utilized Solo Pomodoro Mutti tomatoes)
- 2 huge carrots, diced
- 2 red shepherd peppers, seeded + diced
- 1/4 cup greens of decision (I utilized swiss chard), cut up into little strings or diced
- 1 tbsp smoked paprika
- 1/2 tbsp onion powder
- 1/2 tbsp garlic powder
- 1/4 tsp dried cumin
- 2 tbsp apple juice vinegar
- 1/2-1 tsp ocean salt, dark salt or pink Himalayan salt
- 4 cups custom made stalk, bone stock or water
- Olive oil
- S+P to taste

METHOD

1. Attachment in the Instant Pot and press the "Sauté" work.
2. Include the olive oil, onions, carrots, shepherd peppers, and garlic to the pot and sauté until they start to mellow and turn translucent. Add a spot of salt to bring out flavors and discharge juices.
3. When the veggies are delicate mix in the flavors to cover.
4. Include the ACV and join well. Give the vinegar a chance to cook off for a moment or two, blending persistently. Scrape up any darker bits joined to the base of the pot.
5. Include the container of tomatoes and the cleaved up simmered red peppers to the pot, mix well, and let the tomato blend cook for a moment.
6. Add the greens to the pot just as the cauliflower florets, mix to consolidate, trailed by 4 cups of water (or stalk bone juices).
7. Press the "Keep Warm/Cancel" catch to stop the sauté mode.
8. Mix and afterward place the top on the Instant Pot and lock the top. Curve the steam discharge handle on the top to "Fixing".
9. Press the "Soup" catch to switch the cooking mode. The cooking time will set for 30 minutes. Note that the soup will cook for longer than 30 minutes as it requires some investment for the compel cooker to arrive at the wanted weight. The brief clock will begin once an appropriate weight is accomplished.

More directions to follow:

1. When the soup is finished cooking the Instant Pot will naturally change to the "Keep Warm" mode and will flag finished with signals. When you hear the blares, the soup has cooked for the full 30 minutes at full weight. Give the soup a chance to stay in the "Keep Warm" mode for 10 minutes and afterward press "Drop."
2. Curve the steam discharge handle on the top to "Venting". I generally put on my broiler glove as a safeguard as a limited quantity of steam will escape from the venting gap.
3. When the weight has discharged, cautiously open the Instant Pot.
4. Test for flavoring. Include progressively pink salt, fresh split pepper, and new pressed lemon juice to taste.
5. Utilize a potato masher to separate the lumps of cauliflower to arrive at desired consistency or mix for a smooth consistency.
6. Scoop soup into bowls. Top with some newly slashed chives and hot red pepper chips if so wants!

Eggplant Sauce

SERVINGS
5

INGREDIENTS

80 MINUTES

- 1 pound ground meat of decision (I utilized ground pork)
- 28 Oz jar of tomatoes, depleted + tenderly pureed
- 5.5 Oz jar of tomato glue
- 5 garlic cloves, crushed
- 1/2 enormous sweet onion, hacked
- 1 eggplant, cut into equal parts and diced
- 1/2 cup olive oil
- 1 cup separated water (or bone soup)
- 1/2 tsp turmeric
- 1/2 tsp dried dill
- 1 tbsp apple juice vinegar
- 1/4 cup crisp parsley, hacked
- 1 tsp Himalayan pink salt
- S + P to taste
- Crisp Lemon to serve

METHOD

1. Attachment in the Instant Pot and press the "Sauté" work. Include the ground meat of decision to the tempered steel cooking addition and keep on carmelizing meat until never again pink. Evacuate the meat and cooking fluid and put it in a safe spot.
2. Include the olive oil and onions to the pot and sauté until they start to relax and turn translucent. Add a spot of salt to bring out flavors and discharge juices.
3. Add the eggplant to the pot. Keep sautéing until onions and eggplant are delicate.
4. Include the crushed garlic and cook for one moment until garlic is fragrant.
5. Include the ACV and join well. Give the vinegar a chance to cook off for a moment or two, blending always. Scrape up any darker bits appended to the base of the pot. On the off chance that the nourishment begins to darker also rapidly include a limited quantity of water or progressively olive oil to anticipate consuming.
6. Include the jar of tomato glue to the pot, mix well, and let the tomato glue cook off for a moment or two to relax the flavor.
7. Include the jar of murmured tomatoes, flavors, 1 tsp salt, new parsley and the ground meat (with any juices on the plate) and mix to consolidate, trailed by 1 cup water (or bone juices).
8. Press the "Keep Warm/Cancel" catch to stop the sauté mode.
9. Mix and afterward place the top on the Instant Pot and lock the cover. Wind the steam discharge handle on the cover to "Fixing".

More recipes:

1. Press the "Manual" catch to switch the cooking mode. Utilize the "+/ - " catches to set the cooking time to 15 minutes. Note that the sauce will cook for longer than 15 minutes as it requires some investment for the constrain cooker to arrive at the wanted weight. The brief clock will begin once the appropriate weight is accomplished.
2. When the sauce is finished cooking the Instant Pot will consequently change to the "Keep Warm" mode and will flag finished with blares. When you hear the blares, the soup has cooked for the full 15 minutes at total weight. Give the sauce a chance to stay in the "Keep Warm" mode for 10 minutes and afterward press "Drop."
3. Contort the steam discharge handle on the cover to "Venting". I generally put on my stove glove as a precautionary measure as a modest quantity of steam will escape from the venting opening.
4. When the weight has discharged, cautiously open the Instant Pot.
5. Test for flavoring. Include increasingly pink salt, crisp broke pepper and new crushed lemon juice to taste.
6. Appreciate with avocado pieces, crisp split pepper, and new lemon wedges or served over pasta, rice or spiralized veggies of decision.

30 DAY MEAL PLAN

The 30 days meal plan is a simple, healthy meal plan to heal the Immune System from oxidative pressure. In case you're scared by good dieting or confounded by the word anti-inflammatory, these anti-inflammatory meal plans are for you! Learn what foods heal the Immune System and get tasty plans that are without gluten, refined sans sugar, and dairy-free friendly to go along with it!

WEEK 1

MONDAY

BREAKFAST — Squash and Corn Chowder

Nutritional Information

Serves	Preparation Time	Calories	Protein	Fat	Carbs
7	5	35g	27	6g	32g

Ingredients

- 3 tablespoons extra-virgin olive oil
- 1 cup diced onion
- 1 cup diced celery
- ½ cup generally useful flour
- 1½ teaspoons dried marjoram
- ¼ teaspoon salt
- ¼ teaspoon ground pepper
- 4 cups decreased sodium chicken soup
- 1 cup entire milk
- 3 cups diced summer squash
- 2 cups diced red potatoes
- 1 cup of corn parts
- ¾ cup diced ham
- Cut scallions for decorate
- Shredded pepper Jack cheddar for decorate

Method

1. Heat oil in a large pot over medium warmth.
2. Include onion and celery; cook, blending as often as possible until mollified and starting to dark-colored, 5 minutes.
3. Sprinkle flour, marjoram, salt and pepper over the vegetables and cook, mixing, for brief more. Include soup and milk; bring to a delicate bubble, mixing continually.
4. Mix in squash, potatoes, and corn; carry just to a stew. Stew, revealed, mixing once in a while, until the potatoes are delicate, 14 minutes.
5. Include ham and cook, mixing much of the time, until warmed through, around 2 minutes.
6. Serve bested with scallions and cheddar, whenever wanted.
7. To make ahead: Cover and refrigerate for as long as 4 days, gradually warm over medium-low or microwave on Medium power.

LUNCH Lemon Chicken & Rice

Nutritional Information

Serves	Preparation Time	Calories	Protein	Fat	Carbs
3	8	50g	71	9g	37g

Ingredients

- 2 tablespoons olive oil, separated
- 8 boneless, skinless chicken thighs (1¼-1½ lbs. complete), cut
- 2 big onions, meagerly cut
- ½ teaspoon salt, separated
- 3 cloves garlic, minced
- 2 teaspoons ground turmeric
- 1 teaspoon paprika
- A liberal squeeze of saffron (discretionary)
- 3 cups destroyed cabbage (about ½ little head)
- 4 cups cooked dark colored rice, ideally basmati or jasmine
- ¼ cup lemon juice
- 2 tablespoons slashed new Italian parsley (discretionary)
- 1 lemon, cut (discretionary)

Method

1. Preheat broiler to 375°F.
2. Coat two 8-inch-square preparing dishes or foil skillet with cooking splash.
3. Heat 1 Tbsp. oil in a huge nonstick skillet over medium-high warmth. Include 4 chicken thighs, and cook, turning once, until the two sides are softly caramelized, around 4 minutes.
4. Move the chicken to a plate and put it in a safe spot. Rehash with the staying chicken thighs.
5. Pour off everything except around 1 Tbsp. fat from the dish. Include the staying 1 Tbsp. oil and onions to the container and sprinkle with ¼ tsp. salt.
6. Cook, blending, until delicate and brilliant, 12 to 15 minutes. Mix in garlic, turmeric, paprika, and saffron, if utilizing; cook, combining, for 2 minutes. Move the onions to a plate and put it in a safe spot. Return the dish to medium-high warmth and include cabbage — Cook, mixing, until dried, around 3 minutes.
7. Mix in rice, lemon squeeze, the remaining ¼ tsp. salt, and half of the held onion. Keep cooking until the rice is all around covered and warmed through, 6 minutes.
8. Gap the rice blend between the readied heating dishes; settle 4 of the held chicken thighs in each dish. Top each with half of the staying cooked onions. Spread the two plates with foil.
9. Mark one and stop for as long as multi-month. Heat the rest of the dish, secured, for 30 minutes. Reveal and keep preparing until a thermometer embedded in the thickest piece of the chicken registers 165°F and the onions are beginning to dark-colored around the edges, 5 to 10 minutes more. Topping with parsley and lemon cuts.

DINNER

Cheesy Chipotle-Cauliflower Mac

Nutritional Information

Serves	Preparation Time	Calories	Protein	Fat	Carbs
7	10	35g	71	40g	22g

Ingredients

- 3 cups cauliflower florets
- 8 ounces entire wheat fusilli or rotini pasta
- 1 cup nonfat milk
- 1 chipotle pepper in adobo, minced, in addition to 1 tablespoon adobo sauce
- 1 tablespoon olive oil
- ¼ cup finely hacked yellow onion
- 2 cloves garlic, minced
- 4 cups hacked new spinach
- ¼ teaspoon salt
- 1 tablespoon entire grain Dijon mustard
- 4 ounces decreased fat cheddar, destroyed (around 1 cup)
- 2 ounces part-skim mozzarella cheddar, destroyed (about ½ cup)
- Ground pepper (discretionary)
- Paprika (discretionary)

Method

1. Spot a steamer crate in a huge pot, add water to simply underneath the container and heat to the point of boiling.
2. Add cauliflower to the bin; spread, diminish warmth to medium and steam until delicate, 8 to 10 minutes. In the interim, heat a huge pot of water to the point of boiling.
3. Cook pasta for 2 minutes, not precisely the bundle bearings. Channel the pasta and move to a huge bowl. Move the cauliflower to a nourishment processor or blender. Include milk, chipotle and adobo sauce; puree until smooth.
4. Dry the enormous pot. Include oil and warmth over medium warmth. Include onion and cook until relaxed and straightforward, 2 to 3 minutes. Include garlic and cook until fragrant, 1 moment. Include spinach and cook until gently withered, 2 minutes.
5. Reduce heat to medium-low, cautiously include the cauliflower blend and mix to join. Mix in salt and mustard. Slowly race in Cheddar and mozzarella just until smooth, around 1 moment.
6. Remove from heat. Pour the sauce over the pasta and tenderly mix to join. Embellishment with pepper and paprika, whenever wanted.

TUESDAY

BREAKFAST   Organic vegetable broth

Nutritional Information

Serves	Preparation Time	Calories	Protein	Fat	Carbs
8	10	315g	20	22g	32g

Ingredients

- 4 medium tomatillos, husked, washed and coarsely hacked (8 ounces)
- ¼ cup hacked new cilantro
- 1 medium new jalapeño pepper, seeded and finely hacked (see Tip)
- 1 clove garlic, minced
- ¼ teaspoon salt, separated
- 1 (1¼ to 1½ pound) meat flank steak, 1 inch thick
- 1 teaspoon bean stew powder
- ¼ teaspoon ground cumin
- ¼ teaspoon garlic powder
- ¼ teaspoon ground pepper
- ¼ cup disintegrated queso fresco or ground Monterey Jack cheddar (1 ounce) (discretionary)

Method

1. For tomatillo salsa, consolidate the tomatillos, cilantro, jalapeño, garlic, and ⅛ teaspoon salt in a nourishment processor. Cover and procedure until the blend are slashed.
2. Put in a safe spot. Cut back excess from steak. Score the two sides of the steak in a jewel design; put in a safe spot. Mix together stew powder, cumin, garlic powder, ground pepper, and the remaining ⅛ teaspoon salt (see Tip) in a little bowl. Sprinkle uniformly over the two sides of the steak.
3. For a charcoal flame broil, place the steak on the barbecue rack legitimately over medium coals. Flame broil, revealed, for 17 to 21 minutes for medium (160°F), turning once part of the way through barbecuing. (For a gas flame broil, preheat the barbecue.
4. Spot the steak on the flame broil rack over the warmth. Cover and barbecue as coordinated.) Transfer the steak to a cutting board. Spread freely with foil; let represent 4 minutes.
5. Daintily cut the steak corner to corner over the grain. Present with the saved tomatillo salsa. Sprinkle with queso fresco (or Monterey Jack).

LUNCH

Chicken & Broccoli Casserole

Nutritional Information

Serves	Preparation Time	Calories	Protein	Fat	Carbs
10	10	38g	20	7g	20g

Ingredients

- 1 tablespoon canola oil
- 1 pound boneless, skinless chicken bosoms, cut
- ⅓ cup generally useful flour
- 4 cups decreased fat milk, separated
- 2 (9 ounce) bundles precooked dark colored rice
- 3 cups broccoli florets
- 1½ cups destroyed decreased fat sharp cheddar
- ½ teaspoon legitimate salt
- ½ teaspoon ground pepper
- ½ cup locally acquired firm seared onions

Method

1. Preheat stove to 400°F. Warmth oil in a huge ovenproof skillet over high warmth. Include chicken and cook until all-around seared, around 4 minutes for every side.
2. Move to a spotless cutting board and let it represent 5 minutes. Cut into 1-inch 3D shapes.
3. Whisk flour and ⅔ cup milk in a little bowl. Include the rest of the 3⅓ cups milk to the skillet; heat to the point of boiling over medium-high warmth — step by step speed in the flour-milk blend.
4. Come back to a bubble and cook, regularly mixing, until thickened, 2 to 3 minutes. Mix in rice and broccoli; come back to a bubble and cook until the broccoli is delicate around 2 minutes.
5. Mix in the chicken, cheddar, salt, and pepper. Sprinkle onions on top. Move the dish to the oven. Prepare until the dish is sautéed and foaming, 9 minutes. Let cool for 5 minutes before serving.

DINNER

Greek Turkey Burgers with Spinach, Feta & Tzatziki

Nutritional Information

Serves	Preparation Time	Calories	Protein	Fat	Carbs
7	15	30g	27	6g	32g

Ingredients

- 1 cup solidified cleaved spinach, defrosted
- 1 pound 93% lean ground turkey
- ½ cup disintegrated feta cheddar
- ½ teaspoon garlic powder
- ½ teaspoon dried oregano
- ¼ teaspoon salt
- ¼ teaspoon ground pepper
- 4 little cheeseburger buns, ideally entire wheat, split
- 4 tablespoons tzatziki
- 12 cuts cucumber
- 8 thick rings red onion (about ¼-inch)

Method

1. Preheat flame broil to medium-high.
2. Crush abundance dampness from spinach. Consolidate the spinach with turkey, feta, garlic powder, oregano, salt and pepper in a medium bowl; blend well. Structure into four 4-inch patties.
3. Oil the barbecue rack. Flame broil the patties until cooked through and never again pink in the inside, 4 to 6 minutes for every side.
4. Assemble the burgers on the buns, beating each with 1 tablespoon tzatziki, 3 cucumber cuts, and 2 onion rings.

WEDNESDAY

BREAKFAST — Cheesy Spinach and Artichoke Stuffed Spaghetti Squash

Nutritional Information

Serves	Preparation Time	Calories	Protein	Fat	Carbs
20	12	35g	27	90g	32g

Ingredients

- 1 (2½ to 3 pound) spaghetti squash, cut down the middle the long way and seeds evacuated
- 3 tablespoons water, isolated
- 1 (5 ounce) bundle infant spinach
- 1 (10 ounces) bundle solidified artichoke hearts, defrosted and slashed
- 4 ounces diminished fat cream cheddar, cubed and relaxed
- ½ cup ground Parmesan cheddar, isolated
- ¼ teaspoon salt
- ¼ teaspoon ground pepper
- Squashed red pepper and cut crisp basil for embellish

Method

1. Spot squash chop side down in a microwave-safe dish; include 2 tablespoons water. Microwave, revealed, on High until delicate, 10 to 15 minutes. (On the other hand, place squash parts chop side down on a rimmed preparing sheet.
2. Prepare at 400°F until delicate, 40 to 50 minutes.) Meanwhile, join spinach and the staying 1 tablespoon water in a huge skillet over medium warmth. Cook, mixing once in a while, until withered, 3 to 5 minutes. Deplete and move to an enormous bowl.
3. Position rack in the upper third of stove; preheat the oven. Utilize a fork to scratch the squash from the shells into the bowl. Spot the shells on a heating sheet. Mix artichoke hearts, cream cheddar, ¼ cup Parmesan, salt and pepper into the squash blend.
4. Divide it between the squash shells and top with the remaining ¼ cup Parmesan.
5. Cook until the cheddar is brilliant darker, around 3 minutes. Sprinkle with squashed red pepper and basil, whenever wanted.

LUNCH

Prosciutto Pizza with Corn & Arugula

Nutritional Information

Serves	Preparation Time	Calories	Protein	Fat	Carbs
10	15	40g	27	57g	22g

Ingredients

- 1 pound pizza mixture, ideally entire wheat
- 2 tablespoons extra-virgin olive oil, isolated
- 1 clove garlic, minced
- 1 cup part-skim destroyed mozzarella cheddar
- 1 cup crisp corn bits
- 1 ounce meagerly cut prosciutto, attacked 1-inch pieces
- 1½ cups arugula
- ½ cup torn crisp basil
- ¼ teaspoon ground pepper

Method

1. Preheat barbecue to medium-high. Roll the mixture out on a daintily floured surface into a 12-inch oval.
2. Move to a delicately floured enormous preparing sheet. Join 1 tablespoon oil and garlic in a little bowl.
3. Bring the mixture, the garlic oil, cheddar, corn and prosciutto to the barbecue. Oil the flame broil rack
4. Move the outside layer to the barbecue. Flame broil the mixture until puffed and delicately caramelized, 1 to 2 minutes.
5. Flip the outside layer over and spread the garlic oil on it. Top with the cheddar, corn, and prosciutto.
6. Flame broil, secured until the cheddar is dissolved and the outside layer is delicately caramelized on the last, 4 minutes more.
7. Return the pizza to the preparing sheet. Top the pizza with arugula, basil and pepper. Shower with the staying 1 tablespoon oil.

DINNER — Cauliflower Chicken Fried "Rice"

Nutritional Information

Serves	Preparation Time	Calories	Protein	Fat	Carbs
5	5	35g	220	122g	32g

Ingredients

- 1 teaspoon shelled nut oil in addition to 2 tablespoons, isolated
- 2 enormous eggs, beaten
- 3 scallions, meagerly cut, whites and greens isolated
- 1 tablespoon ground crisp ginger
- 1 tablespoon minced garlic
- 1 pound boneless, skinless chicken thighs, cut and cut into ½-inch pieces
- ½ cup diced red chime pepper
- 1 cup snow peas, cut and split
- 4 cups cauliflower rice (see Tip)
- 3 tablespoons decreased sodium tamari or soy sauce
- 1 teaspoon sesame oil (discretionary)

Method

1. Heat 1 teaspoon oil in a huge level bottomed carbon-steel wok or huge substantial skillet over high warmth. Include eggs and cook, without mixing, until completely cooked on one side, around 30 seconds.
2. Flip and cook until simply cooked through, around 15 seconds. Move to a cutting board and cut into ½-inch pieces.
3. Add 1 tablespoon oil to the skillet alongside scallion whites, ginger and garlic; cook, mixing, until the scallions have relaxed, around 30 seconds. Include chicken and cook, blending, for 1 moment.
4. Include ringer pepper and snow peas; cook, mixing, until simply delicate, 2 to 4 minutes. Move everything to an enormous plate.
5. Include the staying 1 tablespoon oil to the skillet; include cauliflower rice and mix until starting to relax around 2 minutes.
6. Return the chicken blend and eggs to the skillet; include tamari (or soy sauce) and sesame oil (if utilizing) and mix until very much joined — embellishment with scallion greens.

THURSDAY

BREAKFAST Cobb Salad with Herb-Rubbed Chicken

Nutritional Information

Serves	Preparation Time	Calories	Protein	Fat	Carbs
11	20	35g	27	100g	40g

Ingredients

CHICKEN:
- 1 tablespoon extra-virgin olive oil
- 1 teaspoon garlic powder
- 1 teaspoon dried thyme
- ½ teaspoon dried oregano
- ½ teaspoon dried rosemary
- ½ teaspoon ground pepper
- ¼ teaspoon fit salt
- 2 (8 ounce) boneless, skinless chicken bosoms, cut

VINAIGRETTE:
- ⅓ cup extra-virgin olive oil
- ¼ cup lemon juice
- 2 teaspoons champagne vinegar
- ½ teaspoon legitimate salt
- ¼ teaspoon ground pepper

PLATE OF MIXED GREENS:
- 6 cups child kale
- 2 medium ready avocados, cut
- 2 huge hard-bubbled eggs, cut
- 2 cuts cooked bacon, disintegrated
- ½ cup disintegrated feta cheddar
- 10 strawberries, quartered

Method

1. Preheat flame broil to medium-high. To get ready chicken: Combine 1 tablespoon oil, garlic powder, thyme, oregano, rosemary, ½ teaspoon pepper, and ¼ teaspoon salt in a little bowl.
2. Rub the blend over chicken. Oil the barbecue rack. Flame broil the chicken until a moment read thermometer embedded in the thickest part enlists 160°F, 5 to 6 minutes for every side.
3. Move the chicken to a perfect cutting board and let rest for 10 minutes. Cut. To get ready vinaigrette: Whisk oil, lemon juice, vinegar, salt and pepper in a little bowl.
4. To gather serving of mixed greens: Arrange kale, avocados, eggs, bacon, feta, strawberries and the chicken on an enormous platter. Present with the vinaigrette.

LUNCH

Superfood Chopped Salad with Salmon

Nutritional Information

Serves	Preparation Time	Calories	Protein	Fat	Carbs
15	30	80g	45	120g	400g

Ingredients

- 1 pound salmon filet
- ½ cup low-fat plain yogurt
- ¼ cup mayonnaise
- 2 tablespoons lemon juice
- 2 tablespoons ground Parmesan cheddar
- 1 tablespoon finely cleaved new parsley
- 1 tablespoon clipped new chives
- 2 teaspoons diminished sodium tamari or soy sauce
- 1 medium clove garlic, minced
- ¼ teaspoon ground pepper
- 8 cups cleaved wavy kale
- 2 cups cleaved broccoli
- 2 cups cleaved red cabbage
- 2 cups finely diced carrots
- ½ cup sunflower seeds, toasted

Method

1. Organize rack in the upper third of the oven. Preheat grill to high. Line a preparing sheet with foil. Spot salmon on the readied preparing sheet, skin-side down.
2. Cook, pivoting the dish from front to back once, until the salmon is obscure in the middle, 8 to 12 minutes. Cut into 4 segments.
3. In the meantime, whisk yogurt, mayonnaise, lemon juice, Parmesan, parsley, chives, tamari (or soy sauce), garlic and pepper in a little bowl. Join kale, broccoli, cabbage, carrots and sunflower seeds in a huge bowl. Include ¾ cup of the dressing and hurl to cover.
4. Gap the serving of mixed greens among 4 supper plates and top each with a bit of salmon and around 1 tablespoon of the rest of the dressing.

DINNER   Macaroni with Sausage & Ricotta

Nutritional Information

Serves	Preparation Time	Calories	Protein	Fat	Carbs
12	21	32g	20	200g	20g

Ingredients

- 2 tablespoons extra-virgin olive oil
- 6 tablespoons finely hacked yellow onion
- 6 ounces gentle pork wiener, housings expelled
- 1 14-ounce can no-salt-included entire stripped tomatoes, hacked, with their juice
- ¼ teaspoon ground pepper
- ⅛ teaspoon salt in addition to 1 tablespoon, partitioned
- 12 ounces slight cylinder molded pasta, for example, pasta al ceppo
- 6 tablespoons part-skim ricotta cheddar
- 10 crisp basil leaves, daintily cut
- ¼ cup naturally ground Parmigiano-Reggiano cheddar

Method

1. Put 2 quarts of water on to bubble in an enormous pot. In the interim, join oil, onion, and hotdog in a huge skillet over medium-high warmth.
2. Cook, mixing and disintegrating the hotdog with a spoon, until the onion is brilliant, 4 to 5 minutes.
3. Include tomatoes, pepper, and ⅛ teaspoon salt; cook until the tomatoes have diminished and isolated from the oil, 5 to 10 minutes.
4. Remove from heat. Include the staying 1 tablespoon salt to the bubbling water, mix in pasta and cook as indicated by bundle directions until merely delicate. Just before the pasta is done, return the sauce to medium-low warmth. Include ricotta and basil and mix until consolidated. At the point when the pasta is done, channel well and hurl with the sauce and Parmigiano. Serve without a moment's delay.

FRIDAY

BREAKFAST Asian Beef Noodle Bowls

Nutritional Information

Serves	Preparation Time	Calories	Protein	Fat	Carbs
10	22	30g	21	202g	202g

Ingredients

1. 4 ounces dried multigrain high-protein spaghetti or rice noodles
2. 2 tablespoons rice vinegar
3. 2 tablespoons diminished sodium soy sauce
4. 1½ tablespoons lime juice
5. 1 tablespoon sesame oil
6. 1 tablespoon canola oil
7. 1 tablespoon nectar
8. 1 tablespoon ground crisp ginger
9. 2 cloves garlic, minced
10. ¼ teaspoon salt
11. ⅛ teaspoon squashed red pepper
12. Nonstick cooking shower
13. 12 ounces hamburger flank steak, cut and cut corner to corner into slender reduced down strips
14. 1 cup cleaved English cucumber
15. 1 cup destroyed red cabbage
16. ½ cup slight reduced down strips carrot or bundled crisp julienned carrots
17. 2 tablespoons destroyed crisp basil
18. Lime wedges

Method

1. Cook pasta as indicated by bundle headings, discarding any salt; channel. Come back to skillet; cover and keep warm. In the meantime, for sauce, in a little bowl whisk together the following 10 recipes (through squashed red pepper).
2. Coat a 10-inch nonstick skillet with a cooking splash; heat over medium-high. Include meat, half at once, and cook 1 to 2 minutes or just until caramelized.
3. Remove from skillet. Lessen warmth to medium. Include ¼ cup of the sauce to skillet; cook 1 to 2 minutes or until fluid is almost vanished, mixing to scrape up hard darker bits.
4. Return meat with any juices; cook and mix 1 to 2 minutes more or until warmed through.
5. Separation pasta among unique dishes and shower with outstanding sauce. Top with meat, cucumber, cabbage and carrot and sprinkle with basil.
6. Top with extra basil, whenever wanted, and present with lime wedges.

LUNCH

Slow-Cooker Brisket Sandwiches with Quick Pickles

Nutritional Information

Serves	Preparation Time	Calories	Protein	Fat	Carbs
7	6 hours	90g	20	200g	20g

Ingredients

- 2 tablespoons smoked paprika
- 2 teaspoons genuine salt
- 1 teaspoon garlic powder
- 1 teaspoon onion powder
- 1 teaspoon coarsely ground pepper
- 3¼ pounds brisket, cut
- 1 tablespoon extra-virgin olive oil
- 1 16-ounce bottle rauchbier or 2 cups diminished sodium meat juices
- ½ cup white vinegar
- ½ cup juice vinegar
- 2 tablespoons light darker sugar
- 1 teaspoon pickling zest
- 1 teaspoon fit salt
- 2 pickling or smaller than expected cucumbers, cut
- 1 medium sweet onion, meagerly cut into rings
- 2 cloves garlic, slashed
- ½ teaspoon fit salt
- ½ cup low-fat mayonnaise
- 8 entire wheat buns

Method

1. To plan brisket: Combine paprika, salt, garlic powder, onion powder and pepper in a little bowl. Rub all over brisket.
2. Heat oil in an enormous, substantial skillet over medium warmth. Include the brisket and dark-colored the two sides, 3 to 5 minutes for every side. Move to a 6-quart moderate cooker.
3. Include lager (or juices) to the container alongside any residual flavor mix from your cutting board; increment warmth to high. Cook for 5 minutes, scraping up sautéed bits with a wooden spoon.
4. Pour over the brisket. Cover and cook on High for 6 hours or Low for 9 hours. To get ready pickles: Meanwhile, join white vinegar, juice vinegar and dark-colored sugar in a little pan; heat to the point of boiling over high warmth and cook for 1 moment.
5. Include pickling zest and 1 teaspoon salt. Fill an enormous, heatproof glass bowl and include cucumbers and onion.
6. Refrigerate, sometimes mixing, for in any event 1 hour or until prepared to serve. To plan garlic mayo: Mash garlic and ½ teaspoon salt into glue in a mortar and pestle or with the back of a spoon on a cutting board.
7. Consolidate the garlic blend with mayonnaise in a little bowl. Cover and refrigerate until prepared to serve. At the point when the brisket is done, move to a spotless cutting board and let rest for 10 minutes.
8. Maneuver the brisket separated into shreds with 2 forks and afterward coarsely hack the destroyed meat. Join the cleaved brisket with the fluid in the moderate cooker. To serve, channel the cured vegetables. Spread every bun with 1 tablespoon garlic mayo and top with about ¾ cup brisket and ½ cup pickles.

DINNER — Chicken Enchiladas Verdes

Nutritional Information

Serves	Preparation Time	Calories	Protein	Fat	Carbs
6	45	90g	55	232g	70g

Ingredients

- ¼ cup universally handy flour
- 1 cup unsalted chicken juices, isolated
- 2 cups tomatillo salsa
- 1 teaspoon ground cumin
- ½ cup slashed crisp cilantro, isolated
- 3 cups destroyed cooked chicken bosom
- 1 (15 ounces) can no-salt-included dark beans, flushed
- 3 ounces diminished fat cream cheddar
- 12 (5 inch) corn tortillas
- ½ cup destroyed Mexican cheddar mix
- ½ cup slashed tomato
- 6 tablespoons diminished harsh fat cream

Method

1. Preheat grill to 425°F. Whisk flour and ½ cup juices in a little bowl. Join the remaining ½ cup stock, salsa, and cumin in a medium pot. Heat to the point of boiling and race in the flour blend.
2. Cook over medium warmth, mixing once in a while until decreased to about 2½ cups, 6 to 8 minutes.
3. Mix in ¼ cup cilantro. Spread ½ cup of the salsa blend in a 9-by-13-inch ovenproof preparing dish. Join chicken, beans, cream cheddar and ½ cup of the salsa blend in an enormous bowl.
4. Spoon ¼ cup of the chicken blend onto the focal point of every tortilla and fold it up into a stogie shape.
5. Organize, crease side down, in a solitary layer over the salsa blend in the heating dish. Top the enchiladas with the rest of the salsa blend.
6. Heat until rising, around 15 minutes. Expel from broiler; increment stove temperature to sear. Sprinkle the enchiladas with cheddar.
7. Cook 8 creeps from the warmth source until the cheddar are dissolved 2 to 3 minutes. Top with tomato and the remaining ¼ cup cilantro and present with harsh cream.

SATURDAY

BREAKFAST Chickpea Curry (Chhole)

Nutritional Information

Serves	Preparation Time	Calories	Protein	Fat	Carbs
8	22	12g	40	400g	200g

Ingredients

- 1 medium serrano pepper, cut into thirds
- 4 enormous cloves garlic
- 1 2-inch piece crisp ginger, stripped and coarsely hacked
- 1 medium yellow onion, hacked (1-inch)
- 6 tablespoons canola oil or grapeseed oil
- 2 teaspoons ground coriander
- 2 teaspoons ground cumin
- ½ teaspoon ground turmeric
- 2¼ cups no-salt-included canned diced tomatoes with their juice (from a 28-ounce can)
- ¾ teaspoon legitimate salt
- 2 15-ounce jars chickpeas, washed
- 2 teaspoons garam masala
- New cilantro for decorating

Method

1. Heartbeat serrano, garlic and ginger in a nourishment processor until minced. Scratch down the sides and heartbeat once more. Include onion; beat until finely cleaved, however not watery.
2. Heat oil in a huge pot over medium-high warmth.
3. Include the onion blend and cook, mixing once in a while, until mellowed, 3 to 5 minutes. Include coriander, cumin and turmeric and cook, blending, for 2 minutes.
4. Heartbeat tomatoes in the nourishment processor until finely slashed. Add to the skillet alongside salt. Diminish warmth to keep up a stew and cook, sometimes mixing for 5 minutes. Include chickpeas and garam masala, diminish warmth to a delicate casserole, cover, and cook, blending at times, for 7 minutes more.
5. Serve beat with cilantro, whenever wanted.

LUNCH   Quick Shrimp Puttanesca

Nutritional Information

Serves	Preparation Time	Calories	Protein	Fat	Carbs
12	35	32g	20	400g	250g

Ingredients

- 8 ounces refrigerated crisp linguine noodles, ideally entire wheat
- 1 tablespoon extra-virgin olive oil
- 1 pound stripped and deveined enormous shrimp
- 1 (15 ounces) can no-salt-included tomato sauce
- 1¼ cups solidified quartered artichoke hearts, defrosted (8 ounces)
- ¼ cup slashed set Kalamata olives
- 1 tablespoon escapades, washed
- ¼ teaspoon salt

Method

1. Heat an enormous pot of water to the point of boiling. Cook linguine as per bundle guidelines.
2. Channel. In the interim, heat oil in a huge skillet over high warmth. Include shrimp in a solitary layer and cook, undisturbed, until sautéed on the last, 2 to 3 minutes.
3. Mix in tomato sauce. Include artichoke hearts, olives, escapades, and salt; cook, frequently blending, until the shrimp is cooked through and the artichoke hearts are hot, 2 to 3 minutes longer.
4. Add the depleted noodles to the sauce and mix it to consolidate. Partition among 4 pasta bowls serve hot.

DINNER

Creamy White Chili with Cream Cheese

Nutritional Information

Serves	Preparation Time	Calories	Protein	Fat	Carbs
8	22	32g	20	200g	120g

Ingredients

- 2 (15 ounces) jars no-salt-included incredible northern beans, flushed, isolated
- 1 tablespoon canola oil
- 1 pound boneless, skinless chicken thighs, cut and cut into scaled-down pieces
- 1½ cups hacked yellow onion (1 medium)
- ¾ cup hacked celery (2 medium stalks)
- 5 cloves garlic, hacked (2 tablespoons)
- 1 teaspoon ground cumin
- ¼ teaspoon salt
- 3 cups unsalted chicken stock
- 1 (4 ounces) can hack green chiles
- 4 ounces decreased fat cream cheddar
- ½ cup approximately pressed crisp cilantro leaves

Method

1. Crush 1 cup beans in a little bowl with a whisk or potato masher. Warmth oil in an enormous substantial pot over high warmth.
2. Include chicken; cook, turning once in a while, until seared, 4 to 5 minutes. Include onion, celery, garlic, cumin, and salt. Cook until the onion is translucent and delicate, 6 minutes. Include the staying entire beans, the squashed beans, stock, and chiles. Heat to the point of boiling.
3. Reduce heat to medium and stew until the chicken is cooked through, around 3 minutes.
4. Remove from heat; mix in cream cheddar until dissolved. Serve bested with cilantro.

WEEK 2

MONDAY

BREAKFAST Mini Meatloaves with Green Beans and Potatoes

Nutritional Information

Serves	Preparation Time	Calories	Protein	Fat	Carbs
10	21	32g	20	300g	70g

Ingredients

- ½ teaspoon paprika
- ½ teaspoon garlic powder, separated
- ¾ teaspoon salt, separated
- ¾ teaspoon ground pepper, separated
- 1 pound Yukon Gold or red potatoes, scoured and cut into 1-inch wedges
- 2 tablespoons extra-virgin olive oil, separated
- 1 pound lean (90% or less fatty) ground hamburger
- 1 huge egg, gently beaten
- ¼ cup finely hacked onion
- ¼ cup Italian-prepared panko breadcrumbs
- 3 tablespoons ketchup, separated
- 1 tablespoon Worcestershire sauce
- 1 pound green beans, cut

Method

1. Position racks in upper and lower thirds of the stove; preheat to 425°F. Coat 2 large rimmed heating sheets with cooking shower. Join paprika and ¼ teaspoon every garlic powder, salt, and pepper in a huge bowl. Add potatoes and hurl to cover.
2. Sprinkle with 1 tablespoon oil, hurl once more, at that point spread the potatoes in a solitary layer on one of the readied preparing sheets. (Hold the bowl.) Place on the lower rack to broil for 10 minutes.
3. Then, join meat, egg, onion, breadcrumbs, 2 tablespoons ketchup, Worcestershire and ¼ teaspoon every garlic powder, salt, and pepper in the enormous bowl. Structure the blend into 4 little portions around 2 by 4 inches each and place on the other arranged heating sheet.
4. Brush the tops with the staying 1 tablespoon ketchup. Remove the potatoes from the broiler and put the meatloaves on the lower rack. Hurl green beans with the staying 1 tablespoon oil and ¼ teaspoon each salt and pepper.
5. Move the potatoes to the other side of their skillet and add the green beans to the opposite side.
6. Cook the vegetables on the upper rack until the green beans are delicate and a moment perused thermometer embedded into the focal point of the meatloaves registers 165°F, 25 minutes more.

LUNCH   Salmon-Stuffed Avocados

Nutritional Information

Serves	Preparation Time	Calories	Protein	Fat	Carbs
11	22	32g	202	300g	210g

Ingredients

- ½ cup nonfat plain Greek yogurt
- ½ cup diced celery
- 2 tablespoons cleaved crisp parsley
- 1 tablespoon lime juice
- 2 teaspoons mayonnaise
- 1 teaspoon Dijon mustard
- ⅛ teaspoon salt
- ⅛ teaspoon ground pepper
- 2 (5 ounces) jars salmon, depleted, chipped, skin and bones expelled
- 2 avocados
- Hacked chives for decorate

Method

1. Join yogurt, celery, parsley, lime juice, mayonnaise, mustard, salt, and pepper in a medium bowl; blend well.
2. Include salmon and blend well. Divide avocados the long way and evacuate pits.
3. Scoop around 1 tablespoon tissue from every avocado half into a little bowl. Crush the scooped-out avocado tissue with a fork and mix it into the salmon blend.
4. Fill every avocado half with about ¼ cup of the salmon blend, mounding it over the avocado parts. Embellishment with chives, whenever wanted.

DINNER

Stetson Chopped Salad

Nutritional Information

Serves	Preparation Time	Calories	Protein	Fat	Carbs
12	50	322g	203	200g	20g

Ingredients

- ¾ cup of water
- ½ cup Israeli couscous (see Tips)
- 6 cups child arugula
- 1 cup new corn portions (from 2 ears of corn)
- 1 cup split or quartered cherry tomatoes
- 1 firm ready avocado, diced
- ¼ cup toasted pepitas
- ¼ cup dried currants
- ½ cup cleaved new basil
- ¼ cup buttermilk
- ¼ cup mayonnaise
- 1 tablespoon lemon juice
- 1 little clove garlic, stripped
- ¼ teaspoon salt
- ¼ teaspoon ground pepper

Method

1. Heat water to the point of boiling in a little pot. Include couscous, diminish warmth to keep up a delicate stew, cover, and cook until the water is assimilated 8 to 10 minutes.
2. Move to a fine-work filter and flush with cold water.
3. Channel well. Spread arugula on a serving platter. Include the couscous, corn, tomatoes, avocado, pepitas, and currants in improving lines over the arugula.
4. Consolidate basil, buttermilk, mayonnaise, lemon juice, garlic, salt, and pepper in a small scale nourishment processor or blender; beat until smooth.
5. Top the plate of mixed greens with the dressing just before serving.

TUESDAY

BREAKFAST — Zucchini Noodles with Avocado Pesto & Shrimp

Nutritional Information

Serves	Preparation Time	Calories	Protein	Fat	Carbs
5	29	799g	500	208g	203g

Ingredients

1. 5-6 medium zucchini (2¼-2½ pounds aggregate), cut
2. ¾ teaspoon salt, separated
3. 1 ready avocado
4. 1 cup stuffed crisp basil leaves
5. ¼ cup unsalted shelled pistachios
6. 2 tablespoons lemon juice
7. ¼ teaspoon ground pepper
8. ¼ cup extra-virgin olive oil in addition to 2 tablespoons, separated
9. 3 cloves garlic, minced
10. 1 pound crude shrimp, stripped and deveined, tails left on whenever wanted
11. 1-2 teaspoons Old Bay flavoring

Method

1. Utilizing a winding vegetable slicer or a vegetable peeler, cut zucchini longwise into long, flimsy strands or strips. Stop when you arrive at the seeds in the center.
2. Spot the zucchini "noodles" in a colander and hurl with ½ teaspoon salt. Let channel for 15 to 30 minutes, at that point tenderly crush to evacuate any overabundance water.
3. Then, consolidate avocado, basil, pistachios, lemon juice, pepper and the remaining ¼ teaspoon salt in a nourishment processor. Heartbeat until finely hacked. Include ¼ cup oil and process until smooth. Warmth 1 tablespoon oil in a large skillet over medium-high warmth include garlic and cook, mixing, for 30 seconds.
4. Include shrimp and sprinkle with Old Bay; cook, blending once in a while until the shrimp is nearly cooked through, 3 to 4 minutes.
5. Move to an enormous bowl. Include the staying 1 tablespoon oil to the skillet.
6. Include the depleted zucchini noodles and delicately hurl until hot, around 3 minutes. Move to the bowl, include the pesto and tenderly hurl to join.

LUNCH

Roasted Salmon with Smoky Chickpeas and Greens

Nutritional Information

Serves	Preparation Time	Calories	Protein	Fat	Carbs
4	5	32g	1.1	100g	800g

Ingredients

- 2 tablespoons extra-virgin olive oil, partitioned
- 1 tablespoon smoked paprika
- ½ teaspoon salt, partitioned, in addition to a squeeze
- 1 (15 ounces) can no-salt-included chickpeas, washed
- ⅓ cup buttermilk
- ¼ cup mayonnaise
- ¼ cup cleaved crisp chives or potentially dill, in addition to additional for embellish
- ½ teaspoon ground pepper, separated
- ¼ teaspoon garlic powder
- 10 cups packed kale
- ¼ cup of water
- 1¼ pounds wild salmon, cut into 4 segments

Method

1. Position racks in the upper third and center of the oven; preheat to 425°F. Join 1 tablespoon oil, paprika, and ¼ teaspoon salt in a medium bowl. Thoroughly pat chickpeas dry, at that point hurl with the paprika blend. Spread on a rimmed heating sheet.
2. Prepare the chickpeas on the upper rack, mixing twice, for 30 minutes. In the interim, puree buttermilk, mayonnaise, herbs, ¼ teaspoon pepper and garlic powder in a blender until smooth.
3. Put in a safe spot. Warmth the staying 1 tablespoon oil in a large skillet over medium heat. Include kale and cook, blending once in a while, for 2 minutes. Add water and keep cooking until the kale is delicate, around 5 minutes more.
4. Remove from warmth and mix when there's no other option of salt.
5. Remove the chickpeas from the stove and push them to the other side of the dish — Spot salmon on the opposite side and season with the remaining ¼ teaspoon each salt and pepper.
6. Prepare until the salmon is simply cooked through, 5 to 8 minutes. Sprinkle the saved dressing on the salmon, embellish with more herbs, whenever wanted, and present with the kale and chickpeas.

DINNER

Slow-Cooker Mediterranean Chicken and Chickpea Soup

Nutritional Information

Serves	Preparation Time	Calories	Protein	Fat	Carbs
5	35	210g	400	100g	220g

Ingredients

- 1½ cups dried chickpeas splashed medium-term
- 4 cups of water
- 1 huge yellow onion, finely hacked
- 1 (15 ounces) can no-salt-included diced tomatoes, ideally fire-broiled
- 2 tablespoons tomato glue
- 4 cloves garlic, finely slashed
- 1 cove leaf
- 4 teaspoons ground cumin
- 4 teaspoons paprika
- ¼ teaspoon cayenne pepper
- ¼ teaspoon ground pepper
- 2 pounds bone-in chicken thighs, skin evacuated, cut
- 1 (14 ounces) can artichoke hearts, depleted and quartered
- ¼ cup divided set oil-restored olives
- ½ teaspoon salt
- ¼ cup slashed new parsley or cilantro

Method

1. Channel chickpeas and spot in a 6-quart or bigger moderate cooker. Include 4 cups water, onion, tomatoes and their juice, tomato glue, garlic, cove leaf, cumin, paprika, cayenne and ground pepper; mix to consolidate. Include chicken.
2. Cover and cook on Low for 8 hours or High for 4 hours. Move the chicken to a spotless cutting board and let cool somewhat.
3. Dispose of narrows leaf. Include artichokes, olives, and salt to the moderate cooker and mix to join.
4. Shred the chicken, disposing of bones. Mix the chicken into the soup.
5. Serve bested with parsley (or cilantro).

WEDNESDAY

BREAKFAST   Pork Chops with Garlicky Broccoli

Nutritional Information

Serves	Preparation Time	Calories	Protein	Fat	Carbs
9	57	320g	200	800g	20g

Ingredients

- 1½ pounds broccoli with stems, cut and cut into lances
- 6 tablespoons extra-virgin olive oil, isolated
- 1 cup panko breadcrumbs, ideally entire wheat
- ¼ cup ground Parmesan cheddar, in addition to additional for serving
- ¼ cup entire wheat flour
- 1 huge egg, delicately beaten
- (4 ounces) boneless pork slashes, cut
- ¾ teaspoon salt, isolated
- 1 teaspoon lemon juice
- 4 cloves garlic, meagerly cut
- ¼ teaspoon squashed red pepper
- 2 tablespoons red-wine vinegar
- Hacked crisp thyme for decorating (optional)

Method

1. Position rack in the upper third of stove; preheat grill to high. Line a rimmed heating sheet with foil. Hurl broccoli with 1½ tablespoons oil on the readied container and spread in an even layer.
2. Sear, blending once until burned in spots, around 10 minutes. Move to a bowl and put in a safe spot. Then, consolidate breadcrumbs and Parmesan in a shallow dish. Spot flour in another shallow dish and egg in a third shallow dish. Sprinkle pork with ¼ teaspoon salt, at that point dig in the flour, shaking off overabundance; dunk in the egg, allowing abundance to trickle off; and cover with the breadcrumb blend.
3. Heat 3 tablespoons oil in an enormous nonstick skillet over medium-high warmth. Include the pork and cook, turning once, until brilliant dark colored and a moment read thermometer embedded in the thickest segment registers 145°F, around 6 minutes all out.
4. Transfer to a plate and sprinkle with lemon juice. Tent with foil wipe the skillet clean. Include the rest of the 1½ tablespoons oil, garlic, and squashed red pepper and cook over low warmth, mixing, until the garlic is sizzling around 3 minutes.
5. Remove from warmth and mix in vinegar and the remaining ½ teaspoon salt. Shower over the saved broccoli and hurl to cover. Serve the pork and broccoli with more Parmesan and thyme.

LUNCH   Zucchini Lasagna

Nutritional Information

Serves	Preparation Time	Calories	Protein	Fat	Carbs
12	21	320g	20	220g	240g

Ingredients

- 3 huge zucchini (3 pounds), cut the long way into ¼-inch-thick strips
- 1 tablespoon extra-virgin olive oil
- 12 ounces lean ground meat
- 1 cup hacked onion
- 2 cloves garlic, minced
- 1 (28 ounces) can no-salt-included squashed tomatoes
- ¼ cup dry red wine
- 1 teaspoon dried basil
- 1 teaspoon dried oregano
- ¾ teaspoon salt
- ¼ teaspoon ground pepper
- 1½ cups part-skim ricotta
- 1 huge egg, daintily beaten
- 1 cup destroyed part-skim mozzarella cheddar, separated
- Hacked new basil for decorate

Method

1. Preheat stove to 400°F. Coat 2 huge heating sheets with cooking splash. Mastermind zucchini cuts in a solitary layer on the readied preparing sheets.
2. Cook until naturally delicate, around 20 minutes. In the interim, heat oil in a large skillet over medium-high warmth. Include meat and onion; cook, mixing and disintegrating with a wooden spoon until the hamburger is seared, 6 to 8 minutes. Include garlic and cook for one more moment. Include tomatoes, wine, basil, oregano, salt, and pepper; bring to a stew.
3. Reduce heat to medium-low and cook, mixing at times, until thickened, around 8 minutes.
4. Consolidate ricotta and egg in a little bowl. Spread around 1 cup of the tomato sauce in a 9-by-13-inch heating dish. Top with one-fourth of the zucchini cuts and afterward 1 cup sauce.
5. Touch one-fourth of the ricotta blend over the top and sprinkle with ¼ cup mozzarella. Rehash to make 3 additional layers with the rest of the zucchini, sauce, ricotta blend and mozzarella.
6. Prepare until the sauce is rising around the edges, around 30 minutes. Let represent 10 minutes before serving and trimming with basil.

DINNER

Roasted Cauliflower and Potato Curry Soup

Nutritional Information

Serves	Preparation Time	Calories	Protein	Fat	Carbs
10	17	120g	80	700g	120g

Ingredients

- 2 teaspoons ground coriander
- 2 teaspoons ground cumin
- 1½ teaspoons ground cinnamon
- 1½ teaspoons ground turmeric
- 1¼ teaspoons salt
- ¾ teaspoon ground pepper
- ⅛ teaspoon cayenne pepper
- 1 little head cauliflower, cut into little florets (around 6 cups)
- 2 tablespoons extra-virgin olive oil, partitioned
- 1 enormous onion, cleaved
- 1 cup diced carrot
- 3 enormous cloves garlic, minced
- 1½ teaspoons ground crisp ginger
- 1 crisp red chile pepper, for example, serrano or jalapeño, minced, in addition to additional for embellish
- 1 (14 ounce) can no-salt-included tomato sauce
- 4 cups low-sodium vegetable juices
- 3 cups diced stripped chestnut potatoes (½-inch)
- 3 cups diced stripped sweet potatoes (½-inch)
- 2 teaspoons lime pizzazz
- 2 tablespoons lime juice
- 1 (14 ounces) would coconut be able to drain
- Slashed crisp cilantro for embellishing

Method

1. Preheat broiler to 450°F.
2. Consolidate coriander, cumin, cinnamon, turmeric, salt, pepper and cayenne in a little bowl.
3. Hurl cauliflower with 1 tablespoon oil in a huge bowl, sprinkle with 1 tablespoon of the zest blend and hurl once more. Spread in a solitary layer on a rimmed heating sheet.
4. Cook the cauliflower until the edges are caramelized, 15 to 20 minutes. Put in a safe spot. In the meantime, heat the staying 1 tablespoon oil in a huge pot over medium-high warmth.
5. Include onion and carrot and cook, frequently mixing, until beginning to darker, 3 to 4 minutes. Decrease warmth to medium and keep cooking, mixing regularly, until the onion is delicate, 3 to 4 minutes. Include garlic, ginger, chili and the rest of the flavor blend. Cook, blending, for brief more.
6. Mix in tomato sauce, scraping up any cooked bits, and stew for 1 moment. Include stock, potatoes, sweet potatoes, lime get-up-and-go, and squeeze.
7. Cover and heat to the point of boiling over high warmth. Lessen warmth to keep up a delicate stew and cook, mostly secured and blending every so often, until the vegetables are delicate, 35 to 40 minutes. Mix in coconut milk and the roasted cauliflower. Come back to a stew to warm through. Serve embellished with cilantro and chiles, whenever wanted.

THURSDAY

BREAKFAST Crispy Oven-Fried Fish Tacos

Nutritional Information

Serves	Preparation Time	Calories	Protein	Fat	Carbs
20	1 hour -20 minutes	32g	100	900g	420g

Ingredients

- Cooking shower
- 1 cup entire grain oat chips
- ¾ cup dry entire wheat breadcrumbs
- ¾ teaspoon ground pepper, isolated
- ½ teaspoon garlic powder
- ½ teaspoon paprika
- ½ teaspoon salt, isolated
- ½ cup universally handy flour
- 2 enormous egg whites
- 2 tablespoons water
- 1 pound cod, cut into ½-by-3-inch strips (cut down the middle on a level plane, if thick)
- 2 tablespoons avocado oil
- 2 tablespoons unseasoned rice vinegar
- 3 cups coleslaw blend
- 1 avocado, diced
- 8 corn tortillas, warmed
- Pico de gallo

Method

1. Preheat broiler to 450°F. Set a wire rack on a preparing sheet; cover with cooking shower.
2. Spot oat chips, breadcrumbs, ½ teaspoon pepper, garlic powder, paprika, and ¼ teaspoon salt in a nourishment processor and procedure until finely ground. Move to a shallow dish. Spot flour in a subsequent shallow dish. Whisk egg whites and water together in a third shallow dish.
3. Dig each bit of fish in the flour, dunk it in the egg white blend and afterward cover on all sides with the breadcrumb blend.
4. Spot on the readied rack. Coat the two sides of the breaded fish with cooking shower. Prepare until the fish is cooked through and the breading is brilliant dark-colored and fresh around 10 minutes. In the meantime, whisk oil, vinegar and the remaining ¼ teaspoon each pepper and salt in a medium bowl.
5. Add coleslaw blend and hurl to cover. Gap the fish, coleslaw blend and avocado uniformly among tortillas. Present with pico de gallo, whenever wanted.

LUNCH

Broccoli-Cheddar-Chicken Chowder

Nutritional Information

Serves	Preparation Time	Calories	Protein	Fat	Carbs
12	21	332g	240	700g	220g

Ingredients

- 3 tablespoons extra-virgin olive oil
- 1 cup diced onion
- 1 cup diced celery
- ½ cup generally useful flour
- 1 teaspoon dry mustard
- ¼ teaspoon salt
- ¼ teaspoon ground pepper
- 4 cups decreased sodium chicken stock
- 1 cup entire milk
- 3 cups hacked broccoli florets
- 2 cups diced Yukon Gold potatoes
- 1 pound boneless skinless chicken bosoms, cut into scaled-down pieces
- 1 cup destroyed cheddar, in addition to additional for embellish
- Finely diced red onion for embellish

Method

1. Heat oil in an enormous pot over medium warmth. Include onion and celery; cook, mixing much of the time, until relaxed and starting to darker, 3 to 6 minutes.
2. Sprinkle flour, dry mustard, salt and pepper over the vegetables and cook, blending, for brief more. Include soup and milk; bring to a delicate bubble, mixing continually.
3. Mix in broccoli and potatoes and carry just to a stew. Stew, revealed, blending at times until the potatoes are delicate, 12 to 15 minutes.
4. Include chicken and 1 cup Cheddar and cook, blending as often as possible, until cooked through, 4 to 6 minutes.
5. Serve bested with somewhat more Cheddar and red onion, whenever wanted.

DINNER — Chicken and Spinach Skillet Pasta with Lemon and Parmesan

Nutritional Information

Serves	Preparation Time	Calories	Protein	Fat	Carbs
10	45	321g	220	209g	209g

Ingredients

- 8 ounces sans gluten penne pasta or entire wheat penne pasta
- 2 tablespoons extra-virgin olive oil
- 1 pound boneless, skinless chicken bosom or thighs, cut, if vital, and cut into reduced down pieces
- ½ teaspoon salt
- ¼ teaspoon ground pepper
- 4 cloves garlic, minced
- ½ cup dry white wine
- Squeeze and pizzazz of 1 lemon
- 10 cups cleaved new spinach
- 4 tablespoons ground Parmesan cheddar, partitioned

Method

1. Cook pasta as indicated by bundle bearings. Deplete and put in a safe spot. In the interim, heat oil in a large high-sided skillet over medium-high warmth. Include chicken, salt and pepper; cook, sometimes mixing, until cooked through, 5 to 7 minutes.
2. Include garlic and cook, blending, until fragrant, around 1 moment. Mix in wine, lemon squeeze and pizzazz; bring to a stew.
3. Remove from heat. Mix in spinach and the cooked pasta. Cover and let remain until the spinach is withered.
4. Gap among 4 plates and top each presenting with 1 tablespoon Parmesan.

FRIDAY

BREAKFAST — Vegan Mango Almond Milkshake

Nutritional Information

Serves	Preparation Time	Calories	Protein	Fat	Carbs
2	4	311g	290	109g	29g

Ingredients

- 1 ripe of mango, must be pulp
- 3/4 cup of almond milk, must be unsweetened
- Ice

Method

1. Put all the ingredients in a blender & blend until smooth.
2. Drink immediately after preparation.

LUNCH

Peanut Butter Mocha Espresso Shake

Ingredients

- 1/2 solidified banana
- 1 tablespoon nutty spread
- 1 tablespoon unsweetened cocoa powder
- 1/2 cup almond milk
- 1/2 cup solid fermented espresso, chilled
- 3/4 cup ice

Method

1. Consolidate all fixings in a blender. Mix until smooth.

DINNER

Chocolate Chip Banana Pancakes

Ingredients

- 1/2 cups date, pit expelled
- 1/2 cup nutty spread
- 1/2 cup antiquated moved oats

Method

1. Line a 8x8 preparing dish with material paper. Put in a safe spot.
2. Spot the dates in a nourishment processor and procedure until generally hacked. Note: if dates are not sodden and clingy before being cleaved, absorb the entire dates warm water for around 10 minutes.
3. After the dates have been slashed, include the nutty spread and the oats. Heartbeat until just combined. Press the blend into the readied heating dish. Spot in the cooler until set, around 60 minutes.
4. Cut and serve. Store in the cooler.

SATURDAY

BREAKFAST — Peanut Butter Mocha Espresso Shake

Ingredients

- 1 enormous excessively ready banana, crushed
- 2 tablespoons coconut sugar
- 3 tablespoons coconut oil, liquefied
- 1 cup coconut milk
- 1/2 cups entire wheat flour
- 1 teaspoon heating pop
- 1/2 cup veggie lover chocolate chips, we utilized Enjoy Life Mini Chips

Method

1. In an enormous blending bowl, consolidate the banana, sugar, oil, and milk. Blend well to join. Include the flour and heating pop, cautiously mix until simply joined. Be mindful so as not to over blend. Delicately overlap in the chocolate chips.
2. Gently splash a skillet with non-stick shower and warmth on medium warmth. Pour around 1/4 cup of the player into the dish. Cook around 3 to 4 minutes, or until hotcakes start to rise in the middle. Cautiously flip and cook for another 2 to 3 minutes. When cooked, expel flapjack from the skillet and rehash the procedure until all the hitter has been utilized. Oil the skillet varying with non-stick shower in the middle of cooking the hotcakes.
3. Serve hot, whenever wanted top with maple syrup, nectar, coconut margarine, new natural product, or your preferred jam!

LUNCH

Banana Smash Oatmeal

Ingredients

- 1/4 cup antiquated oats
- 1/4 teaspoon cinnamon
- 1/2 cup in addition to 1 tablespoon almond milk, unsweetened
- 1 formula Roasted Banana Smash

Method

1. Make the Roasted Banana Smash formula.
2. Meanwhile, add the initial 3 fixings to a pot and heat to the point of boiling.
3. Diminish heat to a low bubble and cook 5 minutes, or adhere to the directions on the oat's.
4. Expel from warmth and mix in the simmered banana crush, being certain to include all the sweet squeezes.

DINNER

Six Plants Based Oil-Free Salad Dressing

Ingredients

- Tamari Vinaigrette
- 1/4 cup tamari
- 1/4 cup balsamic or red wine vinegar
- 2 teaspoons Dijon mustard
- 1001 Islands
- 6 tablespoons luxurious tofu
- 3 tablespoons stone ground mustard
- 3 tablespoons ketchup
- 1 teaspoon crisply pressed lemon juice
- touch of salt
- touch of naturally ground pepper
- Agave Mustard
- 1/4 cup stone ground mustard
- 1/4 cup smooth tofu
- 3 tablespoons agave syrup
- touch of salt, or to taste
- touch of naturally ground dark pepper, or to taste
- Strawberry Vinaigrette
- 4 huge strawberries
- 1 tablespoon red wine vinegar
- 2 tablespoons agave syrup
- touch of naturally ground dark pepper
- Smooth Italian
- 6 tablespoons delicate, smooth tofu
- 4 tablespoons water
- 2 teaspoons new crushed lemon juice
- 1/2 teaspoons every garlic powder, onion powder, oregano chips, rosemary drops, basil pieces, and salt
- touch of newly ground dark pepper
- Sesame umami
- 1/4 cup tamari or soy sauce
- 2 tablespoons toasted sesame seeds
- 2 tablespoons rice vinegar
- 2 tablespoons water
- 1 huge clove finely squashed garlic

Method

1. Tamari Vinaigrette: Whisk and blend in with a plate of mixed greens.
2. 1001 Islands: Puree utilizing submersion blender or whisk energetically until smooth.
3. Agave Mustard: Puree utilizing submersion blender or whisk energetically until smooth.
4. Strawberry Vinaigrette: Mix in nourishment processor or heartbeat in a rapid blender to hold surface whenever wanted.
5. Velvety Italian: Puree tofu and water utilizing a little nourishment processor or drenching blender at that point beat mix in different fixings to hold bits of shading from herb pieces.
6. Sesame umami: Toast sesame seeds in a skillet over medium-high warmth until they pop, at that point granulate seeds in flavor processor and whisk together with different fixings.

SUNDAY

BREAKFAST   Fusion Lunch Burritos

Ingredients

- 18 rice paper wrappers
- 8 ounces dark colored rice noodles, suggest Annie Chun's Maifun Brown Rice Noodles
- 5 ounces blended child greens, natural if conceivable
- 1 avocado
- 1 cucumber
- 2 chime peppers, your decision of shading
- 2 cups destroyed carrots
- 2 cups destroyed purple cabbage
- 1 (16 ounces) bundle firm or excessively firm square of tofu
- Veggie lover sans oil plate of mixed greens dressing – your decision

Method

1. Prepare rice noodles as per bundle guidelines and afterward channel.
2. Peel and cut avocado, cucumber, and chime peppers into matchstick width strips.
3. Prepare tofu boards as portrayed in this formula, without the marinade, and afterward cut into matchstick width strips.
4. Add the vegetable fillings to an enormous bowl, at that point prepare and cover generously with the vegetarian sans oil serving of mixed greens dressing of your decision.
5. Prepare moves independently by submerging each sheet of rice wrapper in turn in a bowl of warm water for 10 seconds, at that point place on a cutting board or other clean level work surface.
6. Layer an even measure of plate of mixed greens filling crosswise over lower third of rice wrapper, leaving room on sides to fold edges for your burrito spring rolls.
7. Layer an even measure of tofu strips and rice noodles over plate of mixed greens filling, at that point overlay over edge folds and fold your burritos into completely encased cylinders.
8. The fixings recorded should make around 18 completed rolls. Spot completed moves on a serving plate, and be certain not to stack them, as they will stay together.
9. Eat, grin, and feel sound!

LUNCH   Avocado Hummus Bowl

Ingredients

- 1/2 ready avocado, stripped, pitted, and thickly cut
- 1/2 cup chickpeas (from a 15-ounce can), depleted and washed
- 1/2 medium estimated cucumber, meagerly cut
- 2/3 cup grape or cherry tomatoes
- 1 cup child carrots
- 10 spinach leaves, well-cleaned
- 1/3 cup clean eating hummus, any assortment, locally acquired or handcrafted
- 2 tablespoons pumpkin or shelled sunflower seeds, discretionary
- 1/4 teaspoon genuine or ocean salt
- 1/4 teaspoon dark pepper

Method

1. Line a bowl with spinach leaves, layering if vital.
2. Add avocado cuts to one corner, chickpeas to another, grape tomatoes to another, and infant carrots to another.
3. Add hummus to the inside and top with sunflower or pumpkin seeds, if utilizing.
4. Sprinkle entire dish with salt and pepper and appreciate!
5. This is extraordinary for a to-go lunch when made in a compact holder with a top.

DINNER

Slow Cooker Pumpkin Chili

Ingredients

- 1 onion, diced
- 2 (14 ounces) jars squashed tomatoes
- 2 (14 ounces) jars dark beans, depleted
- 1 carrot, destroyed
- 1 chime pepper, diced
- 1 jalapeno, veins and seeds expelled and minced
- 2 cloves garlic, minced
- 1 1/2 cups pumpkin puree
- 1 cups low sodium vegetable soup
- 2 tablespoons stew powder
- 1 teaspoon pumpkin pie flavor
- 1 teaspoon Kosher salt
- 1/2 teaspoon dark pepper

Method

1. Add everything to your moderate cooker and mix to consolidate.
2. Cook on low for 5 to 6 hours or high for 2 to 3 hours. Present with a bit of Greek yogurt or bested with avocado cuts.

WEEK 3

MONDAY

BREAKFAST Butternut Squash & and Cranberry Quinoa Salad

Ingredients

- 3 cups butternut squash, diced little
- 5 tablespoons extra-virgin olive oil
- 2 cups cooked quinoa
- 1/2 cup dried cranberries
- 1/3 cup pecans pieces
- 1 tablespoon newly slashed basil
- 1/4 teaspoon legitimate or ocean salt
- 1/4 teaspoon dark pepper

Method

1. Pour 3 tablespoons of extra-virgin olive oil into a medium pot. Sauté the squash over medium-low warmth until cooked through and delicate.
2. In an enormous bowl, blend the cooked squash, quinoa, cranberries, pecans, basil, salt, pepper, and the staying 2 tablespoons of additional virgin olive oil.

LUNCH

Herbed Wild Rice Stuffed Potatoes

Nutritional Information

Serves	Preparation Time	Calories	Protein	Fat	Carbs
11	22	32g	202	300g	210g

Ingredients

· 4 enormous chestnut potatoes
· 2 tablespoons olive oil, partitioned
· 1/2 teaspoon coarse ocean salt, partitioned
· 1 shallot, minced
· 1 clove garlic, minced
· 4 cups infant spinach
· 1 cup wild rice or wild rice mix, cooked by bundle headings
· 2 tablespoons crisp slashed parsley
· 2 tablespoons crisp slashed basil
· 1 teaspoon minced chives
· 1 tablespoon crisp lemon juice
· 1/4 teaspoon new ground dark pepper

Method

1. Preheat stove to 350 degrees F. Coat the potatoes in 1/2 tablespoon of the oil and rub with a large portion of the salt. Lay on a preparing sheet and heat for 1/2 hour. Expel from the stove and prick with a fork, and set back in the broiler. Keep heating until potatoes are delicate, around 45 minutes more.
2. While the potatoes are preparing, make the filling.
3. Heat the rest of the oil in a skillet over medium warmth. Include the shallots and garlic and cook until delicate. Include the spinach and cook until simply withered. Mix in the cooked rice and mood killer the warmth. Mix in the herbs, lemon juice, staying salt and pepper.
4. When the potatoes are done, they divided each into equal parts. Stuff each with about a half cup of the rice blend and serve.

DINNER

Spicy Kale Salad with Chickpeas and Maple Dijon Dressing

Ingredients

FOR THE SALAD
- 1 (15 ounces) can chickpeas, depleted and flushed
- 1/2 teaspoon cayenne pepper
- 1/4 teaspoon red pepper pieces
- 3 cups kale, generally cleaved
- 1/2 cup carrot, destroyed
- 1/2 cup red onion, cut into slight strips
- 1 jalapeno pepper, cut into small strips (for additional zest, utilize a habanero pepper!)

FOR THE DRESSING:
- 1/4 cup apple juice vinegar
- 2 tablespoons unadulterated maple syrup
- 1 tablespoon dijon mustard
- 1 teaspoon orange get-up-and-go

Method

FOR THE SALAD
1. In a medium bowl, join the chickpeas, cayenne pepper, and red pepper pieces. Hurl well to cover the chickpeas in the flavors.
2. 2In an enormous bowl, consolidate the chickpeas and the rest of the plate of mixed greens fixings. Prepare well to join and place the blended plate of mixed greens into serving bowls. Sprinkle with around 3 teaspoons of dressing and serve.

FOR THE DRESSING
1. Combine all fixings and whisk well. Let sit for 5 minutes. Give the dressing a brisk mix before sprinkling over the serving of mixed greens.

TUESDAY

BREAKFAST Gluten-Free Mango and Black Bean Tacos

Ingredients

- 2 Roma tomatoes, diced little
- 2 tablespoons red onion diced little
- 1/4 cup orange ringer pepper, diced little
- 1 tablespoon lime juice
- 2 tablespoons new cilantro, hacked
- 1/2 teaspoon Kosher salt
- 1 (15 ounces) can dark beans, depleted and washed
- 1/4 cup vegetable soup
- 6 gluten-free corn tortillas
- 1 ready mango, cut into strips
- 1 avocado, pit and strip expelled, cut into little pieces

Method

2. In a blending bowl, consolidate the tomatoes, onion, chime pepper, lime juice, cilantro, and salt. Blend to consolidate. Spread and put aside to rest.
3. Meanwhile, in a little bot, heat the dark beans and vegetable juices, bring to a stew and cook for around 5 minutes. Expel from warm and delicately squash, making a point to leave a few beans entire and the blend exceptionally stout.
4. Heat a large skillet on high warmth, an iron fry dish works extraordinarily! At the point when the skillet is hot, include one corn tortilla. Cook for around 30 seconds, or until caramelized and go over to cook the second side for around 30 seconds. Spot the seared tortilla on a warm plate. Rehash with outstanding tortillas.
5. Place the tortiallas on a level surface and spread with the dark beans. Top the beans with mango and avocado. Spoon the tomato blend on top. Serve and appreciate!

LUNCH

Spicy Kale Salad with Chickpeas and Maple Dijon Dressing

Ingredients

FOR THE SALAD:
- 1 (15 ounce) can chickpeas, depleted and washed
- 1/2 teaspoon cayenne pepper
- 1/4 teaspoon red pepper pieces
- 3 cups kale, generally cleaved
- 1/2 cup carrot, destroyed
- 1/2 cup red onion, cut into slender strips
- 1 jalapeno pepper, cut into slender strips (for additional zest, utilize a habanero pepper!)

FOR THE DRESSING:
- 1/4 cup apple juice vinegar
- 2 tablespoons unadulterated maple syrup
- 1 tablespoon dijon mustard
- 1 teaspoon orange get-up-and-go

Method

Directions For the Salad:
1. In a medium bowl, consolidate the chickpeas, cayenne pepper, and red pepper drops. Hurl well to cover the chickpeas in the flavors.
2. In a huge bowl, join the chickpeas and the rest of the plate of mixed greens fixings. Prepare well to consolidate and put the blended plate of mixed greens into serving bowls. Sprinkle with around 3 teaspoons of dressing and serve.

For the Dressing:
1. Combine all fixings and whisk well. Let sit for 5 minutes. Give the dressing a snappy mix before sprinkling over the plate of mixed greens.

DINNER

Old-Fashioned Potato Salad

Ingredients

- 2 pounds red potatoes, with skins
- 1 tablespoon fit or ocean salt
- 1/2 cup diced celery
- 1/2 cup diced red onion
- 1/2 paprika (for decorate), discretionary
- Plant-Based Mayonnaise
- 1 cup crue cashews + 2 cups water for drenching
- 3/4 cup water
- 2 tablespoons newly crushed lemon juice
- 2 tablespoons white wine vinegar
- 1 teaspoon garlic powder
- 1/2 teaspoon onion powder
- 1 teaspoon ocean salt
- 1/2 teaspoon dark pepper
- 2 tablespoons Dijon mustard
- 2 tablespoons entire grain mustard
- 1/3 cup hacked dill weed

Method

2. Wash and clean potatoes, cut into 3D shapes, around 1-1/2 inches. Include potatoes and 1 tablespoon salt to an enormous pot, totally spread potatoes with water and heat to the point of boiling. Lessen warmth to a low-bubble. Cook until potatoes are delicate when penetrated with a fork, 15-20 minutes. Channel potatoes, spread and put in a safe spot.
3. While potatoes are cooking, add cashews to a huge bowl, spread with 2 cups water and permit to set 15 minutes. Channel and flush cashews.
4. Include flushed cashews and 3/4 cup water to a blender, beat until a smooth consistency. Empty blend into a blending bowl.
5. Include remaining fixings, aside from red onions and celery, to the cashew/water blend. Rush until all around consolidated. Note: mayo will thicken up following a few hours, and is best when made the prior night.
6. Add onions and celery to potatoes, hurl to join.
7. Pour around 1 cup mayo over the potatoes, hurl to join. Include extra mayo for a definitive smooth potato serving of mixed greens. Include extra salt whenever wanted. Softly sprinkle the top with paprika.
8. Cover and refrigerate 2-3 hours before serving.

WEDNESDAY

BREAKFAST

Three Bean Salad: This dish is unquestionable requirements have at any braai however can likewise be presented with flame-broiled chicken bosoms as a light summer supper alternative!

SERVINGS: 6-8

PREPARATION TIME: 20 MIN.

Ingredients

- 1 red onion, finely cut
- 1 tin chickpeas, depleted and flushed
- 1 tin kidney beans, drained and washed
- 250 g cherry tomatoes, divided
- 150 g green beans, toped and followed
- 30 g rocket, washed
- 30 ml KNORR Light Greek Salad Dressing

Method

1. Place every one of the fixings together in a bowl and blend well to join.
2. Serve right away.

LUNCH

Greek Chicken, Tomato & Feta Bake: This simple-to-make heated chicken and feta dish will dazzle family, companions and fans the same.

SERVINGS: 4-6

PREPARATION TIME: 60 MIN.

Ingredients

- 500 g Baby potatoes, divided
- 6 Small chicken thighs on the bone, skin on
- 1 KNORR Brown Onion Gravy
- 1 tsp Robertsons Paprika
- 2 Red onions, cut into eighths
- 1 Red pepper, cut into strips
- 1 Yellow pepper, cut into strips
- 3 Garlic cloves, squashed
- 2 tbsp Olive oil
- 1 tsp Robertsons Origanum
- Robertsons Salt and Pepper
- 200 g Tin diced tomatoes
- 12 Black olives
- Chopped level leaf parsley
- 250 ml Feta cheddar, disintegrated

Method

1. Preheat broiler to 200°C.
2. In an enormous container of bubbling water cook potatoes for 10 minutes.
3. Drain and put aside to cool.
4. Place chicken in an enormous preparing dish.
5. Sprinkle with KNORR Brown Onion Gravy and paprika.
6. Add onions, peppers, garlic and potatoes.
7. Drizzle with oil, sprinkle with origanum and season well. Bake for 30 minutes. Add tomatoes and olives, seasoning chicken with the juices.
8. Cook for 15 additional minutes.
9. Serve sprinkled with parsley and feta cheddar.

DINNER

Butternut & Leek Soup: Customary butternut soup plans are an absolute necessity have on your winter feast organizer, so here's a delectable one made with leek and green apple.

SERVINGS: 4-6

PREPARATION TIME: 40 MIN.

Ingredients

- 15-milliliter oil
- 3 Leeks, cut
- ½ Onion slashed
- 1 kilogram Butternut, cubed
- 1 Green Apple, cored and slashed
- ½ teaspoon Black pepper
- 1 KNORR Vegetable Stock Pot
- 300 millimeter Milk
- 200 millimeter Water
- 1 A swirl of Cream to serve

Method

1. Heat oil in an enormous pot; include leeks and onion and sauté until they mellow.
2. Add butternut, apple and dark pepper.
3. Add KNORR Vegetable Stock Pot, milk and water, and add to the soup blend.
4. Simmer for 25-30 min until the butternut is delicate.
5. Once cooked, place in a liquidizer and puree until smooth.
6. Serve with a whirl of cream and topping gently with dark pepper.

THURSDAY

BREAKFAST   Chicken Vinaigrette

SERVINGS: 4

PREPARATION TIME: 60 MIN.

Ingredients

- 1 oven/fryer chicken (3 pounds), cut up and skin expelled
- 1 teaspoon vegetable oil
- Salt and pepper to taste
- 1 huge onion, hacked
- 1 garlic clove, minced
- 4 medium carrots, cut
- 4 medium red potatoes, split
- 1/2 cup water
- 1 tablespoon minced new parsley
- 1 teaspoon dried basil
- 1/2 teaspoon chicken bouillon granules
- Pinch dried thyme
- 1/2 cup each cleaved sweet red and yellow pepper (1-inch pieces)
- 2 green onions cut
- 1/4 cup juice or red wine vinegar

Method

1. In a nonstick skillet, dark-colored chicken in oil. Sprinkle with salt and pepper. Expel and keep warm. In the drippings, saute onion and garlic until delicate.
2. Mix in the carrots, potatoes, water, and seasonings; top with chicken.
3. Reduce heat; spread and stew for 25 minutes, mixing every so often. Mix in extra water if necessary. Include peppers and green onions.
4. Spread and cook until chicken juices run clear and vegetables are delicate around 5 minutes. Mix in vinegar; heat through.

LUNCH

Hearty Beef Stew with Mushrooms and Mash: Use red wine, button mushrooms, and cubed beef to make this tasty stew ideal for a hearty family feast.

SERVINGS: 4

PREPARATION TIME: 45 MIN.

Ingredients

- 150 g Pickling onions, peeled
- 15 ml oil
- 3 ml crushed garlic
- 500 g Cubed lean beef
- 100 ml Red wine (optional)
- 1 Red pepper, cut into strips
- 150 g Button mushrooms, whole
- 1 KNORR Hearty Beef Stew with Rosemary Dry Cook-in-Sauce
- 400 ml of cold water
- 45 ml Chopped fresh Italian flat-leaf parsley
- 350 g potatoes, cubed and boiled
- 50 ml Milk
- 20 g Stork Margarine

Method

1. In a large pot, brown onions in oil and add garlic and beef cubes.
2. Fry until the meat is browned, then add the wine, red pepper and mushrooms and fry for 2 min.
3. Add 400 ml cold water to the pot and stir in the contents of the KNORR Hearty Beef Stew sachet.
4. Bring to the boil while stirring.
5. Simmer uncovered for 20 min, stirring occasionally and add parsley.
6. Prepare mashed potatoes by mixing potato, milk and Stork margarine.
7. Serve stew with potato as a side dish.

DINNER

Easy Seafood Breyani With Prawns, Hake And Calamari: Use prawns, hake, and calamari to make this unusual seafood breyani dish

SERVINGS: 4

PREPARATION TIME: 30MIN.

Ingredients

- 2 tomatoes, cubed
- 30 ml Fresh coriander, chopped
- 300 g Hake fillet, cubed
- 200 g Prawns, deveined and shelled
- 800 ml Water
- 1 box KNORR Rice Mate Mild Breyani
- 15 ml of oil
- 200 g Calamari rings

Method

1. In a large saucepan, fry the hake and calamari in oil for 3 min.
2. Add the sachet of seasoning mix, 800 ml hot water, and the uncooked rice and bring to the boil.
3. Reduce the heat and simmer for 15 min, stirring occasionally.
4. Stir in the prawns and tomato, and simmer for a further 5 min.
5. Top with chopped coriander.

FRIDAY

BREAKFAST
Portuguese-Style Chicken: A nice and spicy chicken dish with the flavors of Portugal all cooked together in one bag!

SERVINGS: 4-6

PREPARATION TIME: 60 MIN.

Ingredients

- 1 KNORR Cook-in-Bag Spicy Roast Chicken
- 10 skinless chicken thighs
- 1 red pepper, sliced
- 1 punnet mange tout
- 700g sweet potatoes, cubed with skin intact
- 15 ml of lemon juice
- 1 clove roughly chopped garlic
- 5 ml Robertsons Portuguese Chicken Spice

Method

1. Preheat oven to 180°C.
2. Place chicken thighs, red pepper, mange tout, sweet potatoes, lemon juice, garlic and Portuguese Chicken Spice into the cooking bag.
3. Sprinkle the seasoning mix inside the bag, hold the bag closed and roll gently to coat the ingredients evenly.
4. Place the cooking bag onto a baking tray.
5. Knot the bag loosely to seal and pierce the top of the bag 3 times with a knife for the steam to escape.
6. Place the baking tray in the center of the oven and bake for 40-45 minutes. Ensure that the grill is off at all times.
7. Cut the bag open and transfer to a serving dish with any sauce that is in the bag.

Chef Wendy

Cooking With Lentils

Dried lentils are a fantastic ingredient when it comes to 'stretching' family meals - they're inexpensive, packed with fiber, and so versatile because they have a mild, neutral taste that can be combined with many interesting flavors to create memorable and comforting dishes! They're lovely in stews, curries, soups and bakes, and you can also use them to make excellent warm winter salads.

Buying Lentils

- Ordinary brown lentils cost very little and can be found in all supermarkets, in the aisle where the dried beans and pulses are.
- You can also use whole green lentils, or split red or yellow lentils.
- If you're in a hurry, you can use tinned, drained lentils in any of the recipes below (these are already cooked).

How to cook lentils

- Lentils do not need to be soaked before they are cooked, although by soaking them ahead you can reduce the cooking time by about half.
- First, rinse the lentils very well in a sieve to remove any little stones or shriveled lentils.
- Put 1.5 liters cold water into a pot and add 2 cups of dried lentils.
- Bring the pot quickly to the boil, and then turn down the heat and cook, uncovered, over medium-low heat, until the lentils are soft.
- How long they will take to cook depends on the type of lentil. Split red lentils take about 20 minutes, and form a creamy purée, making them ideal for thickening soups and curries. Brown lentils take about 30 minutes, and green lentils a little longer.
- Keep checking the lentils to see whether they are done to your liking. They should be tender you're eating them in a salad or a side dish, and a little softer if they're going into a soup, stew or curry.
- Don't let the lentils get mushy (except if you're cooking split red lentils), and watch the pot closely, so it doesn't dry out.
- Immediately tip the contents of the pot into a large sieve or colander set over the sink, and allow draining for 3-4 minutes. Now add some fabulous flavors...
- You can add some flavoring agents to the boiling water if you like – for example, a slice of onion, a few bay leaves, a cinnamon stick, curry leaves or similar whole spices. Discard these when you drain the lentils.
- Don't add acidic ingredients such as lemon, tomatoes or vinegar to the pot, as these may slow down the cooking process.

How to flavour lentils

- Tip your drained, hot lentils back into the pot in which they boiled and add a Knorr Vegetable or Chicken Stock Pot. Stir until the contents of the stockpot have dissolved. This will add a lovely depth of flavor to the lentils, and will also help season them.
- You can now go ahead and creatively use the cooked lentils as a basic ingredient in a variety of dishes (see our great easy recipes below).
- Or you can create a warm or cold dish to serve on its own as a main course or a side dish.

Here are some other ingredients that go beautifully with a warm or cold lentil salad:
- Cooked beetroot, roasted peppers, roasted butternut
- Chopped fresh herbs such as parsley, chives, mint, basil, spring onions & coriander
- Salad leaves such as wild rocket and watercress
- Feta cheese, Halloumi cheese, goat's cheese and ricotta
- Raw or oven-roasted cherry tomatoes
- Finely chopped cucumber, carrots, peppers and baby marrows
- Garlic, lemon, lemon zest, white-wine vinegar, mustard, olive oil
- Crispy bacon bits
- Toasted sunflower or pumpkin seeds
- Knorr salad dressings of your choice

To make a hot lentil dish, add all or any of the following ingredients:
- A few pinches, to taste, of curry powder, cumin, powdered coriander, cinnamon, chilli powder, turmeric and similar warming spices
- Chopped tomatoes, tinned or fresh
- Fresh chillies, ginger and garlic
- Fried onions and green peppers
- Cooked potato cubes, Tinned chickpeas or beans
- Cooked vegetables such as cauliflower, baby marrow, butternut, spinach and brinjal

LUNCH BAKE DINNER

SERVINGS: 4

PREPARATION TIME: 85 MIN.

Ingredients

- 1 whole chicken, 4 lbs, washed and patted dry
- 2 cloves garlic
- Salt
- Pepper
- Fresh herbs: tarragon, rosemary or thyme
- 6 tablespoons butter
- 1 onion, peeled and halved
- 3 parsnips, peeled and chopped into 3 inch pieces
- 3 carrots, peeled and chopped into 3 inch pieces
- 3 potatoes, quartered
- 2 tablespoons olive oil
- Gravy:
- Splash white wine
- 1 cup chicken stock
- Chopped fresh herbs
- Salt
- Pepper

Method

1. Preheat oven to 425 degrees. Remove giblet bag from chicken's cavity, season cavity well with salt and pepper.
2. Chop up garlic with salt and herbs. Mash garlic mixture with butter. Slide butter mixture under the breast skin of the chicken and next to legs, stuff cavity with onion and whole herbs.
3. Place chicken into roasting pan. Roast for 30 minutes at 425 and then reduce heat to 375. In a large bowl, toss vegetables with olive oil and add to roasting pan. Roast chicken for another 40 minutes. Occasionally baste the chicken with pan juices.
4. To check the chicken for doneness, prick leg with knife and press to see juices. If the juices run clear, then the chicken is done. Remove from the oven and let sit for 15 minutes.
5. Remove roasted vegetables to a side dish and keep warm in the oven. Place roasting pan on a stove burner over medium heat. Add wine and chicken stock. Stir and rub the bottom of the pan to scrape up brown bits, bring to a simmer and season with salt and pepper. Serve hot

DINNER

Vegetable Fried Rice Recipes: This is a basic recipe for fried rice that you can add to as desired. If adding other ingredients, increase the number of eggs to 3. Need a bit of help? Here are step by step photo instructions showing how to make basic fried rice.

SERVINGS: 4-6

PREPARATION TIME: 15 MIN.

Ingredients

- 1 - 2 green onions, as desired
- 2 large eggs
- 1 teaspoon salt
- Pepper to taste
- 4 tablespoons oil for stir-frying, or as needed
- 4 cups cold cooked rice
- 1 - 2 tablespoons light soy sauce or oyster sauce, as desired

Method

1. Wash and finely chop the green onion. Lightly beat the eggs with the salt and pepper. Heat a wok or frying pan and add 2 tablespoons oil.
2. When the oil is hot, add the eggs, cook, stirring, until they are lightly scrambled but not too dry. Remove the eggs and clean out the pan.
3. Add 2 tablespoons oil. Add the rice. Stir-fry for a few minutes, using chopsticks or a wooden spoon to break it apart. Stir in the soy sauce or oyster sauce as desired.
4. When the rice is heated through, add the scrambled egg back into the pan. Mix thoroughly. Stir in the green onion. Serve hot.

SATURDAY

BREAKFAST — MEXICAN HEALTHY DINNERS

SERVINGS: 8

PREPARATION TIME: 15 MIN.

Ingredients

- 2 c. fat free chicken broth
- 1 - 15 oz can white beans OR fat free refried beans (drained)
- 1 - 15 oz can S&W black beans (drained)
- 1 - 15 oz can S&W Stewed Mexican Recipe Tomatoes (barely drained)
- 1 - 15 oz can medium pitted olives (drained)
- 1.5 cups golden hominy
- 1 - 7 oz can diced green chilies
- 1 garlic clove, minced
- 2 tbsp chili powder

Method

1. Open all the cans. Drain the beans and olives, and drain a small amount of liquid off the tomatoes. Pour all the ingredients into a large saucepan. Mince the garlic and add the pot. Season to taste
2. Makes 8 - 1 cup servings of about 153 calories each!
3. Lots of good, healthy nutrients but it is pretty high in sodium.
4. Goes particularly well with a bit of shredded cheddar cheese or a few avocado slices if you have a few more calories to spare for your meal

LUNCH — Fairhaven Fish Chowder

Ingredients

- 3 lbs. (cod, haddock, hake, halibut)
- 1 quart diced potatoes
- 1/4 teaspoon ground cloves (optional)
- 1 tablespoon thyme
- 1 tablespoon marjoram
- 1 bay leaf
- 2 cloves garlic (optional)
- 1 or 2 onions, chopped (optional)
- 1/2 lb lean salt pork, diced
- 1 1/2 cups canned diced tomatoes
- 1 tablespoon sage
- 5 soda crackers (Pilot or Milk Lunch type)
- salt and pepper, to taste

Method

1. Whether prepared in a Crock-Pot or on the stovetop for a winter evening's meal, or over the gas grill's side burner in the dog days of summer, this Fish Chowder is always good.
2. It can be made ahead, and is even better the next day! Unlike the traditional New England clam chowder, this version more resembles what has come to be known as Manhattan Style Clam Chowder.
3. This recipe is a famous Rhode Island recipe circa the early 1800s, which Mrs. Elizabeth Bumpus shared with friends while living in Fairhaven, Massachusetts in 1930.

DINNER

Six Plants Based Oil-Free Salad Dressing

Ingredients

- Tamari Vinaigrette
- 1/4 cup tamari
- 1/4 cup balsamic or red wine vinegar
- 2 teaspoons Dijon mustard
- 1001 Islands
- 6 tablespoons luxurious tofu
- 3 tablespoons stone ground mustard
- 3 tablespoons ketchup
- 1 teaspoon crisply pressed lemon juice
- touch of salt
- touch of naturally ground pepper
- Agave Mustard
- 1/4 cup stone ground mustard
- 1/4 cup smooth tofu
- 3 tablespoons agave syrup
- touch of salt, or to taste
- touch of naturally ground dark pepper, or to taste
- Strawberry Vinaigrette
- 4 huge strawberries
- 1 tablespoon red wine vinegar
- 2 tablespoons agave syrup
- touch of naturally ground dark pepper
- Smooth Italian
- 6 tablespoons delicate, smooth tofu
- 4 tablespoons water
- 2 teaspoons new crushed lemon juice
- 1/2 teaspoons every garlic powder, onion powder, oregano chips, rosemary drops, basil pieces, and salt
- touch of newly ground dark pepper
- Sesame umami
- 1/4 cup tamari or soy sauce
- 2 tablespoons toasted sesame seeds
- 2 tablespoons rice vinegar
- 2 tablespoons water
- 1 huge clove finely squashed garlic

Method

1. Tamari Vinaigrette: Whisk and blend in with a plate of mixed greens.
2. 1001 Islands: Puree utilizing submersion blender or whisk energetically until smooth.
3. Agave Mustard: Puree utilizing submersion blender or whisk energetically until smooth.
4. Strawberry Vinaigrette: Mix in nourishment processor or heartbeat in a rapid blender to hold surface whenever wanted.
5. Velvety Italian: Puree tofu and water utilizing a little nourishment processor or drenching blender at that point beat mix in different fixings to hold bits of shading from herb pieces.
6. Sesame umami: Toast sesame seeds in a skillet over medium-high warmth until they pop, at that point granulate seeds in flavor processor and whisk together with different fixings.

SUNDAY

BREAKFAST Fusion Lunch Burritos

Ingredients

- 18 rice paper wrappers
- 8 ounces dark colored rice noodles, suggest Annie Chun's Maifun Brown Rice Noodles
- 5 ounces blended child greens, natural if conceivable
- 1 avocado
- 1 cucumber
- 2 chime peppers, your decision of shading
- 2 cups destroyed carrots
- 2 cups destroyed purple cabbage
- 1 (16 ounces) bundle firm or excessively firm square of tofu
- Veggie lover sans oil plate of mixed greens dressing – your decision

Method

1. Prepare rice noodles as per bundle guidelines and afterward channel.
2. Peel and cut avocado, cucumber, and chime peppers into matchstick width strips.
3. Prepare tofu boards as portrayed in this formula, without the marinade, and afterward cut into matchstick width strips.
4. Add the vegetable fillings to an enormous bowl, at that point prepare and cover generously with the vegetarian sans oil serving of mixed greens dressing of your decision.
5. Prepare moves independently by submerging each sheet of rice wrapper in turn in a bowl of warm water for 10 seconds, at that point place on a cutting board or other clean level work surface.
6. Layer an even measure of plate of mixed greens filling crosswise over lower third of rice wrapper, leaving room on sides to fold edges for your burrito spring rolls.
7. Layer an even measure of tofu strips and rice noodles over plate of mixed greens filling, at that point overlay over edge folds and fold your burritos into completely encased cylinders.
8. The fixings recorded should make around 18 completed rolls. Spot completed moves on a serving plate, and be certain not to stack them, as they will stay together.
9. Eat, grin, and feel sound!

LUNCH   Avocado Hummus Bowl

Ingredients

- 1/2 ready avocado, stripped, pitted, and thickly cut
- 1/2 cup chickpeas (from a 15-ounce can), depleted and washed
- 1/2 medium estimated cucumber, meagerly cut
- 2/3 cup grape or cherry tomatoes
- 1 cup child carrots
- 10 spinach leaves, well-cleaned
- 1/3 cup clean eating hummus, any assortment, locally acquired or handcrafted
- 2 tablespoons pumpkin or shelled sunflower seeds, discretionary
- 1/4 teaspoon genuine or ocean salt
- 1/4 teaspoon dark pepper

Method

1. Line a bowl with spinach leaves, layering if vital.
2. Add avocado cuts to one corner, chickpeas to another, grape tomatoes to another, and infant carrots to another.
3. Add hummus to the inside and top with sunflower or pumpkin seeds, if utilizing.
4. Sprinkle entire dish with salt and pepper and appreciate!
5. This is extraordinary for a to-go lunch when made in a compact holder with a top.

DINNER   Slow Cooker Pumpkin Chili

Ingredients

- 1 onion, diced
- 2 (14 ounces) jars squashed tomatoes
- 2 (14 ounces) jars dark beans, depleted
- 1 carrot, destroyed
- 1 chime pepper, diced
- 1 jalapeno, veins and seeds expelled and minced
- 2 cloves garlic, minced
- 1 1/2 cups pumpkin puree
- 1 cups low sodium vegetable soup
- 2 tablespoons stew powder
- 1 teaspoon pumpkin pie flavor
- 1 teaspoon Kosher salt
- 1/2 teaspoon dark pepper

Method

1. Add everything to your moderate cooker and mix to consolidate.
2. Cook on low for 5 to 6 hours or high for 2 to 3 hours. Present with a bit of Greek yogurt or bested with avocado cuts.

50 Plant-Based High-Protein

DISCOVER THE BEST 50 PLANT-BASED SOURCES OF PROTEIN TO BOOST YOUR INTAKE AS A VEGAN, INCLUDING PULSES, TOFU, QUINOA, NUTS AND SEEDS, GRAINS, AND VEGETABLES.

Vegan 'Bacon' Strips

SERVES 16

METHOD

Preheat the oven to 250°F. Prepare two baking sheets and line them with parchment paper.
Mix soy sauce, oil, Worcestershire sauce, maple syrup and cumin in a bowl.
Spread the eggplant sticks on the baking sheets in one layer and brush with the mixture from both sides.
Roast for about 45-50 minutes. Let cool slightly before serving. Serve and enjoy!

INGREDIENTS

½ eggplant, cut into strips
1 tablespoon vegan Worcestershire sauce
½ tablespoon maple syrup
1 tablespoon soy sauce
1 teaspoon smoked paprika
1 ½ tablespoons olive oil
A pinch of ground cumin

Fudgy Double Chocolate Apple Muffins

INGREDIENTS

1 1/3 cups whole-wheat flour
1 cup applesauce, unsweetened
2 flax eggs
1/3 cup dairy-free chocolate chips
1/4 cup maple syrup
1/4 cup coconut oil, melted
1/4 cup unsweetened almond milk
1/3 cup brown sugar
1/4 teaspoon sea salt
1 ½ teaspoons baking soda
1/2 cup unsweetened cocoa powder

SERVES 12

METHOD

Preheat the oven to 375°F. Prepare a muffin tin and line the cups with paper liners. Mix applesauce, coconut oil, maple syrup, brown sugar, baking soda and salt in a bowl and stir well to combine. Add the milk and mix well. Add the flours and cocoa powder, stir well until smooth.
Add the chocolate chips and pour the batter into the muffin cups and bake for 20-22 minutes.
Let cool before serving and enjoy!

Salted Caramel Apple

SERVES 10

METHOD

Preheat the oven to 350 F. Mix oat flour, rolled oats, baking powder and salt in a bowl. Stir until well combined. Add the dates, tahini, chia seeds, almond milk and vanilla extract to a blender or a food processor. Blitz until smooth. Add the mixture to the flour mixture along with apples, stir well until combined.
Spread the batter into a baking pan, bake for about 30 minutes. Let cool and cut into bars. Serve and enjoy!

INGREDIENTS

2 apples, grated
3/4 cup Medjool dates, pitted
2/3 cup tahini
1 cup oat flour
1 cup rolled oats
1/4 cup + 2 tablespoons unsweetened almond milk
3 tablespoons chia seeds
1 teaspoon vanilla extract
1 teaspoon baking powder
1/2 teaspoon salt

Lemon Cheesecake

SERVES : 6

METHOD
Combine the biscuits and margarine in a bowl. Transfer the mixture to a springform pan and press it into the bottom. Mix lemon juice, agar-agar and limoncello in a pan and place over low heat. Add a splash of water if the mixture is too thick. Stir until the mixture is smooth and agar is dissolved. Add tofu, cream cheese, sugar, lemon zest, coconut cream, and vanilla to a blender and blitz well until smooth. Pour the mixture over the crust nd spread evenly. Refrigerate for 1 hour and serve topped with fruits or/and berries. Enjoy!

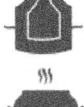

INGREDIENTS
7 oz digestive biscuits, crushed 3 oz vegan margarine, melted 1 block (14 oz) firm tofu 1 tablespoon vegan cream cheese 1 can (14 oz) coconut cream ¼ lb caster sugar
1 lemon, zested an juiced ¾ cup limoncello
2-3 drops vanilla extract
3 tablespoons agar-agar
Berries or fruits of choice, for serving

50 MINUTES

INGREDIENTS
1/2 cup rolled oats
1/2 cup oat flour
1/4 cup quick-cooking oats
4-5 dates, pitted
1/2 cup applesauce, unsweetened
3/4 teaspoon apple cider vinegar
1/3 cup walnuts, chopped
1 lemon, zested
1 teaspoon of cocoa powder
1/2 teaspoon vanilla powder
1/4 teaspoon baking soda
A pinch of salt

Lemon-Oatmeal Cookies

SERVES 7-8

METHOD
Preheat the oven to 275 F. Prepare a baking sheet and line it with parchment paper. oak dates in hot water for about 20 minutes. Drain and add to a blender. Add vinegar and applesauce and blitz until a paste is formed. Combine rolled oats, oat flour, quick-cooking oats, walnuts, lemon zest, cocoa powder, vanilla powder, baking soda and salt in a bowl. Add the date mixture and mix well. Shape the mixture into balls and place them on the baking sheet. Press slightly. Bake for 35-45 minutes. Let cool before serving. Enjoy!

22 MINUTES

Coconut Chocolate Mousse

SERVES 10

METHOD
Combine coconut cream and maple syrup in a bowl. Beat with a mixer until smooth and creamy.
Add cardamom and cacao and stir to combine, beat until smooth.
Cover and refrigerate before serving. Enjoy!

30 MINUTES

INGREDIENTS
Coconut cream from 1 can (14 oz) unsweetened coconut milk
3 tablespoons raw cacao powder
1 tablespoon maple syrup
1/8 teaspoon cardamom

Chocolate Cupcakes

SERVES 12
METHOD

Preheat the oven to 350 F. Prepare a muffin pan and coat it with cooking spray. Bring a pot of water to a boil over medium heat. Put the chocolate to a heatproof bowl and place it on top of the pot. Stir until melted. Remove from heat and let cook for about 5 minutes. Combine milk and vinegar in a bowl. Let rest for 5 minutes. Add maple sugar, vanilla, applesauce, and chocolate and stir well to combine. Mix flour, baking soda, baking powder, cocoa powder and salt in a separate bowl. Now add the flour mixture to the milk mixture and stir well until combined and smooth.
Pour the batter into the muffin pan and bake for 20 minutes.
Let cool before serving. Enjoy!

INGREDIENTS

1 cup whole wheat pastry flour
1 cup unsweetened almond or coconut milk
⅔ cup maple sugar
2 oz unsweetened vegan chocolate
1 teaspoon apple cider vinegar
¼ cup unsweetened applesauce
1 teaspoon vanilla extract
⅓ cup of cocoa powder
¾ teaspoon baking soda
½ teaspoon baking powder
¼ teaspoon salt

Lemon Poppy Seed SconesBars

SERVES 10
METHOD

Preheat the oven to 400 F. Prepare a baking sheet and line it with parchment paper.
Mix flour, poppy seeds, lemon zest, sugar, baking powder, baking soda and salt in a bowl.
Add coconut oil and mix well with a fork until crumbs are formed.
Add milk and stir well to combine. Transfer the dough onto the floured working surface and knead well for about 6-8 minutes. Roll out into 1 inch thick square.
Cut into triangles and place on the baking sheet. Bake for 10 minutes.
Mix all the glaze ingredients in a bowl. Drizzle over scones and serve. Enjoy!

INGREDIENTS

1 3/4 cups all-purpose flour
1 tablespoon poppy seeds
1 lemon, zested
3/4 cup + 1 tablespoon soy milk
1 1/2 tablespoons sugar
1/4 cup coconut oil
1/2 tablespoon baking powder
1/2 teaspoon baking soda
1/2 teaspoon salt
For the Glaze:
2 tablespoons soy milk, warm
1 tablespoon lemon juice
1 tablespoon lemon zest
3/4 cup icing sugar
1 tablespoon coconut oil, melted

Brownies

SERVES 12
METHOD

⏱ 20 MINUTES

Grease a baking tin and line with parchment paper.
Take a bowl and mix 3 tablespoons flaxseeds along with cold water; whisk well; keep aside for 10-15 minutes.
Place a heatproof bowl in hot water pan and melt chocolate in it (water should not be in contact with the bowl). Add margarine when all of the chocolate is melted and turn off the heat. Margarine will melt in hot chocolate.
Add caster sugar, muscovado sugar, vanilla extract, and maple syrup into the chocolate; mix well until smooth.
Now take a bowl and add ½ teaspoon baking powder, a pinch of salt, and flour; mix until all the ingredients are incorporated.
Now transfer the batter to the baking tin; spread evenly; top with chocolate chips; bake in the preheated oven (375 F) for approximately 30 minutes.
Let the brownies cool; transfer to a big board and slice into squares.

INGREDIENTS

1 cup whole wheat pastry flour
1 cup unsweetened almond or coconut milk
⅔ cup maple sugar
2 oz unsweetened vegan chocolate
1 teaspoon apple cider vinegar
¼ cup unsweetened applesauce
1 teaspoon vanilla extract
⅓ cup of cocoa powder
¾ teaspoon baking soda
½ teaspoon baking powder
¼ teaspoon salt

No-Bake Lemon Tarts

SERVES 10
METHOD

⏱ 30 MINUTES

Grease a tart pan with coconut oil. For the crust: Mix ¾ cup raw cashews and 1 cup shredded coconut in a blender/food processor and blend until the cashews are broken into smaller pieces. Now add 2 tablespoons maple syrup, 1 teaspoon lemon zest, 2 tablespoons coconut oil and 2 tablespoons lemon juice; blend until all the ingredients stick together. Pour this mixture into the prepared pan/s; keep it aside. For the filling: Use the same blender and mix all the filling ingredients. Blend until a creamy mixture is obtained for 3-4 minutes. You can also add a little coconut oil to make the mixture smooth. After that, adjust lemon juice and maple syrup according to your taste. Pour this smooth filling over the prepared crust. Make sure that the top must be smooth. Put the pan into the refrigerator for 2-3 hours and then serve immediately. are incorporated. Now transfer the batter to the baking tin; spread evenly; top with chocolate chips; bake in the preheated oven (375 F) for approximately 30 minutes. Let the brownies cool; transfer to a big board and slice into squares.

INGREDIENTS

For the crust
2 tablespoons coconut oil melted
1 teaspoon lemon zest
1 cup coconut, shredded
2 tablespoons lemon juice
¾ cup raw cashews
2 tablespoons maple syrup
For the filling
4 tablespoons canned coconut milk
2 pinches of sea salt
1 cup raw cashews (soaked for at least 4 hours in cold water)
1 teaspoon vanilla extract
½ cup lemon juice
1 tablespoon lemon zest
5 tablespoons coconut oil
4 tablespoons maple syrup

Peanut Butter Caramel Rice Krispies

METHOD

Line a square pan with wax paper/parchment paper. Preheat 3/4 cup brown rice syrup and 4 tablespoons maple syrup in a pot over a medium-high flame; boil and cook for a minute with stirring. Turn off the heat. Add 5 tablespoons peanut butter and 1 teaspoon vanilla extract in the pot and whisk until smooth. Now add 6 cups rice crisp cereal and stir until well combined. Spread this mixture in the pan evenly. Press lightly with a spatula; freeze for 10 minutes. Take another bowl and combine 1 teaspoon maple syrup and 2 tablespoons peanut butter; microwave for 30 seconds. If needed, then add a teaspoon of water. Take out the Krispies from the freezer; drizzle over peanut butter; again freeze until firm for at least 10-12 minutes. Next, slice into cubes. Enjoy the chilled krispies! Leftovers can be stored for 6-7 days in the fridge.

INGREDIENTS

5 tablespoons peanut butter
6 cups rice crisp cereal
3/4 cup brown rice syrup
1 teaspoon vanilla extract
4 tablespoons maple syrup
Peanut butter drizzle
1 teaspoon maple syrup
2 tablespoons creamy peanut butter
1–2 teaspoons water, if needed

Peach Iced Tea

SERVES 10

METHOD

Add peaches and sugar to a pan, cover with water. Simmer for 5 minutes.
Mash the peaches and cook over low heat for 10 minutes more.
Remove from heat; let stand for 30 minutes.
Sieve the mixture. Make the black tea (4 cups) and let cool.
Add peach mixture and tea to the glasses over ice. Serve.

INGREDIENTS

1 ½ peach, sliced
½ cup of sugar
1-2 tea bags
½ cup of water

Guilt-Free Coconut Vanilla Macaroons

SERVES 12
METHOD

⏱ 20 MINUTES

Grease a baking tin and line with parchment paper.
Take a bowl and mix 3 tablespoons flaxseeds along with cold water; whisk well; keep aside for 10-15 minutes.
Place a heatproof bowl in hot water pan and melt chocolate in it (water should not be in contact with the bowl). Add margarine when all of the chocolate is melted and turn off the heat. Margarine will melt in hot chocolate.
Add caster sugar, muscovado sugar, vanilla extract, and maple syrup into the chocolate; mix well until smooth.
Now take a bowl and add ½ teaspoon baking powder, a pinch of salt, and flour; mix until all the ingredients are incorporated.
Now transfer the batter to the baking tin; spread evenly; top with chocolate chips; bake in the preheated oven (375 F) for approximately 30 minutes.
Let the brownies cool; transfer to a big board and slice into squares.

INGREDIENTS

1 cup whole wheat pastry flour
1 cup unsweetened almond or coconut milk
⅔ cup maple sugar
2 oz unsweetened vegan chocolate
1 teaspoon apple cider vinegar
¼ cup unsweetened applesauce
1 teaspoon vanilla extract
⅓ cup of cocoa powder
¾ teaspoon baking soda
½ teaspoon baking powder
¼ teaspoon salt

No-Bake Lemon Tarts

SERVES 10
METHOD

⏱ 30 MINUTES

Grease a tart pan with coconut oil. For the crust: Mix ¾ cup raw cashews and 1 cup shredded coconut in a blender/food processor and blend until the cashews are broken into smaller pieces. Now add 2 tablespoons maple syrup, 1 teaspoon lemon zest, 2 tablespoons coconut oil and 2 tablespoons lemon juice; blend until all the ingredients stick together. Pour this mixture into the prepared pan/s; keep it aside. For the filling: Use the same blender and mix all the filling ingredients. Blend until a creamy mixture is obtained for 3-4 minutes. You can also add a little coconut oil to make the mixture smooth. After that, adjust lemon juice and maple syrup according to your taste. Pour this smooth filling over the prepared crust. Make sure that the top must be smooth. Put the pan into the refrigerator for 2-3 hours and then serve immediately. are incorporated. Now transfer the batter to the baking tin; spread evenly; top with chocolate chips; bake in the preheated oven (375 F) for approximately 30 minutes. Let the brownies cool; transfer to a big board and slice into squares.

INGREDIENTS

For the crust
2 tablespoons coconut oil melted
1 teaspoon lemon zest
1 cup coconut, shredded
2 tablespoons lemon juice
¾ cup raw cashews
2 tablespoons maple syrup
For the filling
4 tablespoons canned coconut milk
2 pinches of sea salt
1 cup raw cashews (soaked for at least 4 hours in cold water)
1 teaspoon vanilla extract
½ cup lemon juice
1 tablespoon lemon zest
5 tablespoons coconut oil
4 tablespoons maple syrup

Peanut Butter Fudge

SERVINGS: 21

METHOD

Take a loaf pan (9x5-inch) and line with parchment paper; keep aside. Add coconut milk in a food processor; blend for about 4 minutes until it becomes a creamy butter. Add coconut oil and peanut butter; blend. Next, add maple syrup (add only 1 tablespoon at a time; it's up to you how much sweetness you need). The mixture can be extra thick if you add too much maple syrup. Add a bit of melted coconut oil if needed. Optional: If you add vanilla and salt, then mix them again.

INGREDIENTS

Fudge
1 teaspoon pure vanilla extract
¼ cup raw cane sugar
2 cups unsweetened coconut, finely shredded
3-5 tablespoon maple syrup (or any other sweetener of choice)
1 cup creamy peanut butter
Coconut oil
Toppings (Optional)
Coconut flakes
Crushed peanuts

INGREDIENTS

50 g cashew nuts
1 onion
2 tbsp. rapeseed or sunflower oil
2 tsp ginger puree
2 tsp garlic puree
3 tsp garam masala
2 tsp turmeric
1 tsp ground cinnamon
250 ml of coconut yogurt
1 tsp salt
25 g sultanas
600 g vegetables and pulses
4 tbsp. dairy-free cream

Takeaway-Style Vegan Korma

SERVINGS: 24

METHOD

Pour 150 ml of warm water into a jar or bowl and add peanut nuts. Soak and reserve.

Peel and chop the onions. Heat the oil in a large or large pot with the pot and cook the onion over medium heat for 4-5 minutes to begin to soften.

Prepare the garlic and ginger and add them to the pot. Continue cooking over medium heat.

Pour peanuts and water into a chopper or blender and add warm masala, turmeric, and cinnamon. Add the ray to a soft paste and then to the pot and simmer for 4-5 minutes, stirring frequently.

Add yogurt, salt and kale, stir and continue cooking for another 4-5 minutes.

Finally, add vegetables or legumes and dairy-free cream and cook for another 4-5 minutes. Serve with rice and in vain.

Black Bean & Avocado Tacos

INGREDIENTS

half a red onion
1 tsp ready-chopped garlic or garlic puree
200 g tinned black beans
5 cherry tomatoes
1 roasted red pepper
half an avocado
juice of half a lime
handful fresh coriander
2 tortilla wraps

SERVINGS: 2

45 MINUTES

METHOD

Heat the oil in a small pan. Peel and chop the onion and add to the pot and then the garlic. Cook for 2 minutes. Wash and wash black beans and put them inside. Mix well with salt and black pepper and cook over medium heat for another 3-4 minutes, stirring occasionally.

Meanwhile, cut the cherry tomatoes in half and chop the peppers into thin strips. Remove the stone from the avocado and cut it into 1 cm pieces. Combine the tomatoes, peppers, and avocado in a small bowl and season with salt and black pepper. Press the lemon juice and pour everything into the mixture.

Heat a second pan and lightly brown the sides of the cream until lightly browned.

Chop the coriander leaves almost and mix them with the tomato and avocado mixture. Place the roasted tortillas in layers with beans and onions, then mix the tomatoes, peppers, and avocado and serve immediately.

Moroccan Stuffed Romano Peppers

SERVINGS: 2

55 MINUTES

METHOD

Heat the oven to 180 degrees Celsius or 350 degrees Fahrenheit and heat 4 times the amount of protein per serving and halve the length of the pepper, brush with a little oil and place on a baking sheet. Roast them for 10 minutes or until they are soft, but still, maintain their shape. Meanwhile, boil a small pot of water with the powdered broth. Add the giant couscous and cook for 6-8 minutes until completely dissolved. Drain and pour into the bowl, squeeze it in lemon juice and add 2 tablespoons of olive oil and baby spinach leaves. Stir well with salt and black pepper and stir well. Heat a little oil in a pan, chop the red onion and chop finely and add to the pot. Cook for 3-4 minutes, then drain and wash the peas and add the tomato puree, harissa paste, boiling water, and powder to the pan. Bring to a boil and simmer for 5 minutes or until the liquid is reduced to a thick, sticky sauce, as necessary.

To assemble, fold the giant couscous in the middle of the pepper, then place the pea on top. Return to the oven for 3-4 minutes to heat, finely chop the cilantro and sprinkle the peppers, then serve immediately.

INGREDIENTS

4 Romano peppers
1 tsp vegetable stock powder
100 g whole-wheat giant couscous
1 lemon
2 tbsp. olive oil
handful of baby spinach leaves
1½2 a red onion
400 g tin chickpeas
1 tbsp. tomato puree
1 tbsp. harissa paste
200 ml of boiling water
1 tsp stock powder
fresh coriander

Spicy Sesame & Edama-

SERVINGS: 21

METHOD

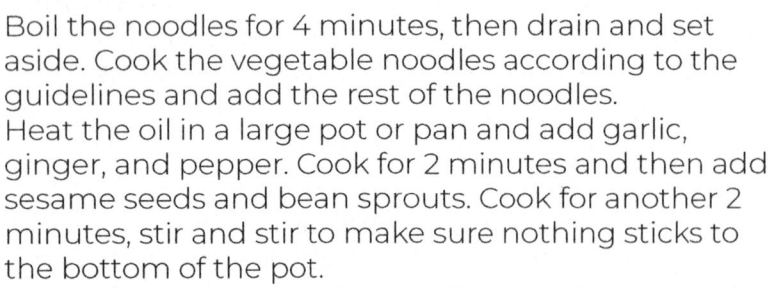

Boil the noodles for 4 minutes, then drain and set aside. Cook the vegetable noodles according to the guidelines and add the rest of the noodles.
Heat the oil in a large pot or pan and add garlic, ginger, and pepper. Cook for 2 minutes and then add sesame seeds and bean sprouts. Cook for another 2 minutes, stir and stir to make sure nothing sticks to the bottom of the pot.
Pour the noodles and the noodles into the pan and cook for 2 minutes.

INGREDIENTS

100 g Blue Dragon Wholewheat Noodles
100 g vegetable 'noodles'
2 tbsp. groundnut or coconut oil
2 shallots, peeled and finely sliced
2 tsp 'lazy' garlic
2 tsp ginger puree
1 red chili, sliced
3 tbsp. sesame seeds
100 g edamame beans, podded
2 tbsp. sesame oil
2 tbsp. Blue Dragon soy sauce
a handful of fresh coriander, roughly chopped
juice of 1 lime

INGREDIENTS

2 tbsp. olive oil
1 onion
1 carrot
1 tsp ready-chopped garlic Protein content per serving garlic purée
1 Protein content per serving2 tsp paprika
400 g tin butterbeans
400 g tin chopped tomatoes
2 tbsp. tomato purée
1 tsp sugar
2 tsp dried oregano
handful baby spinach
handful fresh parsley
8-10 fresh mint leaves

Quick & Easy Tomato and Herb Gigantes Beans

SERVINGS: 2

METHOD

Heat the oil in a large pot or a large bowl with oil. Chop onions and carrots and chop them finely and add them to the bowl with garlic and paprika. Cook over medium heat for 2 minutes.
Rinse and wash the potatoes and add to the pot, then add the greased tomatoes. Fill the empty tomato can in half with water and add it to the bowl with tomato puree, sugar, and oregano. Season well with salt and black pepper, boil, then reduce at dawn, cover and cook for 12-14 minutes.
Chop the baby spinach approximately, then add them to the pot and cook for 2 minutes. Chop the parsley and mint almost and stir just before serving. Taste and adjust the seasoning if necessary, then serve with crusty bread and crispy green salad.

Spelt Spaghetti with Avocado Pesto

INGREDIENTS

- 200 g spelt spaghetti (white or whole-wheat)
- 12 asparagus spears, woody ends removed and sliced into 3-4cm pieces
- 100 g fresh or frozen peas
- 1 avocado
- 75 g brazil nuts
- 1 clove garlic, peeled and crushed
- zest and juice of 1 lemon
- 2 tbsp. extra virgin olive oil
- 50 g fresh basil
- salt

SERVINGS: 2

METHOD

Bring a large pot of boiling water and add spaghetti. After 5 minutes of cooking (or 8 boxes of whole spaghetti), add the peas and asparagus and cook for 2-3 minutes until the pasta is cooked and the asparagus is cooked naturally. He
While preparing the spaghetti, place all remaining ingredients in the blender or meal and cook for a minute. Add 2-3 tablespoons of water and stain again and add a little water once to achieve a thick sauce. Try and add more salt if necessary.
Drain the spaghetti and return them to the pot, then stir over the sauce over low heat to cool.

Vegan Sausage Casserole: Bangers & Borlotti

SERVINGS: 2

METHOD

Fry the oil in a large pan and fry the sausages over medium heat to brown. Peel and chop the red onion and add it to the pot, then finely chop the carrots and cut them in half or a quarter. Add to the pan and cook for 3-4 minutes.
When the onion has softened, add the garlic and paprika to the pot and stir well. Rinse and wash the Borlotti beans and add them to the pan, and then add 250 ml of water and gravitational seeds. Bring to a boil, then reduce to medium heat and cook for 7-8 minutes until the sauce thickens and the carrots are well prepared. Add some salt or black pepper if necessary and try.
Chop the spinach almost and stir only one minute before the end of the cooking time and serve immediately with a baked potato, rice, or noodles.

INGREDIENTS

- 2 tbsp. olive or rapeseed oil
- 6 vegan sausages
- 1 red onion
- 8 baby carrots (e.g. chantenay)
- 1 tsp smoked paprika
- 1 tsp garlic puree
- Protein content per serving ready-chopped garlic
- 400 g tin borlotti beans (drained and rinsed)
- 250 g passata
- 2 tbsp. gravy granules (check they are vegan)
- handful baby spinach

Herby Giant Couscous with Asparagus and Lemon

SERVINGS: 21

METHOD

Bring a large pot of salted water to a boil. Add giant couscous. After 5 minutes, add asparagus and peas and boil for another 4 minutes.

While the couscous is cooking, cook in a mini blender (or directly in a bowl, sharp knife and elbow grease!), Walnut oil, lemon juice, parsley, and mint.

Drain the couscous and immediately stir the dressing of the baby herb and spinach.

Divide between two plates and crush with pine nuts and lemon lotion.

INGREDIENTS

- 150 g giant couscous
- 100 g asparagus tips
- 100 g frozen peas
- 3 tbsp. walnut oil
- Juice and zest of 1 lemon
- Handful fresh parsley
- Handful of fresh mint
- Handful baby spinach
- 2 tbsp. pine nuts

Easy Seitan for Two

INGREDIENTS

- ½ teaspoon freshly ground black pepper
- Pinch of fine sea salt
- 2 (each 4 ounces, or 113 g) Kind-to- Cows Seitan cutlets
- 1/3 cup (80 ml) vegetable broth
- 1 tablespoon (16 g) tomato paste
- 1 teaspoon balsamic vinegar
- 1 teaspoon Dijon mustard
- 1 teaspoon white miso
- 1 tablespoon (15 ml) high heat neutral-flavored oil
- 2 tablespoons (20 g) minced shallot

SERVINGS: 2

METHOD

Rub the pepper and salt evenly into the seitan cutlets. Whisk together the broth, tomato paste, vinegar, mustard, and miso in a small bowl.

Heat the oil over medium-high heat in a large skillet. Put the cutlets into the skillet and cook for 3 to 5 minutes, until browned. Turnover and cook the second side for 3 to 4 minutes until also browned. Remove the cutlets and set aside.

Reduce the heat to medium-low. Add the shallots. Cook and stir for 2 to 3 minutes, until softened. Be careful not to burn them. Scrape up any bits stuck to the skillet.

Pour the broth mixture into the skillet. Bring to a simmer and stir for 3 to 4 minutes. Put the cutlets back into the skillet and turn to coat. Simmer for 3 to 4 minutes to heat the cutlets throughout. Spoon the sauce over the cutlets to serve.

Quit-the-Cluck Seitan

SERVINGS: 2

⏱ 45 MINUTES

INGREDIENTS

1¼ cups (150 g) vital wheat gluten
¼ cup (30 g) chickpea flour
3 tablespoons (22 g) nutritional yeast
1 tablespoon (7 g) onion powder
2 teaspoons dried poultry seasoning
1 teaspoon garlic powder
½ teaspoon ground white pepper
¼ cup (180 ml) vegetable broth
2 teaspoons no chicken bouillon paste
1 tablespoon (15 ml) olive oil
1 tablespoon high heat neutral-flavored oil, for cooking
For the cooking broth:
2 cups (470 ml) vegetable broth
1 tablespoon (8 g) nutritional yeast
2 teaspoons dried poultry seasoning
2 teaspoons onion powder
1 teaspoon Dijon mustard
Salt and pepper

METHOD

Preheat the oven to 300°F (150*C, or gas mark 2). Stir the dry ingredients together in a medium-size bowl. Stir the wet ingredients together in a measuring cup. Pour the wet ingredients into the dry ingredients and stir to combine. Knead with your hands until it forms a cohesive ball. Add tablespoon vital wheat gluten (9 g) or broth (15 ml), if needed, to reach the desired consistency. Divide into 6 equal portions. Sandwich a portion of dough between two pieces of parchment paper. Roll each portion into a cutlet that is no more than 1/2 inch (1.3 cm) thick. Heat the oil in a large skillet over medium-high heat. Cook the cutlets (in batches) for 3 to 5 minutes until browned. Turnover and cook the second side for 3 minutes until browned.

Broccoli, Kale, Chili & Hazelnut Pizza

SERVINGS: 2

⏱ 55 MINUTES

INGREDIENTS

500 g Whole Meal Bread Mix
200 ml Passata with Garlic
1 red onion, peeled and finely sliced
6 sun-dried tomatoes, roughly chopped
75 g fresh curly kale, woody stalks removed and leaves roughly chopped
6-8 stalks purple sprouting broccoli, the lower half of stalks removed
1 red chili, finely sliced
handful hazelnuts, roughly chopped
dried oregano
black pepper
extra virgin olive oil

METHOD

Pack the bread mix according to the instructions. Kneel and let it grow in a warm place for 45.45 minutes.
Meanwhile, prepare the meatballs and heat the oven to 200 degrees Celsius at 400 degrees C with protein content per serving of 6 gasoline and put it in the oven if using a pizza stone. (Check if your stove has a specific pizza setting, many do, and that makes a big difference).
Spread the dough on a floured surface and divide it in two. Insert each section into a ground ball and then roll with a roller in a 30 cm circle.
When all the tanks are ready, and the stove is at maximum temperature, remove the pizza from the oven (or grease a baking sheet) or place the dough on the stone surface. Protein on each plate, cover with half the pasta, then the onion. Sprinkle with cabbage, broccoli, peppers, and hazelnuts, then sprinkle with mint and black pepper and sprinkle with olive oil. Repeat for the second pizza.
Bake for 8-10 minutes until the slices brown and the base is well cooked.

Cassoulet

Yield: 8 to 10 servings

Protein Content Per Serving: 22 g

Ingredients

¼ cup (60 ml) olive oil, divided

4 ounces (113 g) Quit-the-Cluck Seitan, chopped

1/3 of a Smoky Sausage, chopped

1½ cups (240 g) chopped onion

2 ounces (57 g) minced shiitake mushrooms

2 large carrots, peeled, sliced into ¼-inch (6 mm) rounds

2 stalks celery, chopped

1½ cups (355 ml) vegetable broth, divided

1 teaspoon liquid smoke

3 cans (each 15 ounces, or 425 g) white beans of choice, drained and rinsed

1 can (14.5 ounces, or 410 g) diced tomatoes, undrained

2 tablespoons (32 g) tomato paste 1 tablespoon (15 ml) tamari

1 tablespoon (18 g) no chicken bouillon paste, or 2 bouillon cubes, crumbled

2 tablespoons (8 g) minced fresh parsley

2 teaspoons dried thyme

½ teaspoon dried rosemary Salt and pepper

2 cups (200 g) fresh bread crumbs

½ cup (40 g) panko crumbs

Instructions

Preheat the oven to 375°F (190°C, or gas mark 5).

Heat 1 tablespoon (15 ml) of olive oil in a large skillet over medium heat.

Add the seitan and sausage. Cook for 4 to 6 minutes, occasionally stirring, until browned. Transfer to a plate and set aside.

Add the onion and a pinch of salt to the same skillet. Cook for 5 to 7 minutes until translucent. Transfer to the same plate. Add the shiitakes, carrots, and celery to the skillet and cook for 2 minutes. Add 1 tablespoon (15 ml) vegetable broth and the liquid smoke. Cook for 2 to 3 minutes, stirring until the liquid is absorbed or evaporated.

Return the seitan and onions to the skillet and add the beans, tomatoes, tomato paste, tamari, bouillon, parsley, thyme, rosemary, and remaining broth. Cook for 3 to 4 minutes, stirring to combine. Season with salt and pepper to taste and transfer to a large casserole pan.

Toss together the fresh bread crumbs, panko crumbs, and the remaining 3 tablespoons (45 ml) olive oil in a small bowl. Spread evenly over the bean mixture. Bake for 30 to 35 minutes until the crumbs are browned.

Double-Garlic Bean and Vegetable Soup

Yield: 4 servings
Protein content per serving: 21 g

Ingredients
1 tablespoon (15 ml) olive oil
1 teaspoon fine sea salt
1 (240 g) minced onion 5 cloves garlic, minced
2 cups (220 g) chopped red potatoes
⅔ cup (96 g) sliced carrots
Protein content per serving cup (60 g) chopped celery
1 teaspoon Italian seasoning blend
Protein content per serving teaspoon red pepper flakes, or to taste
Protein content per serving teaspoon celery seed
4 cups water (940 ml), divided
1 can (14.5 ounces, or 410 g) crushed tomatoes or tomato puree
1 head roasted garlic
2 tablespoons (30 g) prepared vegan pesto, plus more for garnish
2 cans (each 15 ounces, or 425 g) different kinds of white beans, drained and rinsed
Protein content per serving cup (50 g)
1-inch (2.5 cm) pieces green beans
Salt and pepper

Instructions
Heat the oil and salt in a large soup pot over medium heat. Add the onion, garlic, potatoes, carrots, and celery. Cook for 4 to 6 minutes, occasionally stirring, until the onions are translucent. Add the seasoning blend, red pepper flakes, and celery seed and stir for 2 minutes. Add 3 cups (705 ml) of the water and the crushed tomatoes.
Combine the remaining 1 cup (235 ml) water and the roasted garlic in a blender. Process until smooth. Add to the soup mixture and bring to a boil. Reduce the heat to simmer and cook for 30 minutes.
Stir in the pesto, beans, and green beans. Simmer for 15 minutes. Taste and adjust the seasonings. Serve each bowl with a dollop of pesto, if desired.

Hummus Bisque

Yield: 4 servings
Protein content per serving: 14 g

Ingredients
1 tablespoon (15 ml) toasted sesame oil ¼ cup (40 g) chopped shallot
2 teaspoons grated or pressed garlic 1 teaspoon ground cumin
1 teaspoon sambal oelek or harissa paste, or to taste
⅓ teaspoon smoked paprika
2 cups (328 g) cooked chickpeas ½ cup (80 ml) fresh lemon juice
3 cups (705 ml) vegetable broth, more if needed
⅓ cup (128 g) tahini
Salt and white pepper
¼ cup (4 g) chopped fresh cilantro or (15 g) parsley (or a combination of the two), for garnish
Toasted cumin seeds, for garnish, optional
Lemon zest, for garnish, optional

Instructions
Heat the oil in a large pot. Add the shallot, garlic, cumin, sambal oelek or harissa paste, paprika, and chickpeas. Cook on medium heat, stirring often until the shallot is tender and the preparation is fragrant about 4 minutes. Add the lemon juice, stirring to combine.
Add the broth and bring to a boil. Lower the heat, cover with a lid, and simmer for 10 minutes. Add the tahini, stirring to combine. Note that the tahini might look curdled when you add it, but it will be okay after sim¬merging and blending. Cover with the lid and simmer for another 5 minutes.
Use a handheld blender and blend the mixture until smooth. Be careful: The liquid will be hot, so watch for spatters! You can also use a regular blender to puree the soup, be careful while transferring the hot liquid. If you find the bisque a little thick for your taste once blended, add extra broth as needed.
Adjust the seasonings to taste and serve garnished with cilantro, parsley, cumin seeds, and lemon zest.
Leftovers can be slowly reheated by simmering in a small saucepan for about 6 minutes until heated through. Stir occasionally while reheating and be careful not to scorch what is a rather thick soup.

Mean Bean Minestrone

Yield: 8 to 10 servings
Protein content per serving: 9g

Ingredients
1 tablespoon (15 ml) olive oil
1/3 cup (80 g) chopped red onion
4 cloves garlic, grated or pressed
1 leek, white and light green parts, trimmed and chopped (about 4 ounces, or 113 g)
2 carrots, peeled and minced (about 4 ounces, or 113 g)
2 ribs of celery, minced (about 2 ounces, or 57 g)
2 yellow squashes, trimmed and chopped (about 8 ounces, or 227 g)
1 green bell pepper, trimmed and chopped (about 8 ounces, or 227 g)
1 tablespoon (16 g) tomato paste
1 teaspoon dried oregano
1 teaspoon dried basil
⅓ teaspoon smoked paprika
'⅛ to ¼ teaspoon cayenne pepper, or to taste
2 cans (each 15 ounces, or 425 g) diced fire-roasted tomatoes
4 cups (940 ml) vegetable broth, more if needed
3 cups (532 g) cannellini beans, or other white beans
2 cups (330 g) cooked farro, or other whole grain or pasta
Salt, to taste
Nut and Seed Sprinkles, for garnish, optional and to taste

Instructions
In a large pot, add the oil, onion, garlic, leek, carrots, celery, yellow squash, bell pepper, tomato paste, oregano, basil, paprika, and cayenne pepper. Cook on medium-high heat, stirring often until the vegetables start to get tender, about 6 minutes.
Add the tomatoes and bro
th. Bring to a boil, lower the heat, cover with a lid, and simmer 15 minutes.
Add the beans and simmer another 10 minutes. Add the farro and simmer 5 more minutes to heat the farro.
Note that this is a thick minestrone. If there are leftovers (which taste even better, by the way), the soup will thicken more once chilled.
Add extra broth if you prefer a thinner soup and adjust seasoning if needed. Add Nut and Seed Sprinkles on each portion upon serving, if desired.
Store leftovers in an airtight container in the refrigerator for up to 5 days. The minestrone can also be frozen for up to 3 months.

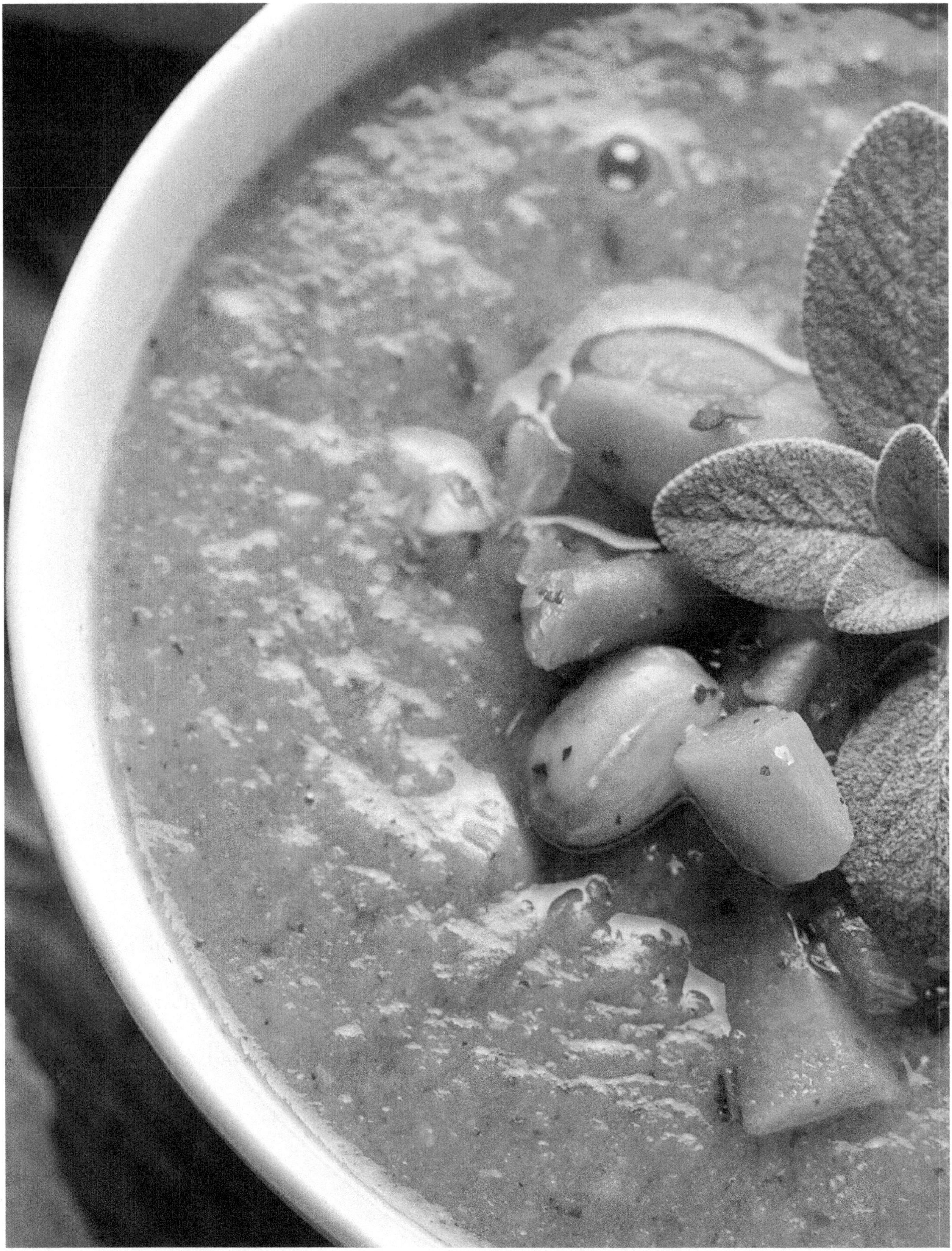

Sushi Rice and Bean Stew

Yield: 4 to 6 servings
Protein content per serving: 11 g

Ingredients
For the sushi rice:
1 cup (208 g) dry sushi rice, thoroughly rinsed until water runs clear and drained
1¾ cups (295 ml) water
1 tablespoon (15 ml) fresh lemon juice
1 teaspoon toasted sesame oil
1 teaspoon sriracha 1 teaspoon tamari
1 teaspoon agave nectar or brown rice syrup
For the stew: 1 tablespoon (15 ml) toasted sesame oil
9 ounces (255 g) minced carrot (about 4 medium carrots)
1/3 cup (80 g) chopped red onion or ¼ cup (40 g) minced shallot
2 teaspoons grated fresh ginger or ⅓ teaspoon ginger powder
4 cloves garlic, grated or pressed
1½ cups (246 g) cooked chickpeas
1 cup (155 g) frozen, shelled edamame
3 tablespoons (45 ml) seasoned rice vinegar
2 tablespoons (30 ml) tamari
2 teaspoons sriracha, or to taste
1 cup (235 ml) mushroom-soaking broth
2 cups (470 ml) vegetable broth
2 tablespoons (36 g) white miso
2 tablespoons (16 g) toasted white sesame seeds

Instructions
To make the sushi rice: Combine the rice and water in a rice cooker, cover with the lid, and cook until the water is absorbed without lifting the lid. (Alternatively, cook the rice on the stove top, following the directions on the package.) While the rice is cooking, combine the remaining sushi rice ingredients in a large bowl. Let the rice steam for 10 minutes in the rice cooker with the lid still on. Gently fold the cooked rice into the dressing. Set aside. To make the stew: Heat the oil in a large pot on medium-high heat. Add the carrots, onion, ginger, and garlic. Lower the temperature to medium and cook until the vegetables start to get tender, stirring often about 4 minutes. Add the chickpeas, edamame, vinegar, tamari, and sriracha. Stir and cook for another 4 minutes. Add the broths, and bring back to a slow boil. Cover with a lid, lower the heat, and simmer for 10 minutes. Place the miso in a small bowl and remove 3 tablespoons (45 ml) of the broth from the pot. Stir into the miso to thoroughly combine. Stir the miso mixture back into the pan, and remove from the heat. Divide the rice among 4 to 6 bowls, depending on your appetite. Add approximately 1 cup (235 ml) of the

stew on top of each portion of rice. Add 1 teaspoon of sesame seeds on top of each serving, and serve immediately.

If you do not plan on eating this dish in one shot, keep the rice and stew separated and store in the refrigerator for up to 4 days.

When reheating the stew, do not bring to a boil. Slowly warm the rice with the stew on medium heat in a small saucepan until heated through.

Giardiniera Chili

Yield: 8 servings
Protein content per serving: 28 g

Ingredients

1 tablespoon (15 ml) neutral-flavored oil
1 medium red onion, chopped
4 carrots, peeled and minced (9 ounces, or 250 g)
2 zucchini, trimmed and minced (11 ounces, or 320 g)
4 Roma tomatoes, diced (14 ounces, or 400 g)
4 cloves garlic, grated or pressed
1 tablespoon (8 g) mild to medium chili powder
1 teaspoon ground cumin
½ teaspoon smoked paprika
½ teaspoon liquid smoke
¼ teaspoon fine sea salt, or to taste
¼ teaspoon cayenne pepper, or to taste
2 tablespoons (32 g) tomato paste
1 can (15 ounces, or 425 g) diced fire-roasted tomatoes
½ cup (120 ml) vegetable broth
½ cup (120 ml) mushroom-soaking broth or extra vegetable broth
1 can (15 ounces, or 425 g) pinto beans, drained and rinsed
1 can (15 ounces, or 425 g) black beans, drained and rinsed
½ cup (60 g) nutritional yeast

Instructions

Heat the oil on medium-high in a large pot and add the onion, carrots, zucchini, tomatoes, and garlic. Cook for 6 minutes, stirring occasionally until the carrots start to get tender. Add the chili powder, cumin, paprika, liquid smoke, salt, cayenne pepper, and tomato paste, stirring to combine. Cook another 2 minutes. Add the diced tomatoes, broths, beans, and nutritional yeast. Bring to a low boil. Lower the heat, cover with a lid, and simmer 15 minutes, stirring occasionally. Remove the lid and simmer for another 5 minutes.

Serve on top of a cooked whole grain of choice or with your favorite chili accompaniments. Leftovers can be stored in an airtight container in the refrigerator for up to 4 days or frozen for up to 3 months.

Shorba (Lentil Soup)

Yield: 4 to 6 servings

Protein content per serving: 10 g

Ingredients

1 tablespoon (15 ml) olive oil

1 medium onion, minced

1 large carrot, peeled and chopped

1 fist-size russet potato, cut into small cubes (about 7 ounces, or 198 g)

4 large cloves garlic, minced

2 teaspoons grated fresh ginger root

1 to 2 teaspoons berbere, to taste

1/3 teaspoon turmeric

1 cup (192 g) brown lentils, picked over and rinsed

6 cups (1.4 L) water, more if desired

1 tablespoon (16 g) tomato paste

1 tablespoon (18 g) vegetable bouillon paste, or 2 bouillon cubes

Salt and pepper

Instructions

Heat the oil in a large soup pot over medium heat. Add the onion, carrot, and potato. Cook for 5 to 7 minutes, stirring occasionally until the onions are translucent. Stir in the garlic, ginger, berbere, turmeric, and lentils and cook and stir for 1 minute until fragrant. Add the water, tomato paste, and bouillon. Bring to a boil, and then reduce the heat to a simmer. Cook for 30 minutes, stirring occasionally until the lentils are tender. Taste and adjust the seasonings.

Split Pea Patties

Yield: 8 patties

Protein content per patty: 10 g

Ingredients

¾ cup (148 g) dry green split peas, cooked al dente (See Recipe Note.), drained

3 tablespoons (45 ml) fresh lemon juice 1 tablespoon (15 ml) neutral-flavored oil 3 cloves garlic, grated or pressed

⅓ cup (53 g) minced red onion

¼ cup (4 g) minced fresh cilantro or (15 g) fresh parsley

1 teaspoon ground cumin

1 teaspoon garam masala

1/3 teaspoon fine sea salt

1/3 teaspoon paprika (smoked or regular)

⅓ teaspoon turmeric

'¼ teaspoon cayenne pepper

⅓ cup (30 g) whole wheat pastry flour or (31 g) all-purpose flour

2 tablespoons (24 g) potato starch or (16 g) cornstarch

1/3 teaspoon baking powder

Water, as needed

Nonstick cooking spray or oil spray

Instructions

Place the cooked split peas in a food processor and pulse about 15 times to break down the peas slightly. You're not looking to puree them, but to make it so the mixture will hold together better to form patties. In a large bowl, combine the split peas with lemon juice, oil, garlic, onion, cilantro, cumin, garam masala, salt, paprika, turmeric, and cayenne pepper until thoroughly mixed. Add the flour, starch, and baking powder on top.

Stir until thoroughly mixed. If the mixture is dry and crumbly, stir water into it, 1 tablespoon (15 ml) at a time until the mixture holds together better. We usually have to add 2 tablespoons (30 ml) of water. Refrigerate for 1 hour.

Preheat the oven to 350°F (180°C, or gas mark 4).

Divide the mixture into 8 patties (each one a scant but packed '¼ cup, or 60 g) of a little under 3 inches (7 cm) in diameter and ^-inch (1.3 cm) in thickness. Place on a baking sheet lined with parchment paper or press into a lightly greased whoopie pie pan. Lightly coat the top with cooking spray.

Bake for 15 minutes on one side, flip, lightly coat with cooking spray, and bake for another 10 minutes until golden brown.

Store leftovers in an airtight container in the refrigerator for up to 4 days. Gently reheat in a pan or in the oven or enjoy cold or at room temperature.

Savory Edamame Mini Cakes

Yield: 14 to 16 cakes, plus ¼ cup (60 ml) sauce

Protein content per cake (with sauce): 3 g

Ingredients

For the sauce:

3 tablespoons (45 ml) tamari

1 teaspoon smooth peanut butter

1 teaspoon seasoned rice vinegar, or to taste

1 teaspoon sambal oelek, or to taste

For the cakes:

1 cup (150 g) frozen, shelled edamame, thawed

¼ cup (36 g) minced bell pepper (any color)

3 tablespoons (30 g) minced red onion

2 cloves garlic, minced

5-spice powder Generous

¼ teaspoon fine sea salt

Pinch of ground black pepper

1 cup (140 g) whole spelt flour

1 ½ cup plus 1 tablespoon (95 ml) unsweetened plain vegan milk

⅔ cup (53 g) panko crumbs

2 tablespoons (16 g) toasted sesame seeds

2 tablespoons (30 ml) high-heat neutral-flavored oil

Instructions

To make the sauce: In a small bowl, whisk together the tamari, peanut butter, rice vinegar, and sambal oelek until smooth. Set aside.

To make the cakes: Put the edamame, bell pepper, onion, garlic, 5-spice powder, salt, and pepper in a medium-size bowl. Stir to combine. Stir in the flour, then the milk to form a dough. It should be shape-able, but some of the edamame may poke out. Combine the panko and the sesame seeds on a shallow plate.

Heat the oil in a large skillet over medium-high heat.

Scoop 1 tablespoon (26 g) of the mixture and shape it into a small round no more than '¼ inch (1.3 cm) thick and about 1¼ inches (3.8 cm) in diameter. Put it in the panko mixture and pat to coat well on both sides, continuing to shape it into a small cake. Repeat until all the cakes have been formed. Put half of the cakes into the skillet and cook for 3 to 5 minutes until golden brown. Turn over to cook the second side for 2 to 4 minutes, until also golden brown. Drain on a paper towel-lined plate. Cook the remaining cakes in the same manner, adding more oil if needed serve with the sauce for dipping.

Quinoa Edamame Rolls

Yield: 14 rolls, plus scant ⅔ cup (175 ml) dressing

Protein content per roll (with dressing): 4 g

Ingredients

For the dressing:

4 Protein content per serving tablespoons (68 ml) fresh lemon juice

1 Protein content per serving tablespoons (23 ml) toasted sesame oil

1 Protein content per serving tablespoons (23 ml) sriracha

1 Protein content per serving tablespoons (23 ml) tamari

1 Protein content per serving tablespoons (30 g) agave nectar or brown rice syrup

1 Protein content per serving tablespoons (12 g) toasted sesame seeds

1 large clove garlic, grated or pressed

For the rolls:

⅔ cup (116 g) cooked shelled edamame

⅔ cup (110 g) packed cooked and cooled quinoa

Protein content per serving cup (45 g) packed minced napa cabbage

¼ cup (27 g) toasted slivered almonds

¼ cup (20 g) chopped scallion

2 tablespoons (2 g) loosely packed chopped cilantro

2 tablespoons (24 g) packed peeled and grated daikon radish, liquid gently squeezed out before measuring

14 spring roll wrappers

Nonstick cooking spray or oil spray

Instructions

To make the dressing: Combine all the ingredients in a small bowl, using a whisk. Set aside. To make the rolls: Combine the edamame, quinoa, napa cabbage, almonds, scallion, cilantro, and daikon radish in a large bowl. Add '¼ cup (60 ml) of the dressing on top, stirring to combine. Set aside the rest of the dressing for serving. Immerse the spring roll wrappers 1 sheet at a time in warm water to soften. Soak for a few seconds, until pliable. Handle carefully because the wraps tear easily. Drain on a clean kitchen towel before rolling. To assemble, place 2 packed tablespoons (30 g) of filling per moistened wrapper. Roll tightly and place on a plate. Repeat with remaining rolls. Be careful when separating the rolls: The wraps might stick to one another a little, but won't tear if you separate them slowly. Heat a large skillet on medium-high heat. Lower the heat to medium, lightly coat with cooking spray or oil spray, away from the heat. Place as many rolls as will fit in your skillet without overcrowding it, and cook the rolls on each side until light golden brown and crisp, about 4 minutes per side. Repeat with remaining rolls. Serve immediately with the remaining dressing. Leftovers can be wrapped tightly and stored in the refrigerator for up to 3 days.

Spicy Chickpea Fries

Yield: About 64 fries, or 4 servings
Protein content per serving: 14 g

Ingredients

4 cups (940 ml) vegetable broth
2 tablespoons (15 g) nutritional yeast
1 teaspoon fine sea salt
1 teaspoon onion powder
1 teaspoon garlic powder
1 teaspoon smoked paprika
1 teaspoon ground cumin
1 teaspoon ground coriander
1 teaspoon garam masala
2 cups (240 g) chickpea flour, sifted
¼ cup (30 g) cornflour, sifted (not cornstarch, preferably organic)
Nonstick cooking spray
Up to ¼ cup (60 ml) olive oil, for brushing

Instructions

Combine the broth, nutritional yeast, salt, onion powder, garlic powder, paprika, cumin, coriander, and garam masala in a large saucepan and bring to a boil. Lower the heat, and then (and this is important to avoid clumping) slowly stream in the flours, whisking constantly. Reduce the heat to medium-low, switch to stirring with a wooden spoon almost constantly, and cook for 6 minutes or until the mixture is so thick that when you slash a line through its center with the spoon all the way to the bottom of the pan, the line remains and the mixture doesn't slide back to cover the bottom of the pan. Be sure to adjust the temperature, if needed, to avoid scorching.

Remove from the heat. Spread evenly in an 8-inch (20 cm) square baking pan coated with cooking spray, using an angled spatula. Do not cover the pan. Once it's cool enough, place it in the refrigerator for at least 2 hours.

Remove the chilled mixture from the pan. Cut into 'Protein content per serving2-inch (1.3 cm) strips, flipping those strips on the side (they will be approximately 1-inch [2.5 cm] wide once flipped) and cutting them in two lengthwise again to obtain two 'Protein content per serving-inch (1.3 cm) wide, 8-inch (20 cm) long strips. Then cut both strips once in the middle widthwise. You should get fries of approximately 4 x 'Protein content per serving inches (10 x 1.3 cm). Preheat the oven to 425°F (220°C, or gas mark 7). Lightly grease a large rimmed baking sheet with olive oil. Lightly brush the fries with oil and space them evenly on the prepared sheet.

Bake for 15 minutes, flip the fries and bake for another 15 minutes or until golden brown and crispy. Serve immediately.

Baked Falafel

Yield: 32 falafels

Protein content per falafel: 2 g

Ingredients

Nonstick cooking spray

3 cups (492 g) cooked chickpeas

¼ cup (60 ml) fresh lemon juice

3 cloves garlic, minced

⅓ cup (20 g) packed fresh parsley

1/3 cup (5 g) packed fresh cilantro

⅓ cup (53 g) minced red onion

2 tablespoons (32 g) tahini

1 tablespoon (15 ml) toasted sesame oil

1 ground cumin

1 Protein content per serving teaspoons ground coriander

¼ teaspoon cayenne pepper

Scant Protein content per serving teaspoon fine sea salt, or to taste

3 tablespoons (23 g) whole wheat pastry flour or all-purpose flour

Protein content per serving teaspoon baking soda

2 tablespoons (30 ml) olive oil

Instructions

Preheat the oven to 400°F (200°C, or gas mark 6). Lightly coat 32 cups out of two 24-cup mini muffin tins with cooking spray.

Place the chickpeas, lemon juice, garlic, parsley, and cilantro in a food processor. Consider doing this in a couple of batches, depending on the size of your food processor. Pulse a few times, stopping to scrape the sides with a rubber spatula: You're looking for a somewhat smooth texture but not precisely a paste. The beans should be broken down, but it's okay if a few pieces remain as long as the mixture is cohesive. Remove from the food processor and place in a large bowl. Add the onion, tahini, sesame oil, cumin, coriander, cayenne pepper, and salt. Stir to combine. Add the flour and baking soda on top and stir until thoroughly combined.

Gather 1 packed tablespoon (18 g) of mixture per falafel, gently shape into a ball and place in the mini muffin tin. Repeat with the remaining dough. Lightly brush the tops with olive oil.

Bake for 15 minutes, carefully flip each falafel, and lightly brush with oil. Bake for another 8 minutes or until golden brown.

Remove from the oven and let stand 5 minutes before serving.

Pudla

Yield: 2 to 4 servings

Protein content per serving: 9 g

Ingredients

¾ cup (180 ml) unsweetened plain vegan milk, plus extra if needed

2 tablespoons (30 ml) fresh lemon juice

1 cup (120 g) chickpea flour

⅓ teaspoon baking soda

⅓ teaspoon ground cumin

⅓ teaspoon ground coriander

⅓ teaspoon garam masala

⅛ to ¼ teaspoon cayenne pepper, or to taste

⅓ teaspoon fine sea salt, or to taste

2 tablespoons (30 ml) olive oil

2 tablespoons (15 g) nutritional yeast

1 tablespoon (16 g) tahini

⅓ cup (40 g) minced red onion

⅓ cup (4 g) fresh cilantro leaves (not packed)

2 cloves garlic, grated or pressed

Nonstick cooking spray or oil spray

Instructions

Combine the milk and lemon juice in a medium bowl. Let stand for two minutes to let the milk curdle. This is your "buttermilk."

In the meantime, whisk together the flour, baking soda, cumin, coriander, garam masala, cayenne pepper, and salt in a large bowl.

Add the olive oil, nutritional yeast, tahini, red onion, cilantro, and garlic to the buttermilk.

Add the wet ingredients to dry thoroughly, but do not overdo it. Let stand for 10 minutes. The dough will thicken. If it is thick enough to be unmanageable, add the milk needed to dilute it in 3 cups (60 ml).

Heat a large skillet over medium heat. Reduce heat to medium. Cover the pan gently and away from the heat of the floor with a baking spray or oil spray. Add the dough (approximately 3.5 ounces or 100 grams), spread it in a circle of just over 5 inches (13 cm). Let cook for about 4 minutes until the center bubbles and is not too dry but not too wet. Lift the edges of the hole carefully to make sure it is light golden brown, which is another sign of being ready to turn.

Carefully fork with a spoon and cook for another 4 minutes or until golden brown on one side.

Before cooking, cover the rest of the dough in three batches. Serve immediately.

The Whole Enchilada

Yield: 12 to 14 enchiladas

Protein content per enchilada: 6 g

Ingredients

For the sauce:

2 tablespoons (30 ml) olive oil 1/3 cup (80 g) chopped red onion 4 ounces (113 g) tomato paste

1 tablespoon (15 ml) adobo sauce

1 tablespoon (8 g) mild to medium chili powder

1 teaspoon ground cumin

3 cloves garlic, grated or pressed

⅓ teaspoon fine sea salt, or to taste

2 tablespoons (15 g) whole wheat pastry flour or (16 g) all-purpose flour

2 cups (470 ml) water

For the filling:

1 Protein content per serving teaspoons olive oil

⅓ cup (53 g) chopped red onion

1 sweet potato, trimmed and peeled, chopped (about 8.8 ounces, or 250 g)

1 yellow squash, trimmed and chopped (about 5.3 ounces, or 150 g)

2 cloves garlic, grated or pressed

1 tablespoon (8 g) nutritional yeast

1 smoked paprika

¼ teaspoon liquid smoke

Pinch of fine sea salt, or to taste

1 (258 g) cooked black beans

3 tablespoons (45 ml) enchilada sauce

12 to 14 corn tortillas

1 recipe Creamy Cashew Sauce

Chopped fresh cilantro, to taste Hot sauce, to taste

Instructions

To make the sauce: Heat the oil on medium heat in a large skillet. Add the onion and cook until fragrant while occasionally stirring, about 2 minutes. Add the tomato paste, adobo sauce, chili powder, cumin, garlic, and salt. Saute for 2 minutes, stirring frequently. Sprinkle the flour on top and cook 2 minutes, stirring frequently. Slowly whisk in the water and cook until slightly thickened, about 6 minutes, frequently whisking to prevent clumps. Remove from the heat and set aside.

To make the filling: Heat the oil in a large skillet on medium heat. Add the onion and sweet potato and cook 6 minutes or until the potato starts to get tender, stirring occasionally. Add the squash and garlic and cook for 4 minutes, stirring occasionally. Add the nutritional yeast, paprika, liquid smoke, and salt, stir to combine, and cook for another minute. Add the beans and enchilada sauce and stir to combine. Cover the pan and simmer until the vegetables are completely tender about 4 minutes. Add a little water if the plants stick to the skillet. Adjust the seasonings if needed.

Preheat the oven to 350°F (180°C, or gas mark 4).

Place the sauce in a large shallow bowl. If you aren't using pre-shaped, uncooked tortillas, follow the instructions in the Recipe Notes to soften the tortillas so that they are easier to work with. Ladle about 1/3 cup (80 ml) of enchilada sauce on the bottom of a 9 x 13-inch (23 x 33 cm) baking dish. Dip each tortilla in the sauce to coat only lightly. Don't be too generous and gently scrape off the excess sauce with a spatula; otherwise, you will run out of sauce. Add a scant ¼ cup (about 45 g) of the filling in each tortilla. Fold the tortilla over the filling, rolling like a cigar. Place the enchiladas in the pan, seam side down. Make sure to squeeze them in tight so that there's room in the dish for all of them. Top evenly with the remaining enchilada sauce. Add the Creamy Cashew Sauce consistently on top. Bake for 20 to 25 minutes or until the top is set, and the enchiladas are heated through. Garnish with cilantro and serve with hot sauce.

Mujaddara

Yield: 4 to 6 servings
Protein content per serving: 11

Ingredients
⅓ cup (144 g) dry green lentils, rinsed and picked through
¼ cup (150 g) dry brown jasmine rice, rinsed and picked through
3 cups (705 ml) vegetable broth
1 tablespoon (15 ml) olive oil or melted coconut oil
2 white onions, chopped (10 ounces, or 340 g)
1 leek, thoroughly cleaned and sliced thinly, white and light green parts (6 ounces, or 170g)
Vegetable broth or water, as needed
4 cloves garlic, grated or pressed
⅓ teaspoon fine sea salt, or to taste
⅓ teaspoon ground cinnamon
⅓ teaspoon ground cumin
⅓ teaspoon ground coriander
⅓ teaspoon paprika
¼ teaspoon cayenne pepper, or to taste
2 tablespoons (12 g) chopped fresh mint
2 tablespoons (8 g) chopped fresh parsley or (2 g) cilantro
Zest and juice of a small organic lemon

⅓ cup (35 g) chopped toasted peanuts, cashews, or pine nuts, optional

Instructions

Place the lentils and rice in a rice cooker. Cover with the broth, and stir to combine. Cover with the lid and cook until tender, 40 to 45 minutes. (Alternatively, cook the lentils and rice on the stovetop, following the directions on the package of rice.)

In a large skillet, add the oil and heat on medium heat. Add the onions and leek and saute until browned, about 15 minutes. Add vegetable broth, 1 tablespoon (15 ml) at a time, as needed, if the onions stick to the pan during that time. Add the garlic, salt, cinnamon, cumin, coriander, paprika, and cayenne pepper, stirring to combine. Stop stirring and cook until the onions are crisped and the spices toasted and fragrant, about 5 minutes.

Place the lentils and rice in a large bowl and add the spiced onions on top; thoroughly and gently fold the onions into the lentils and rice. Once you are ready to serve, fold the mint, parsley or cilantro, zest, and lemon juice into the mujaddara, and garnish each serving with nuts. Adjust the seasonings as needed.

Leftovers can be stored in an airtight container in the refrigerator for up to 4 days. Note that this dish tastes even better when it gets to sit for a while. Gently reheat before serving.

Black Bean and Avocado Salad

Yield: 4 servings

Protein content per serving: 8 g.

Ingredients

1 cup (172 g) cooked black beans

⅓ cup (82 g) frozen corn (run under hot water, drained)

3 tablespoons (15 g) minced scallion

6 cherry tomatoes, cut into quarters

2 cloves garlic, minced

1 teaspoon minced fresh cilantro, or to taste

Pinch of dried oregano 1 chipotle in adobo

1 tablespoon (15 ml) fresh lemon juice

1 tablespoon (15 ml) apple cider vinegar 1 tablespoon (15 ml) vegetable broth

1 teaspoon nutritional yeast

2 tablespoons (15 g) roasted salted pepitas (hulled pumpkin seeds)

2 avocados, pitted, peeled, and chopped

Salt and pepper

Instructions

Combine the beans, corn, scallion, cherry tomatoes, garlic, cilantro, and oregano in a medium-size bowl. Using a small blender or a mortar and pestle, thoroughly combine the chipotle, lemon juice, vinegar, broth, and nutritional yeast to form a dressing. Pour over the bean mixture and stir in the pepitas. Gently stir in the avocados. Season to taste with salt and pepper. Serve promptly so that the avocado doesn't discolor.

Mediterranean Quinoa and Bean Salad

Yield: 6 to 8 servings
Protein content per serving: 6 g

Ingredients
1¾ cups (213 g) dry ivory quinoa, rinsed
2 (590 ml) vegetable broth
2 tablespoons (30 ml) apple cider vinegar
2 tablespoons (30 ml) fresh lemon juice
3 tablespoons (45 ml) extra-virgin olive oil
⅔ cup (40 g) finely chopped red onion
2 to 3 cloves garlic, minced, or to taste
Protein content per serving teaspoon red pepper flakes, or to taste
Salt and pepper
1 (266 g) cooked cannellini beans
24 jumbo pitted kalamata olives, minced
Half of red bell pepper, cored and diced
Half of yellow bell pepper, cored and diced
8 ounces (227 g) mini heirloom tomatoes, halved or quartered depending on size
6 tablespoons (24 g) minced fresh parsley
15 leaves fresh basil, cut in chiffonade

Instructions

Combine the quinoa with the broth in a medium saucepan. Bring to a boil and then reduce the heat to a simmer. Cover and cook until all liquid is absorbed, 12 to 15 minutes. The quinoa should be tender and translucent, and the germ ring should be visible along the outside edge of the grain. Set aside to cool completely.

In a large bowl, combine the vinegar, lemon juice, oil, onion, garlic, red pepper flakes, salt, and pepper. Stir the beans into the dressing. Add the cooled quinoa, olives, bell peppers, tomatoes, and parsley into the bowl with the beans. Fold with a rubber spatula to thoroughly yet gently combine.

Cover and chill for an hour to let the flavors meld. Garnish with basil upon serving. Leftovers can be stored in an airtight container in the refrigerator for up to 4 days.

Tabbouleh Verde

Yield: 4 to 6 servings

Protein content per serving: 9 g

Ingredients

1 cup (186 g) dry whole-wheat couscous

⅓ cup (120 ml) vegetable broth, brought to a boil

3 tablespoons (45 ml) extra-virgin olive oil

2 tablespoons (30 ml) fresh lemon juice

2 tablespoons (30 ml) fresh lime juice

1½ cups (258 g) cooked black beans

1½ cups (225 g) diced heirloom green tomato (Any other color will do.)

1 cup (150 g) diced green bell pepper (Any different color will do.)

⅓ cup (5 g) loosely packed fresh cilantro leaves, minced

⅓ cup (20 g) minced scallion

1 small jalapeno, seeded and minced

⅓ teaspoon toasted cumin seeds

Salt and pepper, optional

Roasted pepitas (hulled pumpkin seeds), for garnish

1 lemon, cut into 4 to 6 wedges

1 lime, cut into 4 to 6 wedges

Instructions

Mix the couscous with the broth in a large glass bowl. Add the oil, lemon juice, and lime juice. Stir well. Cover and let stand 5 minutes until the liquids are absorbed. Fluff with a fork.

Add the beans, tomato, bell pepper, cilantro, scallion, and jalapeno on top. Rub the cumin seeds between your fingers while adding them to release the flavor. Fold to combine with a rubber spatula. Adjust the seasonings to taste. Refrigerate for at least 30 minutes to chill and to let the flavors meld.

Serve and garnish each portion with a small handful of pepitas and a wedge of lemon and lime to drizzle before eating.

Leftovers can be stored in an airtight container in the refrigerator for up to 4 days.

Curried Bean and Corn Salad

Yield: 4 servings

Protein content per serving: 27 g

Ingredients

Protein content per serving cup (90 g) whole freekeh

3 cups (705 ml) salted water

1 can (15 ounces, or 425 g) chickpeas, drained and rinsed

1 cup (164 g) fresh or frozen corn (run under hot water, drained)

¼ cup (40 g) minced red onion

¼ cup (32 g) minced celery

¼ cup (38 g) minced bell pepper (any color)

3 tablespoons (12 g) minced fresh parsley

1 tablespoon (6 g) curry powder (mild or hot)

1 teaspoon ground cumin

1 teaspoon garam masala

1 teaspoon ginger powder

1 teaspoon fine sea salt

1 clove garlic

2 tablespoons (30 ml) seasoned rice vinegar

3 tablespoons (45 ml) olive oil

Instructions

Bring the freekeh and salted water to a boil in a medium-size saucepan. Reduce to simmer and cook for 45 minutes, occasionally stirring, until tender. Drain and run under cold water, draining again. Transfer to a medium-size bowl. Add the chickpeas, corn, onion, celery, bell pepper, and parsley.

Heat the curry powder, cumin, and garam masala in a small skillet over medium heat. Stir and cook for 3 to 4 minutes until fragrant. Do not burn. Transfer to a small blender and add the ginger powder, salt, garlic, and vinegar. Blend until smooth. Add the olive oil and blend again to emulsify. Pour the dressing (to taste) over the bean mixture. Stir to coat and let sit for 15 minutes for the flavors to meld. The salad can also be covered and refrigerated for up to 3 days.

Leek and Lemon Lentil Salad

Yield: 4 servings

Protein Content Per Serving: 16 g

Ingredients

1 cup (192 g) dry French green lentils

¼ cup (60 ml) olive oil

⅔ cup (80 g) chopped leeks (white part only)

1 teaspoon dried thyme

2 cloves garlic, minced

¼ cup (60 ml) fresh lemon juice

1 teaspoon fine sea salt, or to taste

Pinch of ground black pepper, or to taste

1 carrot, peeled, cut into quarters, then thinly sliced

6 small radishes, cut into quarters, then thinly sliced

2 small sunchokes, cut into quarters, then thinly sliced

Instructions

Bring a medium-size pot of water to a boil. Add the lentils. Reduce the heat to simmer. Cook for 25 to 30 minutes until tender. Drain and rinse with cold water. Drain again and then transfer to a medium-size bowl.

Heat the oil in a small skillet over medium heat. Add the leek and thyme. Cook, occasionally stirring, for 3 to 4 minutes until the leek is translucent. Add the garlic and cook for 1 minute longer. Transfer to a small blender. Add the lemon juice, salt, and pepper and process until smooth. Add the vegetables and dressing to the lentils. Stir to combine. Serve immediately or cover and refrig¬erate for up to 3 days. Taste and adjust the seasonings when serving.

Eat-it-Up Edamame Salad

Yield: 4 servings

Protein content per serving: 17 g

Ingredients

2 cups (300 g) frozen, shelled edamame

3 ounces (85 g) somen noodles, broken into 1-inch pieces

Salt, for cooking

⅔ cup (74 g) 'Protein content per serving2-inch (1.3 cm) pieces of snow peas

1 cup (70 g) thinly sliced baby bok choy

1½ cup (27 g) minced scallion

Protein content per serving cup (70 g) minced carrot

2 tablespoons (30 ml) seasoned rice vinegar

2 tablespoons (30 ml) tamari, or to taste

1 tablespoon (15 ml) vegetable broth

2 teaspoons ume plum vinegar

2 teaspoons toasted sesame oil

Protein content per serving teaspoon sambal oelek, or to taste

¼ teaspoon minced garlic

¼ teaspoon grated fresh ginger root

Salt and pepper

Instructions

Bring a large pot of water to boil. Add the edamame, somen, and salt. Cook for 2 minutes or until the noodles are soft but do not overcook.

Drain immediately and rinse under cold water until chilled, draining again. Combine the snow peas, baby bok choy, scallion, and carrot in a medium-size bowl. Add the somen and edamame to the vegetables.

Combine the rice vinegar, tamari, broth, ume plum vinegar, sesame oil, sambal oelek, garlic, and ginger in a small blender. Process until smooth. Pour over the salad and stir to coat. Cover and refrigerate for 1 hour, or longer for the flavors to meld. Taste and adjust the seasonings when serving.

Chapter 9

Crockpot Lasagna with Spinach Tofu

SERVINGS: 1
METHOD

Get a blender. Put silken tofu, firm or extra-firm tofu, soymilk, garlic powder, lemon juice, basil, and salt in the food processor or blender. Grind it together until it is very smooth. After grinding, add thawed spinach to the mixture.

Get a crockpot or slower cooker. Get a cup of tomato sauce. Put the tomato sauce in the bottom of the crockpot or slower cooker. Mix the spinach. Put 1/3 of the lasagna noodles on top of the sauce and 1/3 of the tofu and spinach mixture on top of the noodles. Now repeat the layers. Ensure that the sauce is on top.

In the crockpot, cook the noodles on very low heat between 6 and 8 hours. Or cook the noodles on very low heat till they are soft.

After cooking, put some nutritional yeast on top of the noodles. Serve, and enjoy.

INGREDIENTS

- 1 container of soft (silken) tofu
- 1 container firm or extra firm tofu
- ¼ cup of soy milk
- ½ teaspoon of garlic powder
- 2 teaspoon of lemon juice
- 3 teaspoons of fresh basil (chopped)
- 1 teaspoon of salt
- 2 (10-ounce) packages of frozen spinach (thawed and patted dry)
- 4 cups of tomato sauce
- 1 (10-ounce) box of lasagna noodles

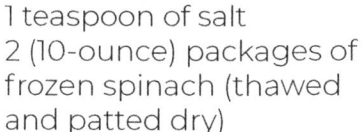

Crockpot Vegetarian Split Pea Soup

SERVINGS: 1
METHOD

Add peas, vegetable broth, and bouillon cubes in crockpot or slow cooker. Stir it and break up the bouillon cubes a bit
Add chopped potatoes, onions, celery, carrot and garlic
Add mustard, cumin, sage, thyme, and bay leaves, and stir
Season soup lightly with salt and pepper
Cook for about 4 hours/till peas split
Taste and check seasoning
Serve, and enjoy!

INGREDIENTS

- 2 cups of split pea soup (uncooked)
- 8 cups of vegetable broth (or water)
- 2 potatoes (chopped)
- 2 cubes of bouillon (vegetarian)
- Optional: 2 ribs of celery (chopped)
- 1 onion (diced)
- 2 cloves of garlic (minced)
- 2 carrots (sliced)
- 1 teaspoon of dry mustard
- 1 teaspoon of sage
- 1 teaspoon of thyme
- 1 teaspoon of cumin

Black Bean Veggie Burger

SERVINGS: 1

METHOD

Grease the bottom of a small frying pan and place it over medium-high heat. Combine onions and sauté and pour it in the small frying pan. Fry them until they are soft. This process usually takes between 3 and 5 minutes.

Get a large bowl. Mash the black beans inside it. Ensure that the beans are almost smooth.

Saute your onions and crumble the bread. In the bowl, add the sautéed onions, mashed black beans, crumbled bread, seasoned salt, garlic powder, and onion powder. Ensure you mix to combine well.

Add some flour to the ingredients by adding a teaspoon per time. Stir everything together until it is well combined. While mixing, make sure that it is very thick. To achieve this, you may want to use your hand to work your flour well.

Make the mixed black beans into patties. Ensure that each of the patties is approximately ½ inch thick. The best way to do this is to make a ball with the black beans. After doing this, flatten the ball gently. Place your frying pan on medium-low heat. Add some oil. Fry your black bean patties in the frying pan until it is slightly firm and lightly browned on each side. This usually takes about 3 minutes. Ensure you adjust the head well because if the pan is too hot, the bean burgers will be brown in the middle and will not be well cooked in the middle.

To serve, assemble your veggie burgers and enjoy it with all the fixings. You can also serve also get a plate, serve them with a little ketchup or hot sauce or no bunds. To increase the nutrition of the meal, you can add a nice green salad.

Serve and enjoy!

INGREDIENTS

- ½ onion (chopped small)
- 1 (14-ounce) can of black beans (well-drained)
- 2 slices of bread (crumbled)
- ½ teaspoon of seasoned salt
- 1 teaspoon of garlic powder
- 1 teaspoon of onion powder
- ½ cup of flour
- Dash salt (to taste)
- Dash pepper (to taste)
- Oil for frying (divide)

Blueberry Tofu Smoothie

SERVINGS: 1

METHOD

Drain the silken tofu in order to remove the excess water (silken tofu as a high water content) Peele and slice the banana. Place the sliced banana on a baking sheet and freeze them. This process usually takes up to 15 minutes. This helps to make the smoothie thicker. Get a blender. Blend the banana, tofu, and soy milk. This usually takes up to 30 seconds.

Add ½ cup of the blueberries to the banana, tofu, and soymilk. Then blend it until it is very smooth. Put the remaining blueberries. Add honey and ice cubes. Blend it until it is well combined. Serve and enjoy.

INGREDIENTS

- 6 ounces of silken tofu
- 1 medium banana
- 2/3 cups of soy milk
- 1 cup of frozen or fresh blueberries (divided)
- 1 tablespoon of honey
- 2-3 ice cubes (optional)

Fluffy 1-Bowl Sugar Cookies

SERVINGS: 4
METHOD

Get an oven, preheat the oven to 350 degrees F (176 C). Put two baking sheets inside the oven

Soften your butter in a large mixing bowl. Beat or whisk the butter until it is creamy and smooth. Do this for about a minutes. Be careful so that the better is not melted or cold.

Add some sugar to the butter. Mix it over medium speed until it becomes and light. This usually takes 1 minute. Add chickpeas brine and vanilla. Mix again until it is very smooth

Add sea salt and baking powder. Blend or whisk to so the ingredients will mix very well. Ass gluten-free flour blend, almond flour, and corn starch and blend. Ensure that the ingredients are well mixed. If desired, you can use a wooden spoon to mix. Add almond milk and stir again.

Now, the dough should be very thick, moldable, and a bit difficult to mix. If it is too soft, add a mixture of the gluten-free flour blend, almond flour, and cornstarchuntil it is thick. If it is too thick, mix with extra almond milk.

20 MINUTES

INGREDIENTS

½ cup of softened butter
½ cup of organic cane sugar
1 tablespoon of vanilla extract
3 tablespoons of aquafupuaba
¾ tablespoon of baking powder
¼ tablespoon of sea salt
1 2/3 tablespoon of gluten-free flour blend
2/3 cups of almond flour
1/3 cup of cornstarch or arrowroot 1 tablespoon of unsweetened almond milk
Frosting (optional) ½ cup of powder 1 ½ cup of sifted organic powdered sugar
¼ tablespoon of vanilla extract 1-3 tablespoon of unsweetened almond milk
Natural food dye

Put the dough in the refrigerator and let it chill. This usually takes 25 minutes. Then use a scooper or a tablespoon to measure out 1 ½ tablespoon of the dough. Roll it carefully to make balls. Be careful because the dough will still be soft. Arrange these balls on the parchment-lined baking sheets. Leave the space of an inch between them. Use your palm to press each of the balls and slightly smash the balls. As an alternative. Make a well-floured surface. Roll the dough on this surface until it is about ¼ inch thick. Press the cookie cutters into the dough. Ensure that the cutters dipped into gluten-free flour. Use the floured spatula to scoop on the baking sheets. This procedure works whether you are using the cut-out method or traditional circles. Bake the cookies. This should take 10 minutes. Make sure they are fluffy and that their edges are starting to become dried out. Leave it on the baking sheet for about 10 minutes for it to cool then transfer it to a plate for it to be completely cool. To make frosting (optiona). Get a mixing bowl. Add softened butter. Whisk or beat it until it is soft and fluffy. This should take about 1 minute. Pour some powdered sugar into the bowl and whip. Add the vanilla extract and whisk. Keep adding sugar and whisking until the frosting can be separated. If you want a thinner frosting, add some almond milk to it. When it is too thick, add more almond milk. If you want, add some food coloring now. Frost the cookies or leave it to be plain.

INGREDIENTS

1 15-oz can of black beans
2 large flax eggs
3 tablespoon of coconut oil
¾ cup cocoa powder
¼ tablespoon of salt
1 tablespoon pure vanilla extract
½ cup of organic cane sugar
1 ½ tablespoon of baking powder Toppings
Crushed walnuts
Pecans
Daily-free semisweet chocolate chips

Gluten-Free Black Beans Brownies

SERVINGS: 1
METHOD

50 - 60 MINUTES

Preheat the oven to 350 degrees F, prepare a baking dish lined with parchment paper. Get a 12-slot standard size muffin pot and grease. Rinse your black beans well and drain. Get the bowl of a food processor and prepare flax egg Leave out walnuts and other toppings and add the remaining ingredients and purre If the batter is too thick, add 1 or 2 tablespoons of water. Get the muffin tin and pour the batter in it. Ensure that the top is smooth

Bake the batter until the tops are dry, and the edges start to pull away from the sides. This takes 25 minutes.

Remove the pan and let it cool

Serve and enjoy!

Tahini Chocolate Banana Soft Serve

SERVINGS: 1
METHOD

Get a high-speed blender. Add sliced frozen bananas. Blend until it is creamy.
Add tahini, cacao powder, and maple syrup and blend. You can also add vanilla extract or a pinch of sea salt for more flavor. Ensure they are well mixed
Transfer it into serving bowls. Serve and enjoy!
cooked in the middle.
To serve, assemble your veggie burgers and enjoy it with all the fixings. You can also serve also get a plate, serve them with a little ketchup or hot sauce or no bunds. To increase the nutrition of the meal, you can add a nice green salad.
Serve and enjoy!

INGREDIENTS

2 cups of ripe sliced frozen bananas
2 tablespoons of tahini
3 tablespoons cacao
1-2 tablespoons of maple syrup
1-2 pitted dates (optional)
1 tablespoon vanilla extract (optional)
1 pinch of salt (optional)
For Toppings (optional)
1-2 tablespoon of magic shell

Raw Oreos

SERVINGS: 1
METHOD

Add coconut butter and vanilla and sweetener to taste. Set it aside
Add nuts and pulse. Add dates, coconut oil, maple syrup, cocoa powder, salt, and blend it well.
Add more cocoa powder for chocolate flavor and dates for sweetness and salt
Get a cutting board, line it with parchment or wax paper. Place dough in the center. Form in a 1-inch disc and top with a piece of wax paper
Roll dough into a ¼-inch-thick rectangle. Remove top wax paper. Use a cookie cutter to cut the dough
Use a spatula to transfer cookie on a flat plate. Put the plate in the freezer for 10-15 minutes
Add coconut butter with half of the cookies. Put it back in the freezer for about some time and add coconut butter to the other half

INGREDIENTS

1 cup of coconut butter
¼ teaspoon of vanilla extract
Organic powdered sweetener (to taste) COOKIE
1 ½ cups of raw almond or walnuts
6-7 whole Medjool or deglet nour dates
3 tablespoon of melted coconut oil
1 tablespoon of syrup
1/3 cup of cocoa powder
1 pinch of sea salt

Peanut Butter Cup Cookies

SERVINGS: 4
METHOD

Pre-heat oven to 375 degrees F (190 C). Put parchment paper on two baking sheets
Get a mixing bowl and add softened butter
Add sugar and mix until it is fluffy. Add vanilla and chickpea, peanut butter, and mix very well. Add baking powder
The dough should be thick by now. Put it in the refrigerator for 5 minutes.
Use a scooper to measure out 1 ½ tablespoon of dough. Roll it into balls and place them on baking sheets. Smash them slightly with your palm
Bake until the edges are starting to dry out. Remove from oven and press an unwrapped peanuts butter in the middle of the cookie. Don't crack too much. Transfer them to a wire rack

20 MINUTES

INGREDIENTS

½ cup of softened butter
2/3 cup of organic cane sugar
1 tablespoon of vanilla extract
3 tablespoons of aquafaba
¼ cup of salted creamy peanut butter
¾ tablespoon of baking powder
1 pinch of sea salt
2/3 cup of almond flour
¼ cup of cornstarch or arrowroot
1 1/3 cup of gluten-free flour blend
15-18 mini peanut butter cups
ned almond milk
Natural food dye

INGREDIENTS

¾ scant cup of unsweetened almond milk
2 tablespoon of organic cane sugar
1 tablespoon of butter
1 packet of active dry yeast
DRY
2 cups of DIY gluten-free flour blend
¾ cup of almond flour
2 tablespoon of sea salt
4 tablespoons of butter
FILLING
3 tablespoons of melted butter
2/3 of organic brown sugar
1 tablespoon of ground cinnamon FROSTING
cream cheese frosting
Simple powdered sugar glaze

Gluten-Free Cinnamon Rolls

50 - 60 MINUTES

SERVINGS: 1
METHOD

Preheat oven to 350 degrees F (176 C). Use butter oil to coat baking dish
Heat the dairy-free milk. Ensure you do not overheat as this may kill the yeast
Add butter and sugar to the dairy milk. Add yeast and stir. Leave it for some time until the surface is puffy
Whisk together gluten-free flour blend, almond flour, cane sugar, baking powder, and sea salt. Use a fork to mix the ingredients
To dry the ingredients, add the almond milk mixture and stir. A dough that looks like moist will be formed. Set it aside
Get a large cutting board and wrap it with a plastic wrap. Clean the surface and add gluten-free flour to it.
Put the dough in the center of the surface and cover it with another plastic wrap. Roll the dough to a large rectangle shape with the rolling pin. Remove the top plastic wrap and brush on the butter. Sprinkle brown sugar and cinnamon on it with your finger. Make sure it is uniform. Remo e the bottom wrap from the cutting board. Use it to roll the dough into a cylinder. Use the serrated knife to cut the dough into equal rolls. Carefully transfer it inside the pie dish or cake pan Cover it with a plastic wrap and towel. Put it in a warm oven and let it rise till the rolls are almost touching. Remove the wrap and towel. Put the rolls on the center rack of the oven. Bake. This usually takes 30-35 minutes. Let the rolls cool for like 20 minutes before frosting.

Conclusion

This book can be your first guide for Plant-Based Diet if you just started your journey. Or it can help you with the recipe choice if you are already following the diet.

The Plant-Based and Alkaline diet is suitable for anyone who wants to improve the quality of everyday life. These diets can help to reduce the risk of heart disease, type 2 diabetes, cancer, premature death, Alzheimer's disease, various cancers, avoid side effects linked to the antibiotics and hormones used in modern animal agriculture, lower body weight and body mass index (BMI).

Usually, people decide to go vegan due to one or several reasons. People might switch to veganism due to their ethical reasons, as they believe all live creatures have a right to live, be free, and fairly treated. You can find your reasons.

There are many sources of healthy nutrients in vegan products. So you don't have to worry about getting enough vitamins to your body. This book will help you to make a healthy vegan Meal Plan for the whole family and spend less time in the kitchen.

Remember that Veganism is not only about the diet, but about changing your lifestyle to a more healthy and balanced one.

And this book will help you with this.

You can choose the recipe you like from a variety of options:
- Breakfast recipes
- Bread and Biscuits
- Salads and Soups
- Main dishes
- Smoothies and Teas
- Sauces and condiments
- Desserts
- Snacks
- Whole Food recipes